Troubleshooting

Microsoft®

Windows® 2000

Professional

Jerry Joyce and Marianne Moon

Microsoft®

PUBLISHED BY
Microsoft Press
A Division of Microsoft Corporation
One Microsoft Way
Redmond, Washington 98052-6399

Library of Congress Cataloging-in-Publication Data
Joyce, Jerry, 1950-
    Troubleshooting Microsoft Windows 2000 Professional / Jerry Joyce, Marianne Moon.
       p. cm.
    Includes index.
    ISBN 0-7356-1165-3
    1. Microsoft Windows (Computer file)   2. Operating systems (Computers) I. Moon, Marianne. II. Microsoft Corporation. III Title.

  QA76.76.O63 J697 2000
  005.4'4769--dc21   00-046056

Printed and bound in the United States of America.

2 3 4 5 6 7 8 9   QWT   6 5 4 3 2 1

Distributed in Canada by Penguin Books Canada Limited.

A CIP catalogue record for this book is available from the British Library.

Microsoft Press books are available through booksellers and distributors worldwide. For further information about international editions, contact your local Microsoft Corporation office or contact Microsoft Press International directly at fax (425) 936-7329. Visit our Web site at mspress.microsoft.com. Send comments to *mspinput@microsoft.com*.

Acquisitions Editors: Chistey Bahn, Alex Blanton
Project Editor: Wendy Zucker
Manuscript Editor: Marianne Moon

Quick contents

Contents

Acknowledgments

This book is the result of the combined efforts of a team of people whose friendship we value highly and whose technical, artistic, and literary skills we've trusted and admired during the many years we've written and produced books together. Ken Sánchez, our talented compositor, meticulously laid out the complex solution spreads; no detail was too small to offend his typographic sensibilities or escape his eagle-eyed scrutiny. Sue Cook produced and refined the decision-tree flowcharts and the interior graphics, and then cheerfully reworked and repositioned as we rewrote and rewrote. We've worked with Alice Copp Smith on so many books. Alice does much more than proofread and copyedit: her gentle and witty chiding on countless yellow sticky notes makes us groan but always teaches us to write better. Jan Wright, indexer *par excellence*, seems to inhale the soul of a book and then magically exhale a comprehensive

and really useful index (but we know there's more than magic to her method). We thank them all for their exceptional work and their good-humored patience under demanding deadlines.

At Microsoft Press, we thank Christey Bahn for making it possible for us to write this book, and we thank our gracious project editor, Wendy Zucker, for patiently answering an endless stream of "questions of the day." Thanks also to Jenny Benson, Alex Blanton, Jana Carter, Kevin Coomes, Candace Jorgensen, Jim Kramer, Joel Panchot, Laura Sackerman, and Tracy Thomsic for all their help.

On the home front, Roberta, Rick, and Zuzu provided love and laughter, and allowed their puppies, Baiser and Pierre, to roam freely on our virtual and literal desktops and to grace some of our pages with their furry little images.

About this book

Troubleshooting Microsoft Windows 2000 Professional presents a new way to diagnose and solve the problems you might have encountered while using Microsoft Windows 2000 Professional. Whether you are a beginning user of Windows or have upgraded to Windows 2000 from an earlier version, the chances are that you bought this book because you want to fix those problems as quickly and easily as possible, without having to read pages of technical background information. Because we know that you don't want to waste a lot of time searching for answers, we wrote this book with three goals in mind: ease of use, simplicity, and speed. We'll show you how to locate your problem, describe what might be causing it without going into too many specifics, and then lead you right to the solution so that you can get back to what you were doing.

How to use this book

Good news! You don't have to read this book in any particular order or even from cover to cover. It's designed so that you can jump in, quickly diagnose your problem, and then get the information you need to fix it, whether you've just begun to learn about operating systems and programs or whether you're knowledgeable enough to get right to the source of the problem. We've grouped the problems you're most likely to encounter into chapters with short, straightforward titles, listed alphabetically, that let you see at a glance what kinds of topics the chapter covers. Each chapter is broken down into two specific elements: the flowchart and the solution spread.

Flowcharts

The first thing you'll see when you turn to a chapter is a dynamic, easy-to-use flowchart. It starts by asking you a broad question about a common problem and then, as you answer a series of yes-or-no questions, guides you toward a diagnosis of the problem. If the solution to your problem is a simple one that requires only a few steps, you'll find a quick fix right there on the flowchart. Take a few minutes to work your way through the steps, and presto—your problem is solved and you're back to work (or play) with a minimum of downtime. If the solution to your problem requires a little more explanation and a few more steps, you'll find a statement that describes the problem, along with the page number of the solution spread you need to go to. And if you can't find your specific problem in the series of questions on the flowchart, look through the list of related chapters for another area where your problem might be addressed.

Solution spreads

The solution spreads are where the real troubleshooting takes place. We provide you with some brief information about the source of the problem you're experiencing and then, with clear, step-by-step instructions, show you how to fix it. The solution spreads contain screen shots that show you what you'll be seeing as you move through the steps, and you'll be happy to see that none of the solutions takes more than two pages.

Although our goal is to give you just the facts so that you can quickly get back to what you were doing, in some cases we've provided more detailed background information that you might or might not want to read, depending on whether you're looking for a deeper understanding of what caused your problem. Also scattered throughout the solution spreads are tips that contain related material or advice that you'll find helpful, and a few warnings that tell you what you should or shouldn't do in a given situation.

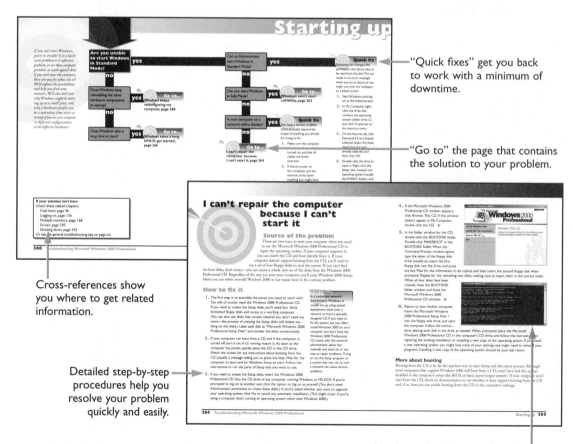

"Quick fixes" get you back to work with a minimum of downtime.

"Go to" the page that contains the solution to your problem.

Cross-references show you where to get related information.

Detailed step-by-step procedures help you resolve your problem quickly and easily.

Handy reader aids provide information to help you avoid additional problems.

Troubleshooting tips

To troubleshoot, as defined by the *Microsoft Press Computer Dictionary*, is to "isolate the source of a problem in a program, computer system, or network and remedy it." But how do you go about isolating the source of the problem in the first place? The source can be difficult to identify even for those well versed in the intricacies of an operating system such as Microsoft Windows 2000 Professional. When the same symptoms are caused by different problems, how do you isolate the real problem? And what if what *you* think is the source of the problem is only a symptom of another problem whose source lies deep in the murky innards of the operating system?

If you can't immediately identify what's wrong, you might be tempted to quote the hardware engineer ("It's a software problem!") or the software engineer ("It's a hardware problem!"). However, blame won't get your computer working properly; information and persistence will. So put on your detective's hat, strap on your virtual toolbelt, and get ready to solve the problem. Note that unlike hardware, which seems to break whenever it feels like it, Windows 2000 is rarely so capricious. In Windows, almost everything has a cause and an effect. You do something wrong, and something in Windows breaks—cause and effect. A program does something evil, and Windows breaks—cause and effect. A chip goes bad on the motherboard, and the computer won't start up—hey, that's a hardware problem; don't blame Windows for that one!

How to troubleshoot

Your objective is to isolate the problem. As soon as you encounter it, write down your observations in the greatest detail possible. (Once you start trying to fix the problem, you probably won't be able to reexamine the symptoms.) Then ask yourself questions, starting with the broadest, and gradually narrow down the scope of the problem. Say, for example, you can't start Windows. Is the computer plugged in, and is the monitor turned on? You can't get much broader than that! If you pass that test, does Windows begin starting up?

Now you can start closing in (this is where you'll appreciate your notes): Can you start up Windows only in Safe Mode? If so, something has messed up your system. Think about what you, or someone else, might have done to cause the problem. Did you install a new piece of hardware? Did you download and/or install a new program? Has someone else been using your machine?

You're now in the final throes of troubleshooting. As you adjust your detective hat, and we sit silently in the drawing room awaiting the denouement, you reveal your theory about the culprit. Swiftly and surely, you open the Control Panel and work your way to the Device Manager, where your theory is confirmed—the modem and driver you just installed aren't working. You disable them, and all is well—cause and effect. Elementary, my dear Watson!

Because the above example was…well, an example, it went quickly to the source of the problem, but your troubleshooting might take you down a few dead ends before it leads you to the source of *your* problem. You're going to need patience and determination to get to the bottom of some problems. If your main method of fixing things is to experiment, be aware that sometimes your "fixes" can cause a second problem, and then you'll have two problems to troubleshoot. Keep detailed notes about what you've done so that you don't travel down the same dead end again, and so that you can reverse, if necessary, any actions you took that might have caused more problems.

Let Windows help

Windows can give you a lot of help by providing a large array of admittedly often obtuse error messages that pop up when a problem is encountered. Windows also provides event logs, diagnostic tools, and reporting tools. These tools, which are described throughout this book, are designed specifically to keep your system running correctly and to help you fix it if it isn't working properly, so don't hesitate to use them.

Although this error message tells you there's a problem, it doesn't tell you that you can't open the file because it was encrypted by someone else.

Windows also provides a set of advanced tools that can help you to diagnose and understand many of those incomprehensible error messages. Using and installing the support tools, located on the Windows 2000 Professional CD, is described in "A program that ran in an earlier version of Windows won't run now" on page 226. The Errors And Events Messages Help—one of the support tools that are installed—provides a huge volume of error messages and event-log messages that include suggested actions to eliminate specific problems.

Do you have permission?

Windows 2000 is extremely self-protective; it's often unwilling to let you meddle with its setup. In some cases, you'll be able to make changes to the system if you're a member of the Users group. To make other changes, you'll need to be a member of the Power Users group. In many instances, however, you must be logged on as a member of the Administrators group, or must run a program or a Control Panel item as a member of the Administrators group, in order to modify the system to fix a problem.

Windows isn't shy about letting you know when you don't have permission to make changes.

Defining what you can do as a member of each of these groups is difficult, because a local or network administrator can easily change the permissions that are granted to a group, and network group policies almost always implement their own sets of permissions. Also, many organizations create their own groups and designate specific permissions for each of these groups. Your best bet is to try a procedure to see whether Windows prevents you from doing it. Don't worry—Windows won't let you do anything you haven't been given permission to do.

There's one special account that exists on most computers. When the computer is first set up, an account with the user name "Administrator" is created, and, not surprisingly, it's a member of the Administrators group for that specific computer. In most cases, if you can log on as this Administrator with the correct password, you'll be able to do almost anything to the computer—unless you're trying to do something that involves the network and that requires a network-wide Administrators account. Again, Windows will quickly tell you if you don't have the proper permission.

Caution rules

No matter how much you grumble about it, it's not for the thrill of absolute power that Windows restricts your right to make changes to your computer. These restrictions are in place for your own good, as your mother might say, because you can really mess up your system if you're not careful. If you're experiencing problems, take precautions before you jump in and make changes. Make sure you keep the backups of your documents and other files up to date. Even if you don't create a problem with your tinkering, the problem you're trying to troubleshoot could suddenly escalate and cause severe difficulty before you can diagnose and fix it. Also, make sure you have a record of your system settings, and that you keep a copy of the settings stored somewhere other than on your computer in case a problem prevents you from accessing your computer. See Appendix C, "Gathering information," on page 299 for information about recording your system settings.

Probably the most important caution we can stress is about making changes to the Windows Registry—the hidden database that stores all the settings for Windows. If you seek help for your problems from sources other than this book, you're likely to encounter advice about editing the Registry. This is because most such advice is voiced or written by software engineers and technicians, who enjoy working in databases and who feel that this is the easiest way to fix problems. Unless you consider yourself to be very tech-savvy, you should investigate all possible alternatives to working directly with the Registry. In most cases the alternative methods are easier, far less intimidating, and much safer. For more information about working with the Registry, see Appendix B, "Editing the Registry," on page 297.

Domains, workgroups, and stand-alone computers

What you can do and how you do it depends very much on your network configuration. If your computer is on a domain, there are many more restrictions as to what you can do than there are if your computer is in a workgroup or if you're working on a stand-alone computer. Much of the control of the computer on a domain is delegated to the network administrator and his or her group of coworkers. In many cases, even if you're allowed to make changes to your computer, you'll be frustrated to discover that the changes are never implemented because network policies and controls take precedence over anything you do. If you find that your efforts to fix a problem are futile, use the opportunity to get help from the network administrator, and take a well-deserved break while the designated authority fixes the problem.

If your computer is in a workgroup (where there's no domain on the network) or if you work on a stand-alone computer, troubleshooting and fixing problems are similar in either situation, except for the additional need to troubleshoot network connections on a workgroup computer. In either case, you'll probably need to do your own maintenance and you'll be able to use the Administrator account when necessary. You won't run into the problem of network policies, although local policies set on your computer can restrict many actions.

Don't fix outdated problems

The best way to fix a problem is to avoid it. Microsoft has a team of crack (no, not crackpot) software engineers and technicians who are dedicated to fixing any known problems in Windows and providing service packs that contain the solutions to those problems. To avoid many of the most serious and/or annoying problems, make sure you install the most recent service pack. Also, keep your programs and software drivers updated when service releases or updated releases become available. See Appendix A, "Installing a service pack," on page 295 for information about obtaining and installing service packs.

If you're still stuck

We've worked hard to address the most common problems you're likely to run into as you use Windows 2000, but, obviously, we can't address every problem. There's even a remote possibility that one of our solutions won't fix your specific problem. If we haven't addressed your problem, make sure that what you've encountered is a real problem rather than your not knowing exactly how to do something in Windows 2000. To figure out how to do things easily and quickly in Windows, you might want to take a look at another of our books, *Microsoft Windows 2000 Professional At a Glance*.

If you do run into a dead end, you can turn to Windows Help; your company's help desk; the manufacturer of your computer, hardware device, or software program; or

Microsoft Product Support. Be cautious, however, about turning to your coworkers for help, unless you're certain they know what they're doing.

If you want to try to search out the information you need yourself, try the following web sites:

- *http://www.microsoft.com/windows2000* for general Windows 2000 information.

- *http://search.support.microsoft.com/kb* for the Microsoft searchable Knowledge Base, where all known problems and solutions are listed.

- *http://windowsupdate.microsoft.com* for assessments of updates that you need and for access to the updates.

- *http://www.microsoft.com/windows2000 /downloads* for available updates and additional downloadable programs.

- *http://www.microsoft.com/hwtest/hcl* to search for hardware that passed testing for compatibility with Windows 2000 and other operating systems.

- *http://www.microsoft.com/windows2000 /upgrade/compat* to determine whether a specific computer, hardware device, or software program has been tested and found compatible with Windows 2000.

- *http://www.microsoft.com/windows2000 /compatible/isp.asp* to determine whether a specific ISP (Internet service provider) uses software that's compatible with Windows 2000. Only major ISPs are listed.

The Troubleshooting web site

If you've found this book so fascinating that you could hardly put it down, you're in luck because…there's more!

With the purchase of this book, you now have access to the Microsoft Press Troubleshooting web site at *http://www.mspress.microsoft.com /troubleshooting*, which complements the book series by offering additional troubleshooting information that's updated monthly. You'll find that some of the flowcharts have been expanded to cover additional problems, and that entirely new flowcharts with accompanying solutions have been created to address some important problems that are perhaps slightly less common than those addressed in this book.

You'll find the Troubleshooting web site as easy to navigate as this book, and it furthers our goal of helping you locate your problem and its solution quickly and easily. To access the site, you need the code number **MSW0079**.

How can you keep your private files from being accessed by other people who either use your computer or have access to it over a network? And what can you do when you want to make changes to your computer settings but don't have permission to do so? It all depends on the access rights you've granted to others, and on the user rights you've been granted.

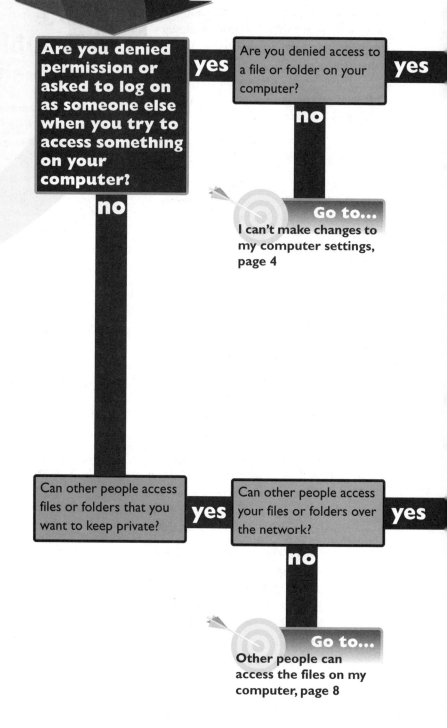

Are you denied permission or asked to log on as someone else when you try to access something on your computer?

yes → Are you denied access to a file or folder on your computer?

yes →

no

Go to...
I can't make changes to my computer settings, page 4

no

Can other people access files or folders that you want to keep private?

yes → Can other people access your files or folders over the network?

yes →

no

Go to...
Other people can access the files on my computer, page 8

When you want to open a file or folder, is its attribute listed as encrypted?

yes

no

Quick fix

Encryption, a security measure available on an NTFS-formatted drive, is designed to prevent anyone other than the person who encrypted the file—or special "recovery agents"—to access it.

1. Ask the person who encrypted the document to provide you with a copy of the file in a decrypted form.

2. If that person isn't available, contact the designated recovery agent to obtain a decrypted copy of the file.

Quick fix

Individual files and folders can have security settings that allow access only to specific individuals or members of certain groups. Although the default is to allow access to everyone, the security settings can be changed.

1. If the item is in a folder that you can't access, ask someone who has access to the folder to move or copy the item you want into a folder that you can access.

2. If the item is a file that you can't open, ask someone who has permission to make security changes to change the security settings for the file.

3. If you need numerous items but are denied access, ask your local or network administrator to add you to a group that has access to the items.

Go to...

Too many people can access my files on the network, page 6

If your solution isn't here
Check these related chapters:
 Encryption, page 52
 Folders, page 76
 Programs, page 220
Or see the general troubleshooting tips on page xiii

Source of the problem

Windows 2000 provides a host of security features that keep your data secure, prevent unauthorized snooping, and eliminate unauthorized changes to the computer setup. However—as with the time-consuming security checkpoints at airports—you'll find yourself occasionally inconvenienced by the security checkpoints in Windows. To further complicate things, not only can security be set up at different levels, but those with the proper authority can modify the settings in almost any way they want. If you're prevented from making some changes to your computer, you can try to get your level of authority changed, you can log on as someone who has more authority, you can have the requirements changed, or—if all else fails—you can simply kick back with a cup of coffee and let the person with the authority make the changes for you.

How to fix it

1. Windows uses a method of assigning individuals to groups and then assigning certain permissions to each group. The combination of which group or groups you're assigned to, and what each of those groups can do, results in what's known as your *user rights*. If you can't make changes to your computer settings, it's because you don't have the user rights to make the changes. To have more permission, you must be added to a group that has more permission. If your computer is on a corporate network that contains a domain, ask the network administrator or whoever assigns user rights to add you to a more powerful group. One or two members of an office or a division are often granted this permission.

2. If your computer is part of a small network (no domain) or isn't connected to a network, your user rights are maintained on your own computer. Therefore you need to get permission from whoever administers the computer or from someone who's a member of the Power Users group. To add you to a group, he or she will need to do the following: Log on, right-click My Computer, and click Manage on the shortcut menu. Double-click the Local Users And Groups item if it isn't expanded, and then click Users.

> **Tip**
> If your computer is on a corporate network but you have a local account on your computer that gives you permission to make changes, log off from the network, and then log on again to the local computer only. Enter your user name and password for the local computer account, and enter the computer's name in the Domain box. You might now be able to make the changes to the computer that you weren't allowed to make when you were connected to the network.

Double-click the user name (yours), and, on the Member Of tab in the Properties dialog box, click Add. In the Select Groups dialog box, click the Power Users group, and then click Add. Click OK, and then click OK again to close the Properties dialog box. Close the Computer Management window. Then the person who's obligingly doing this for you should log off, and you should log on. Say "Thank you!"

Tip

Being a member of the Power Users group grants you additional permission but doesn't allow you to do everything a member of the Administrators group can do. As a security measure, no one should be constantly logged on as an Administrator. Doing so provides too much access for viruses to go about their evil work and for hackers to gain entrance to the network through your computer.

3. Do your work logged on as a Power User. If you need to do something that requires Administrators group permission, you can log on to do that single task if you have an Administrators group account. Ask an Administrator for the user name and password for an account that's a member of the Administrators group. (There are usually accounts designed for just this purpose, and their passwords are changed frequently.) Compliments or cookies might help convince an Administrator that you're worthy of this additional responsibility.

4. If, when you try to run a program or open a Control Panel item, you're asked to log on as an Administrator, use the name and password you were given. In the Domain box, enter the name of the computer if the account is that of an Administrator for this computer only, or enter the network domain name if the account is set up on the network. Click OK.

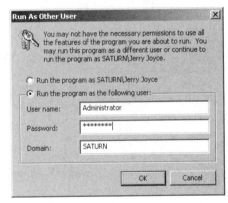

5. If, when you're denied permission or access, you don't see the Run As Other User dialog box, hold down the Shift key; right-click the program, the Start menu item, or the Control Panel item; and click Run As on the shortcut menu. Enter the name, password, and domain or computer name. Click OK, and run the program or item. ▶

More about who can do what, and where

Windows starts with four basic groups: Administrators, who can do almost anything; Power Users, who can do many things but can't change the system too much; Users, who can use the system but have limited permission to make changes; and Guests, who have restricted rights. Other groups exist for administrative purposes, new groups can be created, and existing groups can have their rights changed by an Administrator. To confuse the issue further, the groups can exist in a couple of different areas: as local groups that define permission when you're logged on only to the one computer you're using, and as global groups that—on a network with a domain—define permission to all the resources on your computer and on the network. If you're a member of different groups locally and globally, the global settings are in control when you're logged on to the network.

Too many people can access my files on the network

Source of the problem

When your computer is connected to a network, the folders on your computer can be set for sharing. This means that your folders can be accessed over the network, and that the files in the folders can be opened, copied, modified, and even deleted. If you're worried that the wrong people (or just too many people) are accessing this information, you can monitor who is connecting to your folders. Then you can decide whether you want to restrict who can access the folders and what they can do with them, or whether you'll simply deny access to some or all of the folders.

How to fix it

1. To control sharing, you first need to know exactly what you're sharing. Right-click My Computer, and click Manage on the shortcut menu. In the Computer Management window, double-click the Shared Folders item to expand it, and click Shares. ▶ What you see are the folders on your computer that are being shared with others on the network. If you're horrified that a certain folder is being shared and you know there's no reason to share it, right-click it, and click Stop Sharing on the shortcut menu.

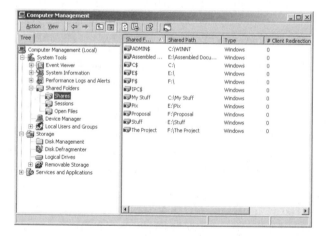

2. In the left part of the window, click Sessions under the Shared Folders item, and note who is connected to your computer and whether anyone you don't want to be connected is connected.

3. In the left part of the window, click Open Files, and note which files are being shared, how long they have been shared and by whom, and from which computer.

Warning

You'll note that some of the items listed under Shares are followed by letters and symbols, such as C$, ADMIN$, and IPC$. These are files that are shared for administrative purposes, and you should not delete or modify the sharing.

4. To prevent future connections to a folder by everyone or by an individual, or to restrict what an individual can do when connected, you need to alter whether the folder is shared and, if so, how. Open My Computer, and navigate to the parent folder or drive of the shared folder. Right-click the folder, and click Sharing on the shortcut menu.

5. If you no longer want to share this folder, click Do Not Share This Folder. If, instead, you just want to restrict access to the folder, click Permissions. ▶

6. To restrict what can be done to items in the folder, click the group (usually Everyone is the only group listed), and clear the check boxes for the actions you don't want people to do. For example, if you want to let people open a file but don't want to let them modify it and save it back to the folder, leave only the Read item selected. ▶

7. To restrict who can make changes, click the current group, and click Remove. Click the Add button to specify who can connect.

8. In the Look In list in the Select Users, Computers, Or Groups dialog box, click the workgroup, domain, or directory that lists the groups or individuals you want to add. Click the names of those you want to add, and click the Add button. Repeat for any other groups or individuals. Click OK when you've finished.

9. In the Permissions dialog box, click each group, and specify the actions you'll allow. Click OK when you've finished, and then click OK to close the Sharing dialog box. Change the sharing of any other folders in the same way.

10. Return to the Computer Management window, and review the connections under the Shared Folders item. If the information doesn't display your changes, press the F5 key to update the information, and then look again to make sure everything is set as it should be.

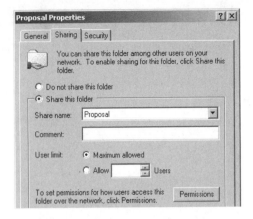

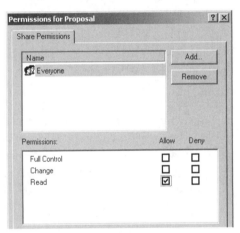

More about specifying who can access your folders

If you're connected to a small network (one without a domain), you won't be able to specify individuals, but you will be able to specify which computers can connect. You can also specify the group Authenticated Users, which is the same as the Everyone group except that it excludes those who sign in as Anonymous Users or as Guests.

Other people can access the files on my computer

Source of the problem

When other people use your computer, they might be able to access your files, even when they log on using their own user names. If your computer uses NTFS (NT file system) drives, you can develop a strategy wherein you maintain the files you want to keep private in folders that are automatically hidden from other users. You can, however, allow designated users access to certain files and folders if you want.

How to fix it

1. This procedure works only on disk drives that are formatted with the NTFS system, which provides a much higher level of security than do other types of disk file systems. If you're not sure whether a disk is in NTFS format, right-click the drive in My Computer, and click Properties on the shortcut menu. On the General tab of the Properties dialog box, under File System, you should see the letters *NTFS*. If you don't, the disk isn't NTFS-formatted, and you'll need to find other ways to protect your private files.

2. Store your private documents in the My Documents folder on the Desktop, or in folders that you create on the Desktop. No other users of your computer, unless they're members of the Administrators group, can access those files.

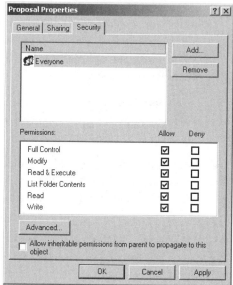

3. To provide limited access to a folder, locate the folder, right-click it, and click Properties on the shortcut menu. On the Security tab, you'll find an option whose tortured language makes all but the most tech-crazed individual cringe: the Allow ▶ Inheritable Permissions From Parent To Propagate To This Object check box! It simply means that if the option is selected, whatever settings are made for the parent folder (the folder that this folder is in) will be copied to this folder. Clear this check box so that you can make different settings for the folder. When the Security dialog box appears, and you're asked what you want to do, click Copy.

4. Back in the folder's Properties dialog box, if you want to change only the basic permissions, clear the check boxes for the permissions you don't want to grant, and click OK. If you want to restrict who can access a folder, click Everyone, click Remove, and then click Add.

5. In the Look In list in the Select Users, Computers, Or Groups dialog box, click the computer, workgroup, domain, or directory that lists the groups or individuals you want to add. Click those you want to add, and then click the Add button. Repeat for any other groups or individuals. Click OK when you've finished.

Tip

When you change the permissions on a folder, make sure that you include yourself, or the group you're a member of, and give yourself full access. Otherwise, you won't be able to access or modify the folder or anything in it without going back and changing the permissions again.

6. Click the name of a group or an individual, and clear or select check boxes to specify what they can do.

7. Click the Advanced button. Select the check box to reset permissions on all child objects. When this option is selected, any subfolders and files in this folder will be given the same permissions you've set for the folder itself. ▶

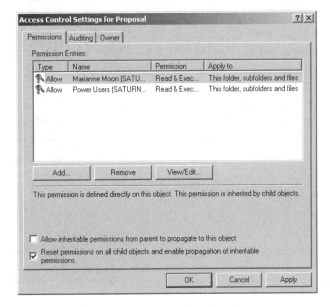

8. To specify the permissions in more detail and control which items within this folder have the same permissions, click the name of the group or individual whose permissions you want to modify, and click the View/Edit button. In the Permission Entry dialog box, select the check boxes for the permissions you want to grant, and clear them for those you want to withhold. Click OK to close the dialog box. Click OK to close the Access Control Settings dialog box, and click OK to close the folder's Properties dialog box. You have now restricted access to that folder.

More about permissions for files and folders

Setting the security for a folder provides reasonably good protection, but be aware that you can set the permissions only for folders you've created yourself—that is, unless you're a member of the Administrators group, in which case even if someone has set the permissions for a folder so that you can't access it, you can change the permissions and grant yourself the access rights. You can also apply security settings to an individual file within a folder. This can cause a few complications, based on that weird stuff about things propagating from parent to child. Also, if you move a file to a disk that isn't formatted in NTFS, you'll lose all the security settings. It's best to set the security for a folder and then keep the documents that you want to keep secure in that folder.

If you're seeing the wrong date/time information displayed on your files and in your e-mail messages, if your faxes aren't being sent when the discount phone rates apply despite being set to do so, or if your maintenance programs are running on the wrong schedule, you need to reset the date and time on your computer. If your date/time format isn't appropriate for the country or region you're in, or if you want a 24-hour clock instead of a 12-hour clock, you need to change the date/time format.

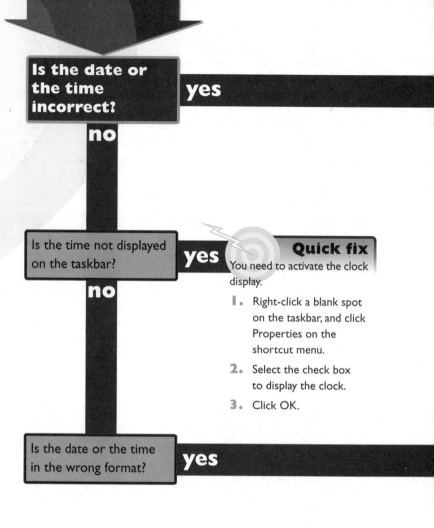

Is the date or the time incorrect?

yes

no

Is the time not displayed on the taskbar?

yes

no

Quick fix

You need to activate the clock display.

1. Right-click a blank spot on the taskbar, and click Properties on the shortcut menu.
2. Select the check box to display the clock.
3. Click OK.

Is the date or the time in the wrong format?

yes

If your solution isn't here
Check these related chapters:
Or see the general troubleshooting tips on page xiii

Date and time

Does the corrected date or time change whenever you log on, or does your computer's time slow down over the first 20 minutes?

yes →

Does this happen only when you're logged on to the network?

yes →

Quick fix

The network system clock is probably adjusting the time on your computer.

1. Double-click the time on the taskbar, make sure you have the correct time zone selected, and click OK.
2. If the time is still incorrect, contact the network administrator.

no ↓

Quick fix

The battery on your computer might need replacing or charging.

1. If your computer is a portable computer with a battery, make sure the battery is fully charged.
2. For all other computers, have the battery checked and replaced if necessary.

no ↓

Go to...
The date or the time is incorrect, page 12

Are you logged on as yourself to a computer you use routinely?

yes →

Go to...
The date or the time is in the wrong format, page 14

no ↓

Quick fix

You need to be correctly logged on for your individual settings to take effect.

1. On the Start menu, click Shut Down, and then click Log Off.
2. Log on using your standard user name. If this isn't the computer you normally use, consult with your network administrator about setting up a roaming profile for you.

The date or the time is incorrect

Source of the problem

Should you really care whether your computer knows the correct date or time? After all, doesn't it work just fine even though the date or the time is off by a few minutes or days or years?

The answer is that having an incorrect date or time on your computer can cause problems you might not even be aware of. One of the obvious ones is having your files stamped with the wrong date and time, which makes it difficult to sort and find them. Those same files could be skipped in routine file backups, and any maintenance programs that were set to run at specific times might not run on the correct schedule. If you've selected to send your faxes only when discount phone rates apply, you might be surprised by your next phone bill! And your e-mail messages might bring a laugh to the recipients when they realize that the sent date is later than the received date. You could encounter many other problems. You might have trouble on a network if your date and time settings are incorrect. If your date is very far off, you might find that some software programs won't run correctly, and that even your security access and your password—not to mention any licenses you have for downloaded music—have all expired.

Whether your computer has the wrong date or time because you've changed time zones or because something went awry with your system, you should always be sure to reset your computer date and time correctly. It's quick and easy to do.

How to fix it

1. Check the time on the taskbar to see whether it's correct. Then point to the time, keeping the mouse pointer steady until the date pops up, and check to see whether the date is correct.

2. Double-click the time on the taskbar.

3. If the time isn't displayed on the taskbar, point to Settings on the Start menu, and click Control Panel on the submenu. In the Control Panel, double-click the Date/Time icon.

4. Click the Time Zone tab. ▶

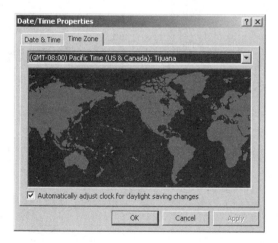

5. Click the time zone you're in. Note that the world map shifts as you click different time zones. Be sure to select the appropriate time zone, because some places within a specific time zone have different rules—for example, whether or not daylight saving time is used.

6. Select or clear the check box to have the time automatically changed for daylight saving time. The check box appears only if the time zone you selected recognizes daylight saving time.

7. Click Apply.

8. Click the Date & Time tab. ▶

9. Click the correct month and year if they're currently incorrect.

10. In the calendar, click today's date if it's not already selected.

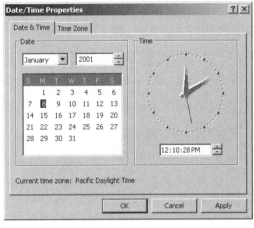

11. If the hour is incorrect, click to select it. Click the up or down scroll arrow at the right of the time to specify the correct hour.

12. Click the minutes, seconds, or the AM and PM symbols if they're incorrect, and use the scroll arrows to correct them.

13. Click OK.

14. Check the date and time on the taskbar to confirm that they're now correct.

More about time and networks

Time is critical on many networks for synchronization. Some networks run special programs that set the time on your computer. If your computer is on a corporate network, and you notice that the time changes after you've reset it or after the next time you log on, discuss the problem with your network administrator.

If the date and time are incorrect on your computer, you could encounter a problem when you try to dial in to a network. An administrator can restrict the times during which you can connect, so if the time on your computer is wrong by an hour or more, and if you're denied access to the network, reset the time and try to connect again.

Warning

Use caution if you're going to substantially advance the date on the computer. When you set your computer to an advanced date, some programs with specific time licenses could expire, and other limited licenses might also expire. Even when you reset the clock to the correct date, some of these licenses might no longer be valid. If this happens, you'll need to contact the issuer of the program or license to see what can be done.

The date or the time is in the wrong format

Source of the problem

Your computer is an accurate (albeit expensive) clock and calendar. You'll see the date and time stamped on each of your files when you view a folder window in Details view, and you'll see the date and time in every e-mail that you send or receive. You can also display the time on the taskbar. As far as your computer is concerned, the date and time are just numbers—for example, January 1, 2001, at 10:15 AM is 36892.042708333 in computer language! Those numbers might work for your computer, but we humans like our date and time in a simpler and more familiar form. And, although computers use a single standard, people in different parts of the world use different layouts to represent the date and time. To avoid confusion, set up your date and time format so that it's appropriate for your location. If you don't like any of the preset formats, you can design your own.

How to fix it

1. On the Start menu, point to Settings, and click Control Panel on the submenu.

2. Double-click the Regional Options icon.

3. On the General tab, click the appropriate region. Note that the choices are arranged by language, with additional entries when one language uses different settings in different locations. Click Apply.

4. On the Time tab, inspect the time formats. To use a different preset format for the time, the time separator, or the AM and PM symbols, click one in the list. The only time formats that are listed are the ones commonly used in the region you've specified. ▶

5. If you want to use a format other than those listed, type it in. For the time, use the codes shown in the dialog box. For example, entering H:m:s would display the time in 24-hour format, with no leading zeros in the hour, minute, or second, and no AM or PM symbol.

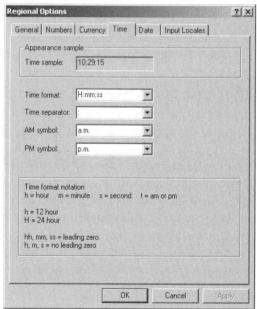

6. On the Date tab, inspect the date formats. The short date is used in file listings. Many programs insert a date into a document for you, using either the short or long date format. Click one of the preset formats if you want to change the existing format. The only date formats that are listed are the ones commonly used in the region you've specified. ▶

7. If you want to use a format other than those listed, type it in. Use the codes in the table to change the date format.

8. Click OK. Point to the time on the taskbar and wait for the date to appear. Make sure that the time and the long date are in the format you want. Take a look at the short date in any folder that shows files in Details view. If you don't like the format, return to the Regional Options dialog box and modify the selection.

More about regional settings

Regional settings do more than change the format or language of the date and time. They also set the default format for numbers and currency. When you add a new locale, Windows 2000 gives you the option of switching to a different keyboard layout. You don't need a second keyboard—instead, some of the keys on your keyboard will produce different characters. For example, if you switch from a U.S.-type keyboard to a Spanish (Argentina) keyboard, pressing the semicolon (;) key produces the ñ character.

Code	Result
M	The month number
MM	The month number, always two digits
MMM	The three-letter month abbreviation
MMMM	The full name of the month
d	The day number
dd	The day number, always two digits
ddd	The three-letter day abbreviation
dddd	The full name of the day
yy	The year number, the last two digits only
yyyy	The full number of the year

How can you prevent your Windows Desktop from becoming a cluttered mess? "Too late!" you say. Whether you're using the plain old standard Desktop or the Active Desktop, or switching between the two, you can keep only what's essential to your work on the Desktop and put the other stuff—folders, icons, the taskbar, scraps of text—neatly out of sight until you need it. And if your Active Desktop isn't working right, this is where you'll find out how to fix it.

Does your Desktop look different from what you expect?

yes

no

Is your Desktop cluttered?

yes

no

Go to...
My Desktop needs some serious house-cleaning, page 20

Are you unable to access folders, documents, programs, or web sites from your Desktop?

yes

Quick fix
You can place shortcuts on the Desktop to almost anything.

1. If it's a Start menu item, hold down the Ctrl key and drag the item from the Start menu onto the Desktop.

2. If it's an item in a folder, locate the item, right-click it, point to Send To on the shortcut menu, and click Desktop (Create Shortcut).

3. If it's a web page, go to Internet Explorer, open the File menu, point to Send, and click Shortcut To Desktop.

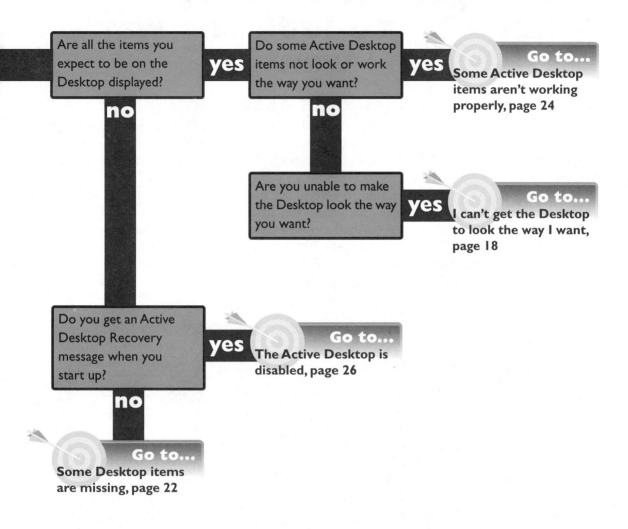

Are all the items you expect to be on the Desktop displayed?

yes → Do some Active Desktop items not look or work the way you want?

yes → **Go to...** Some Active Desktop items aren't working properly, page 24

no ↓

no ↓

Are you unable to make the Desktop look the way you want?

yes → **Go to...** I can't get the Desktop to look the way I want, page 18

Do you get an Active Desktop Recovery message when you start up?

yes → **Go to...** The Active Desktop is disabled, page 26

no ↓

Go to... Some Desktop items are missing, page 22

If your solution isn't here
Check these related chapters:
Internet Explorer, page 104
Screen, page 230
Toolbars, page 286
Or see the general troubleshooting tips on page xiii

I can't get the Desktop to look the way I want

Source of the problem

If you've tried to customize your Desktop but can't get it to look and act the way you want, you might be trying to make your changes to the wrong type of Desktop. Your Desktop can be in either of two states, each with its own pros and cons. You might like the standard Desktop, which provides a simple work surface with icons arranged on top of a solid color background, a pattern, or a picture. Or—with the understanding that it can be a drain on your system resources—you might prefer the Active Desktop, where you can display an assortment of items, including live content from the web, your own web page, links to other locations, or just about anything else that can be put on a web page. If you can't decide which kind of Desktop you want, you can set up both and switch between them, depending on your needs.

How to fix it

1. Start with a clear view of the Desktop. Click the Show Desktop button on the Quick Launch toolbar. If any open windows or dialog boxes aren't minimized, close them.

2. Right-click the Desktop, and click Properties on the shortcut menu. On the Web tab, make sure the Show Web Content On My Active Desktop check box is selected if you're going to design an Active Desktop, or that it's cleared if you're going to design a standard Desktop. Click Apply.

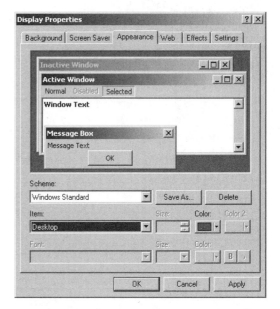

3. On the Appearance tab, click a color scheme in the Scheme list. If you like this scheme and want to use it, click Apply. If you don't want to change the color of all the elements, return to the original scheme, and click Desktop in ▲ the Item list if it's not already selected. Click the Color box, and choose a different color. To change the size of the icons and their fonts, click Icon in the Item list, and make the changes. To change the spacing between the icons when you have Windows arrange them, click Icon Spacing (Horizontal) or Icon Spacing (Vertical), and change the value in the Size box. Click Apply.

4. On the Background tab, click the background picture you want. You can display only bitmap pictures (those with the pen-and-pencil-in-a-cup icon) on the standard Desktop, but you can use any picture or web page (HTML document) in the list on the Active Desktop. If you don't see the item you want, click the Browse button, and locate a file you want to use. In the Picture Display box, specify how you want the picture to be displayed (for a standard Desktop only): ▶

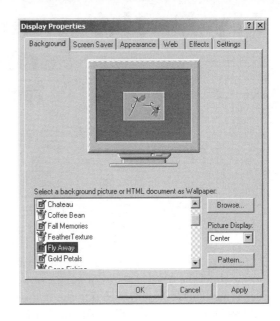

- Center to place the unaltered picture in the center of the Desktop—a good choice for a large picture. With this choice, you can click the Pattern button to specify a pattern that will fill the part of the Desktop that isn't covered by the picture.

- Tile to use multiple copies of the picture to fill the Desktop—a good choice for a small picture designed specifically to be a tiled background picture.

- Stretch to modify a single picture by distorting it horizontally or vertically so that it fills the Desktop. This is effective only for certain pictures, so experiment.

Tip

Be aware that some settings can affect the performance of your computer. See "My screen's performance is really slow" on page 234.

5. To change the picture that's used for an icon, on the Effects tab, click the icon you want to change, and then click Change Icon. Click the replacement picture, and click OK. If you don't see an icon you want, click the Browse button, and locate and select a file. (Try the *shell32.dll* and *moricons.dll* files, both located in the System32 subfolder of the WINNT folder.) Click the icon you want, and click OK. To revert to an original icon picture, click the icon on the Effects tab, and click the Default Icon button. While you're on the Effects tab, you can experiment by smoothing the screen fonts, using large icons (instead of setting the size yourself, as in step 3), or displaying the icons in all possible colors to improve their appearance.

6. If you're setting up the Active Desktop, on the Web tab, select the items you want displayed and clear the items you don't want displayed. If an item you want isn't listed, click the New button, and use the New Active Desktop Item Wizard to add the item. Click OK to apply the changes. Inspect your Desktop to make sure it looks the way you want. To switch from the standard to the Active Desktop, right-click the Desktop, point to Active Desktop on the shortcut menu, and click Show Web Content on the submenu.

My Desktop needs some serious housecleaning

Source of the problem

As you work at your computer, you're probably making slow progress toward that paperless office we're all dreaming of. However, the trade-off might be that your virtual Desktop has become the new storage place for all the junk that used to litter your physical desk! If your Windows Desktop is cluttered with files you store on it, with shortcuts that are automatically placed there when you install a program, with web page links, and with all the other detritus of a busy working life, it's time to do some housecleaning. You can clean up your Desktop by deleting the items you don't need and by moving into the appropriate folders all the items you still need but that really don't have to be on the Desktop. Then you can organize the remaining items into a practical and efficient arrangement.

How to fix it

1. To figure out what you have, clear your work area, sort through the clutter, and group the items by category. ▶ To do so, click the Show Desktop button on the Quick Launch toolbar to minimize any open windows and running programs. Then right-click the Desktop, point to Arrange Icons on the shortcut menu, and click By Type on the submenu.

2. Note the different types of icons. Any icon that displays a little arrow at its bottom left is a shortcut. Many shortcut icons also include the word *Shortcut* as part of the file name. You can delete any shortcuts you don't need without worrying about deleting their actual files. For

example, if you delete the shortcut to a document, the document remains, undisturbed, in its original location. However, if you do delete a shortcut, make sure you know where to locate the original file. To delete a single shortcut, click it, and press the Delete key. To select a group of adjacent icons to delete, drag the mouse around the icons. To select multiple noncontiguous items to delete, hold down the Ctrl key and click each icon. When you're asked to confirm the deletion or deletions, click Yes. After you've deleted all the shortcuts you don't need, right-click the Desktop, point to Arrange Icons on the shortcut menu, and click By Type on the submenu.

3. After you've deleted all the extra shortcuts, you need to decide what you want to do with the remaining Desktop items. You can select and delete almost anything on the Desktop (although you can't delete some of the original icons). Just be aware that if you're not deleting a shortcut, you're deleting a file or a folder. Instead of deleting those items, you might want to move them into folders for safekeeping. To move documents off the Desktop and into your My Documents folder, click the document icons, and drag them onto the My Documents icon. To move items off the Desktop and into a different folder, open the folder from My Computer, resize it if necessary so that you can see both the contents of the folder and the Desktop, and drag the item or items into the folder. If you copy the items into the folder instead of moving them, you can then delete the items from the Desktop.

Tip

If you realize too late that you just deleted or moved something you shouldn't have, right-click the Desktop immediately, and click Undo Delete or Undo Move on the shortcut menu. If you deleted something a while ago, you can recover it from the Recycle Bin. See step 3 in "Some Desktop items are missing" on page 22.

4. If there are still many items that you need to access from the Desktop, you can place them in folders on the Desktop. To do so, right-click the Desktop, point to New on the shortcut menu, and click Folder on the submenu. Give the new folder a name that easily identifies its contents, and then drag the appropriate items onto the folder icon to move them into the folder. Repeat to create as many folders as you need.

5. Once you've deleted and moved all the items you want, right-click the Desktop, point to Arrange Icons, and click a command to order and arrange the icons the way you want them on your Desktop. Click the Auto Arrange command on the shortcut menu (if it's unchecked) if you want Windows to line up the icons any time you add, move, or delete an item. If the Auto Arrange command is checked, click it if you want to be able to move the items wherever you want them on the Desktop and to arrange them only when you choose a command to do so.

There's more to the Desktop than meets the eye

The Desktop is more than just the surface you see on your screen. It's also a folder that contains all the items you've stored on the Desktop. Each person who uses your computer has an individual Desktop folder, so the display of items on the Desktop changes when each user logs on. Windows makes the Desktop folder easy to access by placing it at the top of the Folders list and by providing a Desktop button in the Save As and the Open dialog boxes. However, the Desktop folder actually resides on your main disk drive, under your user name in the Documents And Settings folder.

Some Desktop items are missing

Source of the problem

Windows 2000 is a great magician. No, it doesn't use real magic, despite some claims to the contrary, but it often performs some of those "now-you-see-it-now-you-don't" illusions. Although such tricks can be very useful when you know how they work, they can also cause much frustration and gnashing of teeth when certain items appear or disappear and you don't know why. The Desktop is the main stage for the Windows magic show, so if you discover that items are missing from your Desktop, it's time to look closely to find out how Windows performs these tricks, and then you can master them yourself.

How to fix it

1. Windows uses different tricks (okay, settings) to make specific items disappear. You should expect to see the icons for My Documents, My Computer, My Network Places, the Recycle Bin, and Internet Explorer, plus a few other icons, on your Desktop. If all the icons except the My Documents icon are visible, you can make that icon reappear in a jiffy. To do so, double-click My Computer on the Desktop, and, in the My Computer window, click Folder Options on the Tools menu. On the View tab of the Folder Options dialog box, select the Show My Documents On The Desktop check box, and click OK. ▶

2. If all the icons except the Internet Explorer icon are visible, you need to reset Internet Explorer to display its icon. On the Settings submenu of the Start menu, click Control Panel. In the Control Panel, double-click the Internet Options icon. On the Advanced tab of the Internet Properties dialog box, look through the Settings list, and, in the Browsing section of the Settings list, select the Show Internet Explorer On The Desktop check box. Click OK.

3. If all the standard icons are displayed but items you've added to the Desktop are missing, they've probably been deleted. To try to recover them, double-click the Recycle Bin on the Desktop. Look through the list for the missing item or items. Note the Original Location information. If you can't read the entire location, either point to it and wait until it's displayed, or drag the right border of the box containing the Original

Location title to the right until you can see the entire location. Files that have been deleted from the Desktop show a location in the form *drive:\Documents and Settings\user name\Desktop,* where *user name* is the name you use to log on to the computer. If you find any missing items, click them, and then click the Restore button. Close the Recycle Bin. ▶

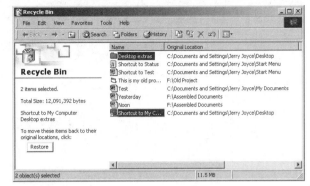

4. If you want to go even further, you can make all the icons disappear. This trick is part of the Active Desktop, whereby Windows turns your Desktop into something like a big web page. And all you have to do to make your icons reappear is right-click a blank spot on the Desktop, point to Active Desktop on the shortcut menu, and click Show Desktop Icons on the submenu.

5. The Active Desktop can display many items that aren't present on the standard Desktop. If any items are missing from your Desktop, right-click the Desktop, and point to Active Desktop on the shortcut menu. If there's a check mark next to Show Web Content, your Desktop is displaying web content. If Show Web Content isn't checked, click it to display web content on your Desktop. Switch between the standard and Active Desktops to see whether the missing items reappear.

6. If items that once appeared on the Active Desktop no longer appear when you switch to the Active Desktop to display web content, right-click the Desktop, point to Active Desktop on the shortcut menu, and look at the list of items at the bottom of the submenu. These are web elements that have been added to the Desktop. Items that are set to be displayed have a check mark next to them. Click an unchecked item to display it. Note that some items designed to be periodically updated, such as web pages, might not be displayed or might function improperly if you're not connected to the Internet or to an intranet where the page can be accessed.

> **Tip**
>
> You can keep your Desktop uncluttered and free of all icons but still access the hidden icons from the Desktop toolbar when you need them. For information about displaying the Desktop toolbar, see "The toolbars are too big or are in the wrong place" on page 292.

Things are not always as they appear

If you're unable to display the items you want after working though the above steps, perhaps the items aren't missing at all. Make sure they're not obscured by elements such as icons or windows. If your computer is set up to use multiple monitors, make sure the monitors are turned on. To verify that certain icons aren't on the Desktop, display the Desktop toolbar from the taskbar, and look through all the items. If an Active Desktop element is missing, make sure it isn't too small to display all its content and that you're not looking for content that might have changed if the element was updated.

Some Active Desktop items aren't working properly

Source of the problem

Your Active Desktop can display many different items. When you install these items, Windows places them on the Desktop in a rather haphazard way, and sets them up with whatever default settings it deems appropriate. Unless you do some resizing and repositioning, some Desktop items will probably be obscured by others, and you won't be able to see the content you want. It's also unlikely, if items are set to be updated, that the schedule will meet your needs. You'll probably want to adjust it—not only so that the new information is available when you need it, but to keep your system from becoming overburdened.

How to fix it

1. Right-click the Desktop, and click Properties on the shortcut menu. On the Web tab, make sure the check box to show web content is selected, and verify that the items you want displayed are listed and that their check boxes are selected.

2. If an item you want displayed isn't listed, click the New button, and use the New Active Desktop Item Wizard to add the item. Click the Visit Gallery button to go to a Microsoft web site and get some interesting Active Desktop items, or enter the address of an Internet or intranet web page, or click the Browse button in the wizard to locate HTML (web page) documents or pictures that are stored on your computer or network. Click OK when you've finished. If prompted, set up a schedule for downloading the item or items.

> **Tip**
> To find a web page that you visited recently, click the Browse button in the wizard, and click History in the Look In list. Click the web page, and click Open.

3. You'll need to reset any automatic scheduling if the updating interferes with your work, or if you find that you're often looking at outdated information. On the Web tab, select the item you want to display, and click the Properties button. On the Schedule tab of the Properties dialog box, make sure the settings are correct. Click the Only When I Choose Synchronize Fom The Tools Menu option if you want to update the information manually, or click the option to use a schedule if you want the item updated automatically. If you chose to have the item updated automatically, specify the schedule to use, and click Edit. If there's no schedule listed, click Add, create a schedule, and then click Edit.

4. Review the settings on all the tabs of the dialog box that appears. You can designate which items you want updated on this schedule; when and how often the updating should occur; whether the

computer should connect if it's not already connected; whether updating should be done only when the computer is idle, isn't running on batteries, or isn't in Standby mode; and how long to try to update if the web site isn't available. Make changes to the settings if the updating is causing problems. Click OK to close the dialog box.

5. On the Web Document tab, clear the check box to have the page available off line if you're concerned about disk space on your computer and if your computer is always connected to the Internet (or whatever connection is required to connect to the page). Select the check box if you want the page available whether or not you're connected.

6. On the Download tab, specify how much information you want downloaded each time the page is updated, and how much disk space the download may use. Specify whether you want to be notified by e-mail when the page is updated, and provide any password required to log on to the web site.

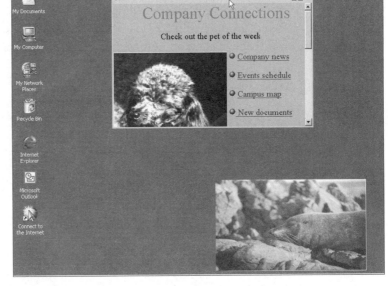

7. Click OK to close the item's Properties dialog box. Repeat steps 3 through 6 for each item you're displaying. Note that some items— pictures on your com- puter, for example— don't have properties that can be set.

8. Now you can reorga- nize your Desktop. To move an item, move your mouse pointer to the top of the item until a title bar appears. Drag the item by its title bar to the location you want. ▲

9. To resize an item, click it, and then move the mouse pointer to an edge of the item. When the pointer changes into a two-headed arrow, you can move the border in either direction the arrow is pointing. If you don't want to move or resize any of the items, right-click the Desktop, point to Active Desktop, and click Lock Desktop Items.

10. To manually update web items on your Active Desktop, whether or not they're set for automatic updating, right-click the Desktop, point to Active Desktop, and click Synchronize on the submenu.

11. To hide an item on the Desktop, or to hide all the items by turning off the Active Desktop completely, right-click the Desktop, point to Active Desktop, and click a selected item to hide it, click a cleared item to display it, or click Show Web Content to turn off the Active Desktop.

The Active Desktop is disabled

Source of the problem

Sometimes, when your computer is misbehaving, or a program isn't responding as it should, or everything has just "frozen" and you can't make a move, your only recourse is to physically turn off the computer instead of using the Shut Down command on the Windows 2000 Start menu. If this was the case, or if Windows was shut down in any other improper way—because of a power failure, for example—and if the Active Desktop was turned on when this happened, the Active Desktop will probably be deactivated when Windows restarts, and you'll also see a rather intimidating message. Don't worry. It's just a security procedure to prevent an item on the Active Desktop from doing any additional damage to your system.

How to fix it

1. When Windows starts and displays the Active Desktop Recovery message, read the text of the message. ▶
If you know what caused the problematic shutdown, and if you know that it wasn't related to any Active Desktop component, click the Restore My Active Desktop button. Figure out what went wrong, and try to fix it. If the problem was caused by your turning off the computer without using the Shut Down command on the Start menu, don't do that again unless you have absolutely no other choice.

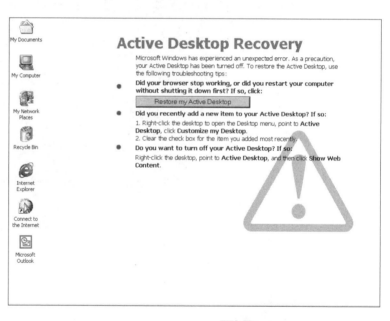

2. If you don't know what caused the problem, or if you suspect the problem might be associated with an item on the Active Desktop, or if you thought you'd fixed the problem but the

Tip
Whenever you encounter an inexplicable problem, it's always a good idea to run a full scan for viruses. Use a good virus-scanning program that has recently been updated.

Active Desktop Recovery message appears the next time you start Windows, right-click the Desktop, point to Active Desktop on the shortcut menu, and click the checked Show Web Content item on the submenu. This turns off the Active Desktop and makes the Active Desktop Recovery message disappear.

3. If you don't encounter any problems as you're using Windows and doing your work, and you want to use the Active Desktop again, you need to deactivate the item that you think caused the original problem. Right-click the Desktop, and click Properties. On the Web tab, select the check box to show web content. Select the check box for any recently installed item, or any item you suspect might have caused the problem. If you think you might want to use the item again in the future, clear the item's check box. If you won't want to use the item again, click the Delete button, and click Yes when you're asked to confirm the deletion. Click Apply. ▶

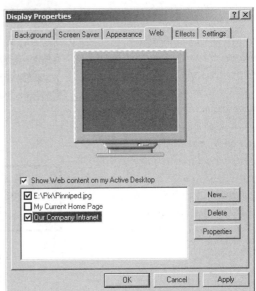

4. On the Background tab of the Properties dialog box, look at the lists of backgrounds. The one you're currently using is highlighted. If your background is anything other than a bitmap picture (one whose name has the pen-and-pencil-in-a-cup icon next to it), it could be what's causing a problem. Click either None (for no background) or a bitmap picture, and click OK.

5. If everything continues to function properly after you've been running your programs for a while, you can return to the Web and the Background tabs to reactivate a web component or to use a different type of picture or document as your background. You should do this one item at a time, though, and run your programs for a while to make sure once again that the component you just activated isn't the source of another problem.

More about breaking the Active Desktop

Windows is concerned about your system when all sorts of web pages and web elements are running on your Desktop. Although most problems you'll encounter are the result of bad programming or programming designed for an earlier operating system, there is a real and constant threat of evil hackers devising new ways to undo your system. You can prevent some problems by increasing the security settings for your Internet connection. For information about changing your security settings, see "It takes so long to download web pages" on page 106. Some words of warning: if you have an Administrators account, don't stay logged on to your computer using that account. If some Active Desktop item tries to do something cataclysmic to your computer, far less damage will occur if the permission you have as a User or Power User doesn't allow system changes.

Connecting to your network from a remote location should be a simple matter, but dialing in can often be a headache because of incorrect settings, an improperly configured computer, or that all-too-familiar nemesis, problems with network security policies. And if you have trouble connecting to an Internet service provider, you might need to install an updated version of its software that's compatible with Windows 2000.

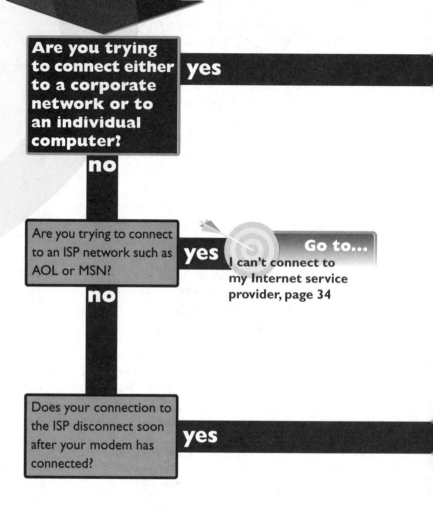

Are you trying to connect either to a corporate network or to an individual computer?

yes

no

Are you trying to connect to an ISP network such as AOL or MSN?

yes

Go to...
I can't connect to my Internet service provider, page 34

no

Does your connection to the ISP disconnect soon after your modem has connected?

yes

If your solution isn't here
Check these related chapters:
    Access to the computer, page 2
    Logging on, page 136
    Modems, page 146
    Starting up, page 260
Or see the general troubleshooting tips on page xiii

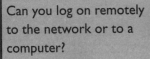

Can you log on remotely to the network or to a computer? **yes**

Are you unable to access network computers after you've logged on? **yes**

Quick fix

You could be experiencing one of two access problems: either your dial-up connection is set for limited access, or the network is failing to provide your computer with the names of all the computers and shared files.

no

no

Go to...

I can't log on remotely, page 30

Can you connect to the network automatically?

no

Go to...

I can't set up an automatic remote connection, page 32

1. Contact the network administrator to make sure your access by dialing up isn't restricted.

2. Use the Address tool-bar to go to a specific computer. If the toolbar isn't displayed, click a blank spot on the taskbar, point to Toolbars on the shortcut menu, and click Address on the submenu.

3. In the box on the Address toolbar, type the name of the computer you're trying to access in the form **\\computer**, where *computer* is the name of that computer. In the window that appears, double-click the folder you want to access.

Quick fix

Either the network protocol or the logon method you're using isn't compatible with that required by the ISP.

1. Right-click My Network Places, and click Properties on the shortcut menu. In the Network And Dial-Up Connections window, right-click the dial-up connection, and click Properties on the shortcut menu. On the Security tab, note the details under Security Options.

2. On the Networking tab, note the type of server and the network protocols that are listed and selected. Click Cancel.

3. Contact your ISP for details about the type of server and the network protocols that are required to connect.

4. If necessary, return to the connection's Properties dialog box and change the options and/or server type, or add protocols. You'll need to be logged on as an Administrator to make these changes.

I can't log on remotely

Source of the problem

Connecting and logging on to a network from a remote location can be a difficult task until you get all the kinks worked out. After you've fixed all the problems and made all the correct settings, logging on from a remote location can be just as easy—although not as fast—as logging on from your office computer. But working out the kinks can be a major chore, especially if you don't know whether the problems arise from the settings on your own computer or the settings on the host computer. With a little exploration and experimentation, as well as a few judicious queries to whoever is running the network, it shouldn't be too long before you can easily log on from a remote location.

How to fix it

1. To avoid the most prevalent problem with remote network connections—that is, the inability to get your computer properly configured for the network—connect directly to the network, if possible, by using a docking station or by using a network card. If necessary, log on to your computer as the Administrator, and, on the Settings submenu of the Start menu, click Control Panel. In the Control Panel, double-click the System icon. On the Network Identification tab of the System Properties dialog box, click the Network ID button. Use the Network Identification Wizard to get the computer up and running on the network. Once you've successfully used the computer on the network, you've solved many of the problems that you're likely to encounter when you first try to use a remote connection. If you can't connect directly, you'll need to go though this process after you connect by dialing in.

> **Tip**
>
> Remote connections are very scary to network administrators, who usually apply some fairly substantial security policies to the connection. Different types of networks also have different connection procedures. Before you try to connect, get detailed information about the required process for remote connection. The procedures detailed here assume that you're connecting to a Windows 2000 Server with no additional security policies in place.

2. Before you attempt to connect remotely, gather all the information you'll need for the connection. If you've been able to connect to the network, verify that your call-in user name, password, and domain are the same as the ones you used to connect directly to the network. If you haven't yet set up your computer on the network, you'll need to know the user name, password, and domain that have been assigned to you, and possibly the computer name, computer domain, and the user name and password of a person who is authorized to add your computer to the network. Check with the network administrator if you'll need that information. Regardless of how your computer is set up, you'll need the phone number you'll use to connect to the network.

3. To connect to the network, you must create a dial-up connection. To do so, right-click My Network Places, and click Properties on the shortcut menu. In the Network And Dial-Up Connections window, double-click the Make New Connection icon. Click Next to step into the Network Connection Wizard. On the Network Connection Type page of the wizard, click Dial-Up To Private Network, and click Next. Complete the wizard, supplying a name for the connection and the phone number you'll use to connect to the network.

4. If you haven't yet connected your computer to the network, in the Connect dialog box, enter the user name and password assigned to you, and click Dial. You'll probably be prompted for more information to complete the connection. When you're connected, use the Network Identification Wizard to join the network. You'll need to reboot the computer to complete the process. When you log on again, log on as a member of the domain. If you have any problems completing the wizard, check with the network administrator to verify that an account for you and your computer has been established.

5. If the Connect dialog box is not still open, in the Network And Dial-Up Connections window, right-click the connection, and click Properties on the shortcut menu. If the Connect dialog box is still open, click the Properties button. Either way, you'll get to the same place. On the Security tab, click Require Secure Password in the Validate My Identity As Follows list. Select the check box to use your logon name and password. On the Options tab, clear the Prompt For Phone Number check box, and click OK. Double-click the connection icon, and wait to be connected.

6. If, when you try to connect, you receive a message telling you that you're denied access, check with the network administrator to verify that your account has been set up to allow a dial-up connection. Many accounts don't permit this type of connection.

7. When you've finished, log off from the computer. If you simply disconnect, the network will list you as still being logged on, which could cause problems when you try to log on later.

8. You have now verified that you can connect to the network. However, unless you log on to the network when you log on to your computer, some network and/or group policies might not implemented. To prevent this problem, when you want to log on to the network, log off if you're working on the computer without the network connection. When you log on to your computer, in the Log On To Windows dialog box, select the Log On Using Dial-Up Connection check box. If you don't see this check box, click the Options button in the dialog box. Click OK, click the dial-up connection to use in the list of connections, and click Dial. You are now logging on to the network as if your computer were physically connected to the network.

Tip

Not all remote connections will work with a secure connection. Other connections require one user name and password to log on to the remote server, and a second user name and password to log on to the network. If you can't connect using the secure password, change the selection to Allow Unsecured Password, and, in the Connect dialog box, enter the user name and password you were assigned to connect to the server.

I can't set up an automatic remote connection

Source of the problem

If you always use a remote connection to connect to your network, you've probably often thought about how convenient it would be if Windows 2000 connected you to the network automatically whenever you logged on to your computer. Well, as you've no doubt discovered, Windows doesn't do that. However, if you're willing to use a little creativity, along with one of the many tools that Windows hides from public scrutiny, you can set up just such a connection. After you've set up the connection, the only thing you'll be bothered by is a Command Prompt window that pops up to display the connection process—a small price to pay for the time and the hassles you'll be saving.

How to fix it

1. To automate the process, you need to establish a connection to your network. If you don't already have one, right-click My Network Places, and click Properties on the shortcut menu. In the Network And Dial-Up Connections window, double-click the Make New Connection icon, and use the wizard to create your connection. After you've created the connection, use it to log on to your network to verify that you're able to connect properly. Log off when you've finished. If you have any problems logging on to the network, see "I can't log on remotely" on page 30. Don't try to automate the process until you've solved any problems that occur when you try to connect to the network manually.

2. Now it's time for some creativity. Right-click a blank spot on the Desktop. On the shortcut menu, point to New, and click Shortcut on the submenu.

3. In the Create Shortcut Wizard, in the Type The Location Of The Item box, type **rasdial.exe** *connection*, where *connection* is the name of the connection you've created to connect to your network. ▶ For example, if your connection is called "Work," you'll type **rasdial.exe work** in

the box. Click Next, type a name for the shortcut, and click Finish to complete the wizard.

4. After you've created the shortcut, you'll want to test it. If you're currently connected to the network, log off, and log on to your computer again without establishing a connection to the network. Double-click the shortcut on your Desktop. A Command Prompt window appears, displaying the progress of the connection. After you're connected, explore the network to make sure that you're connected correctly. Log off when you've finished.

5. Although this process provides a little more automation, it still doesn't connect you to your network automatically. To do this, you have to get the shortcut to run when you start Windows. To do so, drag the connection onto the Start button. While you're still holding down the mouse button, wait for the Start menu to open. Continue holding down the mouse button as you drag the shortcut up the Start menu to the Programs item. Wait for the Programs submenu to appear, and, still holding down the mouse button, drag the shortcut onto the Startup menu item. Wait for the Startup submenu to appear, drag the shortcut onto that submenu, and then release the mouse button. ▶

6. Now to test the setup. Log off, and then log on to your computer again. After you've completed logging on (make sure the Log On Using Dial-Up Connection check box isn't selected), your computer should now dial up the network and connect you. Watch the Command Prompt window for the progress of the connection. If you need to terminate the call before the connection is made, close the Command Prompt window.

7. If you need to use the connection after you've logged on to the computer but terminated the connection to the network, either click the shortcut on the Startup submenu of the Start menu, or double-click the connection in the Network And Dial-Up Connections window.

Tip

If your computer isn't set up as a member of a domain, you can set the computer to start up without requiring you to enter your password. For information about this feature, see "I'm not required to use a password to log on" on page 140. Be cautious about doing this, however, as it violates several security principles that network administrators like to enforce.

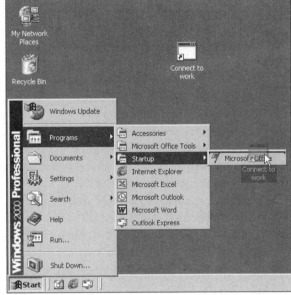

I can't connect to
my Internet
service provider

Source of the problem

There are two main types of Internet service providers (ISPs): those that simply give you access to the Internet, and those that supply you with extensive content in addition to providing Internet access. The latter type of ISP requires you to use its software to view all or part of the content it provides. Unfortunately, because the ISP's software must work very closely with its operating system, most of its software will work only on specific operating systems. To use this type of ISP's program, you'll need to install an updated version of its software that is compatible with Windows 2000. Otherwise, you can use a workaround to access the Internet and possibly some of the ISP's content.

How to fix it

1. The most serious problems are likely to occur after you've upgraded your computer from an earlier version of Windows to Windows 2000. In that case, an incompatible version of the ISP's software might be present on your computer. (If you try to install the software with Windows 2000 already installed, Windows will probably prevent you from installing an incompatible version.) If you use the ISP's software, you could have failures such as repetitive dialing, immediate hang ups, or even a system lockup. If you have a problem with the software, use the Add/Remove Programs Wizard in the Control Panel to remove the software. If you can't remove it, see whether there's an uninstall program for it listed on the program's submenu on the Start menu.

2. Go to *http://www.microsoft.com/windows2000/compatible/isp.asp* to see whether your service provider has an updated version of its software, or contact your service provider directly for updated information if you find nothing in the list or if you're currently without Internet access. For example, AOL (America Online) has issued an update (version 5) that is compatible with Windows 2000. Install the new software, and you should be able to connect to the service provider.

Tip

If you really want access to an ISP whose software is incompatible with Windows 2000, you can set up your computer as a dual-boot computer and use Windows 95/98/Me to access the ISP's services. For information about using a dual-boot setup, see "Dual boot," starting on page 46.

Tip

Make sure your connection problem is caused by the software. Verify that your modem is working properly (see "Modems," starting on page 146) and that you have the correct phone numbers and logon name and password set up for your service.

3. If there is no compatible software to use with Windows 2000, check with your service provider for a possible workaround for a direct connection to the Internet. If you have an MSN (Microsoft Network) account that you used on a different computer or that you used before you upgraded to Windows 2000, you can set up a connection that will give you Internet access. Then you'll be able to use many, but not all, of MSN's features, and you'll also be able to use Outlook Express to send and retrieve your MSN e-mail. To set up a connection to MSN, right-click My Network Places on the Desktop, and click Properties on the shortcut menu. In the Network And Dial-Up Connections window, double-click the Make New Connection icon.

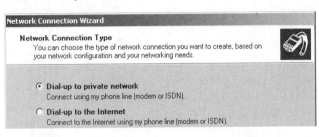

Click Next to step into the Network Connection Wizard. In the Network Connection Type ▲ page of the wizard, click Dial-Up To Private Network, and then click Next.

4. On the Phone Number To Dial page of the wizard, enter the local access number you used to connect to MSN. If you need to use an area code or any special dialing rules, select the Use Dialing Rules check box, and set up the special dialing instructions. Click Next. Complete the wizard, specifying a name for the connection and whether it is to be available only when you log on, or available to all users of the computer.

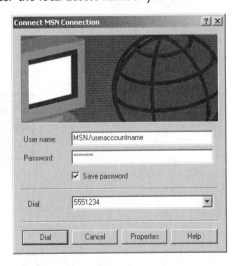

5. In the Connect dialog box for the connection, type **MSN/*username***, where *username* is your MSN account name. Enter your password, and select the Save Password check box. If you selected the Use Dialing Rules check box in the wizard, click the location you're dialing from. (The dialing options appear only if you selected the check box.) ▶

6. Click Dial. Wait for the connection to be completed, and for your user name and password to be verified. Once you're connected, use Internet Explorer to explorer the Internet, or use other tools to make connections over the Internet. Set up and use your e-mail account in Outlook Express just as you did when you used your MSN account on a different computer system. ▶

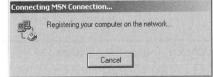

7. When you've finished, click the Dial-Up Connection icon on the taskbar, or double-click the connection icon in the Network And Dial-Up Connections window, and click the Disconnect button to hang up.

You're well aware of how frustrating it can be when Windows won't let you open a file or folder, when you're told that your disk is full, or when you're denied permission to do something as simple as format or label certain removable disks—especially when a cryptic error message doesn't give you much of a clue as to what's going on. You'll find some solutions here. And if your search for a file seems to take forever, you can speed things up with the Indexing Service.

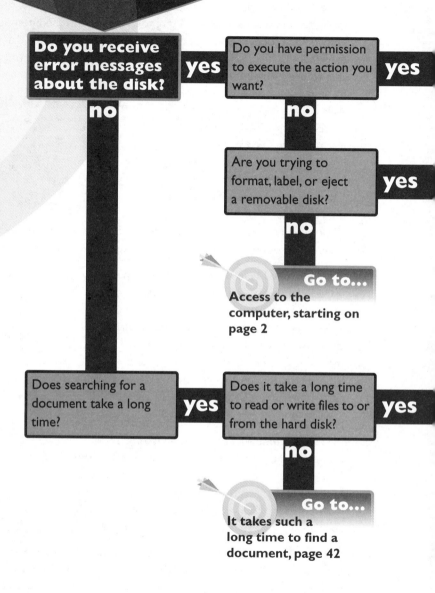

Do you receive error messages about the disk? **yes** → Do you have permission to execute the action you want? **yes**

no

Do you have permission to execute the action you want?
no

Are you trying to format, label, or eject a removable disk? **yes**

no

Go to...
Access to the computer, starting on page 2

Does searching for a document take a long time? **yes** → Does it take a long time to read or write files to or from the hard disk? **yes**

no

Go to...
It takes such a long time to find a document, page 42

If your solution isn't here
Check these related chapters:
Encryption, page 52
Appendix C, page 299
Or see the general troubleshooting tips on page xiii

Disk storage

Are you told that the disk is full or that there isn't enough available disk space?

yes → Go to...
The disk is full, page 38

no

Go to...
I'm denied permission when I'm working on a removable disk, page 44

Are you told that files or folders are corrupted or unreadable?

yes → Go to...
I can't open a file or folder, page 40

Quick fix

After you've added and deleted files over a period of time, they get broken up into small pieces and stored all over the hard disk. By having Windows defragment the files (rearrange them and reassemble the pieces into long, continuous sections), you'll find that your computer can read and write files to the hard disk much faster than before.

1. On the Start menu, point your way through Programs, Accessories, and System Tools, and click Disk Defragmenter on the submenu.

2. Click the drive to be defragmented, if there's more than one.

3. Click Defragment.

4. Go have something to drink—this might take a while!

The disk is full

Source of the problem

As the storage capacity of disks has grown, so have the sizes of programs and the amount of disk space they gobble up. Not only do you need space to store the programs and the documents you've created—you also need room for all the temporary files the programs use, for the web pages you've saved, for the network files stored on your computer for offline use, and for all those huge music and picture files you've downloaded. As if that weren't bad enough, in addition to the enormous amount of disk space the Windows 2000 operating system occupies, it also uses substantial disk space for its own temporary files and to provide extra memory (known as virtual memory) when it's needed. If your computer doesn't have a lot of extra space, you're likely to run into some serious problems, from your system slowing down to operations being canceled or programs stopping. You might even get an error message when you use Help for the first time if your system doesn't have enough room to create the Help index.

How to fix it

1. Double-click My Computer on the Desktop.

2. Right-click the disk that's full or nearly full, and then click Properties on the shortcut menu.

3. On the General tab, note the amount of free space. How much free space you need depends on the program you're using. A program often needs two or three times more disk space for temporary files than it needs to store the final document. You might also need extra free space for other temporary files created by the program.

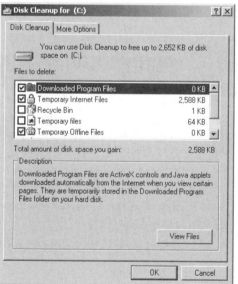

4. Click the Disk Cleanup button. Wait for ▶ Windows to read the disk and determine how much space you can save by removing different types of files.

5. Select check boxes for the types of files you want to remove, and clear check boxes for items you want to keep. If the disk is NTFS-formatted, you have the option of compressing files you haven't used recently. To determine what types of files will be deleted in each category, click the item and read its description. If you're still uncertain about deleting files, click the View Files button (available only for some types of files), and review the list of files to be deleted.

6. Click OK, and then click Yes when prompted to confirm your decision. Wait while the files are deleted.

7. Click OK to Close the disk's Properties dialog box.

8. Right-click the disk in My Computer, and click Properties on the shortcut menu. Note the updated information about free space. Click OK if you now have enough free space on the disk. If the disk is still too full, click the Disk Cleanup button.

9. Select any additional files that you can delete.

10. Click the More Options tab. If you want to remove some optional Windows components or programs that you don't use, click the appropriate Clean Up button. Step through the wizard to remove the items. ▶

11. Click OK to close the Properties dialog box.

12. Click the disk in My Computer, and note how much free space is available. If it's still not enough, double-click the disk and browse through it, moving files to network drives, tape backups, or removable disks. Delete any files you're certain you don't need (but don't delete any program files—use the Add/Remove Programs Wizard to do that).

13. If you still don't have enough room, consider using the Windows compression feature to compress additional folders on an NTFS-formatted disk, buying a file-compression program (such as a ZIP program) to compress large files, or adding a second disk drive or large-capacity removable disk drive to your computer.

Tip
The Properties dialog box for the disk shows the disk's formatting, which will be either FAT, FAT32, or NTFS. An NTFS-formatted disk provides the most options for disk management and security; disks formatted as FAT or FAT32 allow more interoperability with other operating systems.

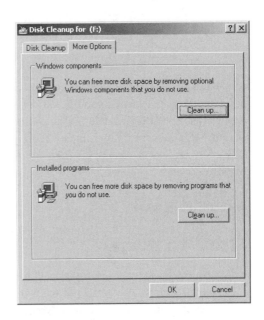

More about temporary Internet files and evil web designers

If you delete those temporary Internet files, your next visit to the web might be a bit slower because some of the files that had been stored on your computer—small graphics files that serve as buttons or other design features, for example—might need to be downloaded. This is a small price to pay, however, because you'll probably never need the majority of the deleted files.

Temporary Internet files are supposed to expire after a set period of time and then be deleted so that—theoretically, anyway—you don't accumulate a massive number of these files. However, some evil web designers have designed their temporary files never to expire, and therefore the temporary files from these sites will come back to haunt you forever, regardless of how long it's been since you visited that site.

I can't open a file
or folder

Source of the problem

Although storing information on a disk seems like a simple thing to do, it's actually a fairly complex process. Windows 2000 needs to know where there's adequate empty space to put the file, and, after it sends the file there, it has to record where the beginning of the file is stored. To do this, Windows uses something like an address book. We've all used address books, so how hard can it be? Well, now we're getting into the tricky stuff. Windows stores files in little blocks on the hard disk and, quite often, many of the separate blocks used to store a single file aren't adjacent to each other. To find all these pieces and put the file back together again when you open it, Windows records the addresses of these blocks. Over time, however, as you add and delete files, some of these blocks get out of whack and either can't be found (Windows has the wrong address) or can't be read (a physical failure of that part of the hard disk). Suddenly everything gets more complicated, and you get an error message telling you that you can't open a file or folder. Now it's time to put on your virtual toolbelt, load it up with the appropriate tools, try to fix the problem and recover what you can, and make sure the same error doesn't happen again.

How to fix it

1. Use the Backup tool to make a full backup of the disk you're going to repair. Be careful not to overwrite your previous backup (you *do* have one, don't you?). If there are corrupted files in this most recent backup, you might need to resort to that previous backup.

2. Log on to the computer as a member of the Administrators group.

Tip

You can start the Backup tool by clicking the Backup Now button on the Tools tab of the disk's Properties dialog box. If your network uses different backup tools, check with your network administrator about which tool to use.

3. Close all the files on the disk you're going to check. Open files can cause incorrect error messages and will prevent you from fixing any problems. If the disk is used by others over the network, make sure that no one is connected and that no one will need anything from the disk for a while—the disk will not be accessible while the test is being run, and the test can take a very long time, depending on the size of the disk and the number of files on it.

4. Double-click My Computer on the Desktop.

5. Right-click the disk that has the problems, and click Properties on the shortcut menu.

6. On the Tools tab of the Properties dialog box, click Check Now.

7. Under Check Disk Options, select the appropriate check box, and then click the Start button: ▶

- Automatically Fix File System Errors to search for and recover any files whose pieces have been broken off and lost

- Scan For And Attempt Recovery Of Bad Sectors to perform a much more rigorous (and time-consuming) test that will also examine the disk surface for bad sectors and try to recover lost files

8. If this is the disk your operating system is on, or if the disk is being used, you'll see a message telling you that the program can't be run now and asking you whether you want to run it the next time you start the computer. Click Yes, and then restart the computer.

9. At some point you might receive a cryptic message telling you that there were some lost allocation units in some chains. This means that some unidentified parts of files have been found. Click Yes to save these files.

10. After the program has finished, double-click the disk in My Computer. Look for files that are in the form *filennn.chk* (they should be in the root directory of the drive you checked). Right-click one of these files, click Open With on the shortcut menu, and open the file in Notepad. Examine the contents to see if there's anything that you can or want to recover. Check each of the *.chk* files that you found. You won't normally find much that you can use.

11. If the corrupted file was of vital importance and you can't recover it from the *filennn.chk* files, take the *.chk* files to a recovery expert, or simply restore the file from one of your most recent backups. Aren't you glad you routinely back up your files?

More about recovering corrupted files

Some third-party tools are available that are highly successful in recovering corrupted files. These tools, however, can be difficult to use and are usually powerful enough that they can cause serious damage to your files and to your system. If critical files are corrupted and you haven't backed up the original files, contact a service person. The recovery can take some time, can cost quite a bit, and might not be successful, depending on the cause of the problem.

Because running the Check Disk program could decrease your chance of recovering the files using other methods, you might need to make available to the service person the backup file that you created in step 1.

If you're having problems with a disk that's formatted as FAT32 and the Check Disk program doesn't work correctly, you'll need to seek help for the repairs. The Check Disk program is unable to run on a FAT32 disk if there are certain errors on the disk.

It takes such a long time to find a document

Source of the problem

When you can't find a document, you can always have the computer search for it. But because today's hard disks are so large, a search of this type can take a long time. And you need to know the name of the file (or at least part of it) and/or the approximate date you saved it. If you're desperate to find a document whose file name you don't remember—and if you have substantial time—you can try searching for the file based on some specific text that you know it contains, but this means that Windows will have to examine the contents of every file. There *is* a better—and faster—way!

Windows 2000 provides a powerful tool called the Indexing Service. You can index all the documents on your computer and then use the index to speed up your searches. You can also search for documents based on their properties—the author, the title, the subject, or even the text contained in the document. Of course, the index can do this only for documents whose properties have been completed and that are in a format the index can read. If your documents were created in Microsoft Office programs, for example, or are in HTML format, you'll find the index to be an almost miraculous tool for locating those missing documents.

How to fix it

1. Check to see whether the Indexing Service is installed by double-clicking the Add/Remove Programs icon in the Control Panel, and then clicking the Add/Remove Windows Components item. If the Indexing Service isn't installed, install it now, and then close the Add/Remove Programs window. You'll need to be logged on as a member of the Administrators or Power Users group to do this.

2. On the Start menu, point to Search, and click For Files Or Folders on the submenu. In the Search area, click Search Options to expand the list of options. If the Indexing Service is disabled, click Indexing Service.

3. Click the option to enable the Indexing Service, and then click OK. ▶

Indexing Service Settings

When Indexing Service is enabled, the files on your computer are indexed and maintained so you can perform faster searches. Indexing Service also provides greater search capabilities. For more information, click Help.

Status: Indexing Service has finished building an index of all the files on your local hard disks and is monitoring changes.

Do you want to enable Indexing Service?
- ⦿ Yes, enable Indexing Service and run when my computer is idle.
- ◯ No, do not enable Indexing Service

OK | Cancel | Advanced | Help

4. Now Windows will start building your index. You can keep working on the computer, and Windows will continue creating the index whenever the computer is idle (except, of course when it's in Standby or Hibernate mode, or is shut down). The text next to the Indexing Service item in the Search area tells you the status of the index. Creating the index can take a long time, especially if you're using your computer while the index is being built. Once the index is completed, it will be updated as you add, delete, or change files.

5. Use the Search area to search for documents. Note that even when you use specific terms and search an entire disk or several disks, the search is very fast. To search for a property of a document, type the property value in the Containing Text box. For example, to search for all documents that contain the name *Jerry Joyce* in any of the property fields (as well as anywhere in the document text), type **Jerry Joyce** in the Containing Text box, and click Search Now. To specify a property, type it in the form **@Doc*property*=*value***, where *property* is the name of the property and *value* is the text or other value

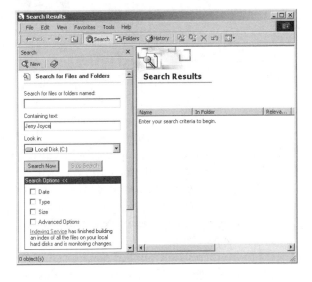

you want to find. For example, to find all documents that contain the Company property *Moon Joyce Resources*, type **@doccompany=Moon Joyce Resources**, and click Search Now.

More about the Indexing Service

If you want to conduct more advanced searches of the index, or if you'd like to see a list of files that have been indexed but that haven't had their contents or properties indexed, click the Advanced button on the Indexing Service Settings dialog box, and, in the Indexing Service window, click Query The Catalog.

The procedure we've described in this section is the basic way to set up the Indexing Service. However, the index can be managed to provide easier and more powerful searching and to allow greater control of the way items are indexed. For example, a network administrator can use the tools in the Windows Software Developer's Kit to create customized index forms and methods, to set which folders and which properties are indexed, and to create different index directories to manage the index. Don't be surprised if your organization provides easier ways to search the index than those we've described here.

Tip

To read more about the document properties you can search for, or to read about using logical statements to improve your search text, click the Indexing Service item in the Search area, and then click the Help button in the Indexing Service Settings dialog box.

I'm denied permission when I'm working on a removable disk

Source of the problem

Some people have extremely peculiar ideas about what other people should be allowed to do. Windows 2000 is set up to allow only those people who belong to the Administrators group to format, label, or eject certain removable disks. (These are the larger disks, such as ZIP disks, not the little floppy disks you use in drive A.) This doesn't make a whole lot of sense, because it's considered a bad security practice to stay logged on as an Administrator. But here comes the really tricky part: some of the actions you take can trigger an error message that doesn't even give you a clue that the problem is caused because you don't have the proper permission! So if you're trying to eject a disk, for example, and you get a cryptic message telling you that Windows "cannot unmount drive," it's time for you to try to fix the problem.

Some progressively minded network administrators have probably already changed the policy that defines access, but if you're faced with this annoying situation, here's what you can do.

How to fix it

1. Verify the problem by placing a disk in your removable drive, double-clicking My Computer on the Desktop, right-clicking the removable drive, and clicking Eject on the shortcut menu. If you get the "Cannot Unmount Drive" error message, you need to change your permission.

2. If you're on a corporate network that uses system policies, contact the network administrator and ask him or her to change your permission to eject removable media. If the administrator doesn't seem to know what you're talking about (or tells you that this is only for NTFS media and that you don't use those media), give him or her a copy of this book!

3. If you need to make these changes on your individual computer, you'll have to edit the local system policy. This isn't as daunting as it sounds. You must have local Administrator permission to make these changes, though, so the first thing to do is log off and then log on again as the local Administrator for this computer.

4. On the Settings submenu of the Start menu, click Control Panel. In the Control Panel, double-click the Administrative Tools icon, and, in the Administrative Tools folder, double-click the Local Security Policy icon. Now you get to play real administrator. The window you just opened is called the Microsoft Management Console, or MMC.

5. Click the plus sign next to Local Policies, and then click the Security Options item. ▶

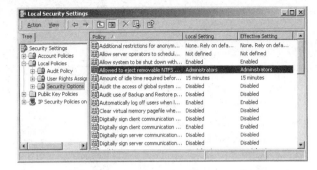

6. In the right part of the window, double-click the Allowed To Eject Removable NTFS Media option. Note that although this option seems to be for NTFS media only and to apply only to removing the media, it really applies to FAT- and FAT32-formatted disks, as well as to NTFS-formatted disks. This item also controls the ability to format and label the disks, as well as to eject them.

7. In the Local Security Policy Setting dialog box, open the list for Local Policy Setting, and specify which groups you want to have permission to eject, format, and label removable disks. Don't forget to include the group that you're a member of, so all this work isn't for nothing. (The confusing term "Interactive Users" is just another name for standard users.) Click OK. ▶

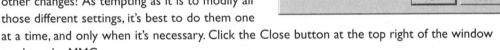

8. Now comes the hardest part: don't make any other changes! As tempting as it is to modify all those different settings, it's best to do them one at a time, and only when it's necessary. Click the Close button at the top right of the window to close the MMC.

9. On the Start menu, click Shut Down, click Log Off, and click OK. Log on using your user name.

10. Open My Computer if it's not already open, right-click the removable drive, and click Eject on the shortcut menu.

More about those security policies

Security policies are powerful tools that customize who can do what. There are two levels of policies: the local policy that is set directly on the computer, and the system-wide policy that is set by those who control the network. The system-wide policy can override the local settings, so if you make changes but the settings revert to the old ones, you know whom to blame (or bribe).

If one operating system isn't enough for you, you can set up your computer as a dual-boot system, and you can then start the computer using whichever operating system you need. However, if you want to keep an earlier version of Windows on your computer in addition to Windows 2000, your computer must be able to support dual booting—that is, it must have at least two hard disks or a large-capacity hard disk that's separated into at least two partitions.

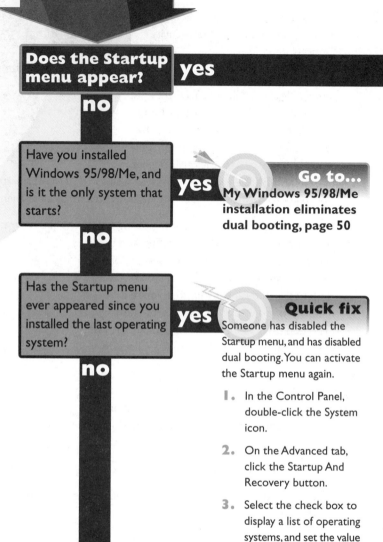

Does the Startup menu appear?

yes

no

Have you installed Windows 95/98/Me, and is it the only system that starts?

yes

Go to...
My Windows 95/98/Me installation eliminates dual booting, page 50

no

Has the Startup menu ever appeared since you installed the last operating system?

yes

Quick fix
Someone has disabled the Startup menu, and has disabled dual booting. You can activate the Startup menu again.

1. In the Control Panel, double-click the System icon.

2. On the Advanced tab, click the Startup And Recovery button.

3. Select the check box to display a list of operating systems, and set the value to 30 seconds. Click OK, and then click OK again.

no

Quick fix
The operating system was either improperly installed, or some files have become corrupted.

1. Back up all the data on the hard disk.

2. Use the operating system's disks to reinstall the operating system, making sure it's installed on a separate disk or partition.

3. Restore the dual-boot setup if necessary.

Dual boot

Did you receive an error message when you tried to start Windows 95/98/Me?

yes → **Go to...**
An operating system won't start, page 48

no

Are you unable to access a disk drive in Windows 95/98/Me that you can access in Windows 2000?

yes → **Quick fix**

The inaccessible drive either is formatted as NTFS and is readable only when you're using Windows 2000, or is on a logical drive created in Windows 2000 that isn't defined in the other system.

1. Start Windows 2000.

2. Move the files you need onto a drive that's accessible by the Windows 95/98/Me operating system.

3. Shut down Windows and restart it using your Windows 95/98/Me operating system.

no

Does the wrong operating system start if you don't specify one on the Startup menu?

yes → **Quick fix**

The wrong system is set as the default operating system.

1. In the Control Panel, double-click the System icon.

2. On the Advanced tab, click the Startup And Recovery button.

3. In the Default Operating System list, click the operating system you want to start. Click OK, and then click OK again.

no

If your solution isn't here

Check these related chapters:

Hardware installation, page 96

Multiple monitors, page 168

Screen, page 230

Starting up, page 260

Or see the general troubleshooting tips on page xiii

An operating system won't start

Source of the problem

When you install Microsoft Windows 2000 Professional on a system that already contains another operating system, several problems can occur during the setup. Some of these problems might be caused by you, others by a problem with your computer, and still others by problems with the Windows 2000 Setup program. The result is that when you start the computer, the Startup menu displays both your Windows 2000 operating system and your old operating system. When you choose the old operating system, however, you get an error message and find that you can only start the computer using Windows 2000. Your solution to this is either to set your system to ignore the other operating system and skip the Startup menu, or to make some serious modifications to system files and to delete the old operating system from the Startup menu. You'll probably want to do the latter to recover all that wasted disk space, or if you're planning to install another operating system to create a multiple-boot system.

How to fix it

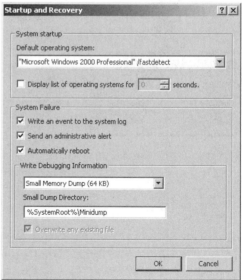

1. The simplest solution is to tell Windows 2000 not to display the Startup menu. To do so, on the Settings submenu of the Start menu, click Control Panel. In the Control Panel, double-click the System icon. On the Advanced tab of the System Properties dialog box, click the Startup And Recovery button.

2. In the Startup And Recovery dialog box, click Microsoft Windows 2000 Professional in the Default Operating System list if it isn't already selected.

3. Clear the Display List Of Operating Systems For [ ] Seconds check box, and click OK. ▶ The next time you start the computer, the Startup menu won't appear and Windows 2000 will start automatically.

4. If you want to fix the problem instead of simply hiding it, you can edit the file that provides the information to the Startup menu. You need to do this carefully, however; editing a system file can be a dangerous process. Windows, with its strong will for self-preservation, fears change and

makes it difficult to modify system files—perhaps justifiably worried that someone will unwittingly turn the entire system into useless junk. To get around these barriers, you need to make the system files available. To do so, open My Computer if it isn't already open, and, on the Tools menu, click Folder Options. On the View tab of the Folder Options dialog box, make the following changes, and then click OK. ▶

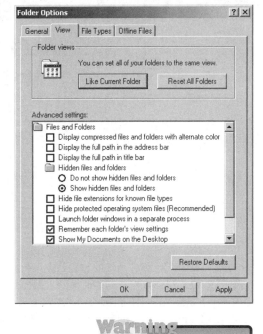

- Under Hidden Files And Folders, click Show Hidden Files And Folders.

- Clear the Hide File Extensions For Known File Types check box.

- Clear the Hide Protected Operating System Files check box. When you're presented with a warning, click Yes to confirm that this is what you want to do.

5. In the My Computer window, double-click the main boot drive (usually drive C). In the window, right-click the *boot.ini* file, and click Copy on the shortcut menu. Right-click a blank spot in the folder, and click Paste on the shortcut menu. You now have a copy of the file in case something goes wrong.

6. Right-click the *boot.ini* file again, and click Open With. In the Open With dialog box, click Notepad, and then click OK.

7. In Notepad, click the entry referencing the file system you want to delete from the Startup menu, and press Delete. On the File menu, click Save, and then close Notepad. ▶

8. In My Computer, on the Tools menu, click Folder Options. On the View tab, change your settings back to

Warning

Modifying system files can cause cataclysmic problems that can't easily be remedied. Don't be tempted to make other changes in the *boot.ini* file, and don't make changes to any other system file you can see. Always keep system files hidden so that you don't accidentally modify or delete a vital file.

rehide hidden files and folders, file extensions, and system files, and then click OK to close the Folder Options dialog box. The next time you start the computer, either the Startup menu won't appear if you have only one operating system installed, or, if you do have other operating systems installed, the one item you deleted won't appear on the Startup menu.

My Windows 95/98/Me installation eliminates dual booting

Source of the problem

If Windows 2000 Professional is installed on your computer, and you then install Windows 95, Windows 98, or Windows Me (Millennium Edition), or if you upgrade your existing Windows 95/98/Me operating system to a newer version, you might not have a system that can boot both Windows 95/98/Me and Windows 2000 Professional. This usually happens when you do a clean installation of the new operating system—that is, when you delete the old system and install a new copy of the new operating system. This procedure modifies the contents of the main boot disk (usually drive C), and, in the process, deletes some of the files Windows 2000 needs to control the dual booting. To fix the problem, you need to restore those deleted boot files.

How to fix it

1. Before you go any further, check to make sure your system is set up to support dual booting and the recovery of the Windows 2000 system.

   - To support both Windows 95/98/Me and Windows 2000, your computer must have at least two separate hard disks or a hard disk that's separated into at least two partitions.

   - Each operating system must be installed on a different hard disk or partition. Installing both systems on a single hard disk or partition can cause the system to become unstable and possibly unusable.

   - The hard disks or partitions must be formatted as FAT or FAT32. To check the formatting, in My Computer, right-click the disk, and click Properties on the shortcut menu. On the General tab, the disk's formatting is shown in the File System item.

   - Make sure you have an up-to-date Emergency Repair Disk for Windows 2000.

2. After you verify all of the above, you're ready to restore the Windows 2000 system. To do so, start your computer with the Windows 2000 Professional CD or with the Windows 2000

> **Tip**
>
> A partition is a part of a hard disk that's turned into a separate section and that has its own drive letter. To create partitions on a hard disk using the Windows tools, you'll end up deleting the contents of the disk, including any operating system that's installed on that disk. Some third-party tools, such as PartitionMagic, allow you to create partitions without losing the contents of the hard disk.

Professional Setup disks. When Windows 2000 starts the setup process, in the "Welcome To Setup" section, press R to use the repair option. Insert the Windows 2000 Professional CD if it isn't already in your computer's CD drive, and, in the Windows 2000 Repair Options section, press R to use the emergency repair process.

3. When you're offered the choice of Automatic or Manual repair, press M to use manual repair. To eliminate an unnecessary check and shorten the length of the repair process, use the Up arrow key to select the Verify Windows 2000 System Files item, and press Enter to clear the check box for that item. This leaves both the Inspect Starting Environment and Inspect Boot Sector check boxes still selected. Use the Down arrow key to move to the Continue item, and then press Enter.

4. When you're asked whether you want to use the Emergency Repair Disk, press L to have Setup locate Windows 2000 for you. Continue through the repair process. When it's completed, the computer is rebooted, and, as it starts, you should see the Startup menu so that you can specify which system you want to start. If your system has problems after this repair, repeat the repair process, using the Emergency Repair Disk to restore your settings.

Tip

Starting your computer by using the Windows 2000 Professional CD is the easiest way to start up your system. Some older computers can't boot from the CD and must be started using the Windows 2000 Professional Setup disks, but most computers that support Windows 2000 will boot from a CD. For more information about starting your computer from the CD or from the Setup disks, and how to create the disks if you don't have them, see "I can't repair the computer because I can't start it" on page 264.

More about dual booting and partitions

Competition isn't always good. For an operating system, competition can come from another operating system that wants to use its own files to run the show. This type of competition can be so confusing to an operating system that it sometimes just gives up and quits. To avoid the problem, just as you separate competing and quarreling children by placing them in separate rooms, you need to separate the quarreling operating systems by placing each one on a separate partition or hard disk. By doing so, you prevent one system from substituting some of its files for those of another system. When you do put these operating systems on different partitions or hard disks, your computer needs to know where to start. Windows 2000 comes with a utility program, called a boot loader, that keeps track of the operating systems and where they're stored. It's this tool that can become lost or deleted when another operating system is installed.

If you've made the mistake of installing more than one operating system on a single partition or disk, you'll need to do some remedial work. Even if one of the systems is working now, you're asking for trouble at some point. The safest remedy is to use the working operating system to back up all your data; create the partitions if you need to, or format the partition that has the multiple operating systems; and reinstall the operating systems on separate partitions or hard disks. Then reinstall all your programs and settings and restore all the backed-up data. A quicker alternative is to remove one of the operating systems, and to use the repair process to fix the Windows 2000 installation. Then you can install the second system on a different partition or hard disk.

Encryption is a powerful security tool that protects your files from unauthorized access. Perhaps you thought your files were encrypted, but now you've discovered that they weren't, or that they were somehow decrypted without your knowing it. Or your files are encrypted but—despite having a "key"—you can't unscramble them. What's going on? Find the solutions, and meet the mysterious "recovery agent," in this chapter.

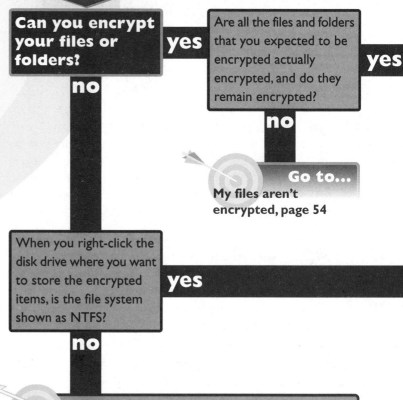

Can you encrypt your files or folders?

yes → **Are all the files and folders that you expected to be encrypted actually encrypted, and do they remain encrypted?**

no

no

Go to...
My files aren't encrypted, page 54

When you right-click the disk drive where you want to store the encrypted items, is the file system shown as NTFS?

yes

no

Quick fix
Items that you want to encrypt using the Windows encryption tools must be on an NTFS-formatted drive.

1. Store the files to be encrypted on an NTFS-formatted drive.

2. If you don't want to format the drive as NTFS, investigate other third-party programs that can encrypt files.

yes

If your solution isn't here
Check these related chapters:
  Access to the computer, page 2
  Outlook Express, page 178
Or see the general troubleshooting tips on page xiii

Encryption

Can you open or decrypt encrypted files, and can you decrypt encrypted folders?

yes

Do you need to store encrypted files or folders on non-NTFS-formatted disks or other media, or do you want to e-mail encryped files?

yes

Quick fix

Either process would decrypt your files. To preserve encryption, use the Windows Backup tool.

1. Start Windows Backup, and back up the files or folders.

2. Copy the backup file to the non-NTFS-formatted media, or send the file as an attachment in an e-mail message.

3. Use Windows Backup to restore the files from the backup file to a disk that uses the NTFS format.

no

Go to...

I can't decrypt my files or folders, page 56

Are you trying to compress and encrypt the same item?

yes

Quick fix

Windows doesn't support compressing and encrypting the same item.

1. In the Advanced Attributes dialog box, select the check box for encryption.

2. Click OK, and click OK again to close the Properties dialog box.

no

Quick fix

You might not have permission to encrypt items, or you might be trying to encrypt items that can't be encrypted.

1. Check with your network administrator to see whether you have permission to encrypt files.

2. Don't attempt to encrypt system files; they can't be encrypted. There are also certain file types that can't be encrypted. You'll just have to live with it!

My files aren't encrypted

Source of the problem

The Windows 2000 encryption feature is a powerful tool that provides great security for your files. It's fairly easy to use, provided you're diligent about following the rules. We're telling you this at the outset because, unfortunately, some of the rules are a bit difficult to remember, especially when most of the encryption activity occurs invisibly behind the scenes and you're probably not even aware of it. What usually happens is you discover that the files you thought had been encrypted either were never encrypted or were decrypted without your realizing it.

Tip

You can convert a disk drive to the NTFS format without losing the information on the drive. However, there are certain circumstances in which you will not want to have your drive formatted as NTFS. Also, once you've converted a drive to the NTFS format, you can't easily convert it back to any other format. See Windows Help for information about converting your disk drive to the NTFS format.

How to fix it

1. The ability to encrypt works only on the version of NTFS (NT File System) that comes with Windows 2000, and you can encrypt only those files that are stored on an NTFS-formatted disk drive. If you're not sure whether your disk drive is NTFS-formatted, right-click the drive in My Computer, and click Properties on the shortcut menu. The Properties dialog box shows the format of the drive on the General tab, under the File System entry. If the drive isn't shown as NTFS, any files or folders you move to that drive cannot be encrypted. Close the dialog box when you've finished. If you must encrypt files on a drive that isn't NTFS-formatted, you might be able to convert your current disk format to NTFS.

2. When you encrypt a folder, you need to make sure that the entire contents of the folder are encrypted. If you encrypt only the folder, any files and subfolders already in it won't be encrypted. Any files or folders that you subsequently add to the folder will, however, be encrypted. To encrypt the entire contents of a folder, right-click the folder, and click Properties on the shortcut menu. On the General tab of the Properties dialog box, click the Advanced button. In the Advanced Attributes dialog box, select the check box to encrypt the contents of the folder, and click OK. ▶

3. In the Properties dialog box, click OK. When the Confirm Attributes dialog box appears, click the option to apply the changes to this folder and to all the subfolders and files contained in it. Click OK, and wait while the attributes are changed for the folder and its entire contents. (This dialog box won't appear if the folder doesn't contain any files or subfolders.) When the attributes have all been changed, every file that can be encrypted has been encrypted. However, there are some files—such as Windows system files, some program files, and some files created by certain programs—that can't be encrypted. ▶

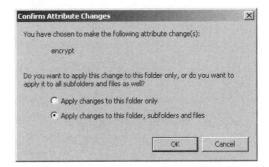

4. As you work with, move, and change files, check to make sure that each file is still encrypted. To do so, locate the file using My Computer, and click it. Provided its folder is set to display web content, the attributes of the selected file will be displayed, including information about encryption. As you work with the files, remember the basic rules about encryption:

● If you move or copy a file to a non-NTFS-formatted drive, the file will not be encrypted. This includes files that you copy to floppy disks, to other types of removable disks, and to network drives.

● If you move or copy an encrypted file to a non-encrypted folder on an NTFS drive, the file remains encrypted. If you move a file that isn't encrypted into a folder that is encrypted, the file becomes encrypted.

● If you move an encrypted file into a compressed folder, the file remains encrypted but is not compressed. If you move a compressed file into an encrypted folder, the file becomes encrypted and is no longer compressed.

Just how secure is encryption?

Encryption is a high-level security system that uses special cryptographic "keys" to scramble and unscramble the file contents. While you work on your computer, all this is invisible—files that you save in an encrypted folder become encrypted, and encrypted files are decrypted when you open them. You have a personal key that's automatically created when you encrypt something, so an unscrupulous person who logs on to your computer can't open your encrypted files (unless he or she uses your user name and password). If your computer is stolen, your encrypted files can't be accessed, even if the thief uses sophisticated tools that directly access your hard disk and bypass the security features of Windows. However, a "recovery agent" who is authorized to use a special key that can decrypt any files can gain access to your private files. There's more about recovery agents in "I can't decrypt my files or folders" on page 56. Note that encryption is designed for security on your computer only—it isn't easily transferable between computers. If you want to send secure e-mail, for example, use the encryption tools that came with the e-mail program. Don't try to send files that you encrypted on your hard disk.

I can't decrypt my files or folders

Source of the problem

The contents of encrypted files and folders are scrambled to the point of being indecipherable to anyone who doesn't have the "key" to unscramble them and put them back together again. And what, exactly, *is* a key? Well, to spare you a string of arcane technicalities, we'll call it a secret cryptographic recipe. The only way files and folders can be decrypted, and thus accessed, is with the key. If you can't access your files or folders because you can't decrypt them, you probably don't have the correct key. You must either obtain the correct key or find a "recovery agent"—someone who has a master key and can decrypt the files or folders for you.

How to fix it

1. If you try to open, move, or copy a file to a location in which it must be decrypted (a non-NTFS-formatted disk, for example), and if you receive a message telling you that you're denied permission to do so, the first thing to do is check to see whether the file really is encrypted. Use My Computer to open the folder window, if it's not already open. Even if the folder is encrypted, you should be able to see its contents. Click the file. The details about the file—its attributes—should be listed in the folder window. If you don't see the file attributes, maximize the window so there's more room to display the information. If you still don't see the file attributes, you'll need to

Despite the suggested causes of the problem, you'll see messages similar to these if you try to open or copy a file that someone else encrypted on a non–NTFS-formatted drive.

switch your view of the window so that it includes web content. For information about changing the view of the window, see "My folder windows don't display all the information I need" on page 80. If the file attributes are listed as anything but Encrypted, the file isn't encrypted.

2. If the file is encrypted, you can decrypt and open it only if you're the one who encrypted it. If you're certain this is the case, make sure you're logged on using the same user name that you used to encrypt the file. To be absolutely certain, click Shut Down on the Start menu, and look at the list of options. If your correct user name is listed in the Log Off option, click Cancel.

If another user name is listed, click Log Off, click OK, and then log on again using the correct user name.

3. If you still can't open and decrypt the file, make sure—unless you're using a roaming profile over a network—that you're working at the same computer on which you encrypted the file. The key that was used to encrypt the file—which is the key that's needed to decrypt the file—will usually be located on that computer. If you're using a roaming profile, however, you should have access to the key from any computer that you're properly logged on to.

4. If none of these suggestions helps, your key might have been damaged or deleted. Don't despair. You do have another recourse. Encrypted files can be decrypted by a person designated as a recovery agent. On a corporate network, the network administrator uses system policies to designate the recovery agents. There will probably be one or two recovery agents per organizational unit. Contact a recovery agent for instructions. In most cases, the recovery agent can decrypt the file directly from his or her computer. If you must e-mail the file to the recovery agent, use the Backup tool to back up the file, and then send the backup copy of the file via e-mail to the recovery agent.

5. On a smaller network (one without a domain server) or on a stand-alone computer, the recovery agent is a local administrator. To decrypt a file, log on as that user. You can then open, copy, or simply change the file's attributes so that it's no longer encrypted.

More about moving and storing encrypted files

When you store an encrypted file in a network folder—and the folder supports encryption—the file can be decrypted by you from your computer only, unless you're using a roaming profile.

If you need to move encrypted files to a different computer so that you can use them on that computer, you must do so carefully. The easiest and safest way is to decrypt the files before you move them, and then, when you're working on the other computer, to encrypt the files again. That way, a new encryption key is created and stored on the other computer. If you have so many files that moving them would be a real hassle, an alternative solution is to use the Backup tool to copy the files. Then you can use the Backup Restore option on the other computer to copy the files from the Backup file. When you use the Backup tool, the encryption key is also backed up. A third option is that, as an Administrator, you can export the encryption key on one computer (known as a certificate) to a file, and then import the certificate on the other computer.

Tip
So who *is* the mysterious recovery agent? If your computer is on a large network, ask the network administrator. To find out who's the local recovery agent for your computer, you'll need to log on as a user with Administrator rights. Open the Administrative Tools folder in the Control Panel, and double-click the Local Security Policy item. Expand the Public Key Policies item, and then click Encrypted Data Recovery Agents. The authorized agent is shown in the right part of the window.

Tip
Even if you can't decrypt a file, you can delete it, or you can move or copy it to another folder on an NTFS-formatted drive.

Receiving and reading a fax on your computer can be a breeze or a nightmare, depending on a bunch of different factors, including the source of the fax and its file type, problems with your phone line or modem, or not having the right permission. Do you want the Fax Service to answer a fax call automatically? And what can you do if your computer doesn't wake up for a fax call? Read on.

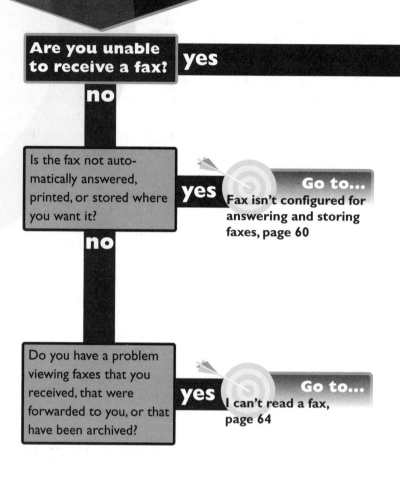

Are you unable to receive a fax?

yes

no

Is the fax not automatically answered, printed, or stored where you want it?

yes

Go to...
Fax isn't configured for answering and storing faxes, page 60

no

Do you have a problem viewing faxes that you received, that were forwarded to you, or that have been archived?

yes

Go to...
I can't read a fax, page 64

Faxes, receiving

Is the Fax printer not displayed in the Printers folder?

yes → **Quick fix**

If your modem isn't installed correctly or isn't fully compatible, Fax will not be installed.

1. Verify that your modem is installed. If it isn't, install it using the Add/Remove Hardware item in the Control Panel.

2. If you can't install the modem, or if the fax printer isn't installed after you've installed the modem, check to make sure the modem is in the Windows 2000 hardware compatibility list and that it has fax capabilities.

no

Is your modem configured to receive faxes, and do you have permission to receive faxes?

yes → **Does the computer fail to come out of Standby mode to answer a fax?**

yes → **Go to...**
A fax call doesn't wake the computer, page 66

no

Go to...
I can't receive a fax, page 62

If your solution isn't here

Check these related chapters:

Or see the general troubleshooting tips on page xiii

Fax isn't configured for answering and storing faxes

Source of the problem

Once you have Fax set up on your system, there are multiple options you need to consider, including whether you want the fax call to be answered manually or automatically, and what actions you want to be taken after the fax has been received. For example, if your computer uses a single phone line for voice and fax communications, you can have Fax set to answer only when you click a button or only after you've given Fax the okay to answer after a specified number of rings. This type of configuration is not very practical, however, unless the only time you ever receive a fax is when you're sitting at your computer. Once the fax has been received, you can print it, store it wherever you want it, and—provided you have the correct setup—even send it to a specific e-mail inbox.

How to fix it

1. On the Settings submenu of the Start menu, click Control Panel. In the Control Panel, double-click the Fax icon.

2. On the Status Monitor tab, clear the check box to enable manual answering if it's checked and if you want the computer to answer automatically. Select the unchecked box if you want a dialog box to appear every time the phone rings, asking you whether you want Fax to answer. Select any other options you want, and then click OK. ▶

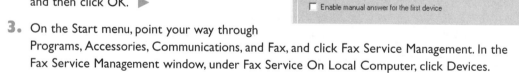

3. On the Start menu, point your way through Programs, Accessories, Communications, and Fax, and click Fax Service Management. In the Fax Service Management window, under Fax Service On Local Computer, click Devices.

4. In the right part of the window, double-click the modem you use to receive the fax to display its Properties dialog box. In the Receive section of the General tab, make sure the Enable Receive check box is selected, and then type a value or use the scroll arrows to specify how many times you want the phone to ring before Fax answers.

5. On the Received Faxes tab, specify what you want done with the fax, and then click OK.

- To print every incoming fax, select the Print On check box, and then click the printer you want to use in the list.

- To save the incoming fax in a folder other than the default Received Faxes folder in the Faxes folder, make sure the Save In Folder check box is selected, and either type the full path to the destination folder or click the Browse button at the right of the folder address box. Use the Browse For Folder dialog box to locate the folder you want, and then click OK.

- To have the fax sent to an e-mail inbox, select the check box to send the fax to an inbox, and click the correct e-mail profile name. If this check box is grayed (unavailable), it means that a compatible MAPI (Messaging Application Programming Interface) e-mail system isn't installed on your computer. ▶ With a system such as Microsoft Exchange 5.5 or later e-mail server on the network and an Exchange client or Microsoft Outlook client installed on your computer, this option should be available. Having only Outlook Express as your mail client will not provide the support for this option.

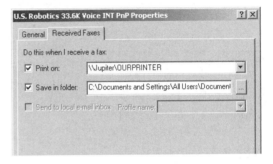

6. Click OK to close the dialog box, and then close the Fax Service Management window.

More about using a phone line for voice and fax

Dialing someone's phone number, only to hear the beeping and screeching of a fax, is one of the more unpleasant forms of noise pollution. To avoid this communications faux pas when someone is calling you, make sure your modem speaker is turned on. That way, if your fax is set to automatically receive a fax call, when someone is calling to chat you'll hear their insistent pleas to be heard. Then you can pick up a phone that's attached to the same telephone line and simply click the End Fax Call button in the Fax Monitor dialog box. This will terminate the call on the modem, ending all that fax noise and letting you and your caller converse in peace.

Tip
If you set the fax to be answered manually, you really don't need to sit up all night waiting for that one fax to arrive. To have the next—but only the next—phone call received automatically, click the Answer Next Call As Fax check box in the Fax Monitor dialog box.

I can't receive a fax

Source of the problem

Receiving a fax on your computer isn't always as simple as receiving a fax on a fax machine. You might need to do a little finagling to get everything to work. Just as you have to make sure that a fax machine is turned on, you have to make sure that fax receiving on your computer is turned on. You also have to make sure that you have the right equipment. Just as you can't substitute an answering machine for a fax machine, you can't use a modem on your computer if the modem isn't designed for receiving faxes and isn't fully compatible with Windows 2000. And, just as you can't receive a fax on a fax machine that's located in a locked room to which you don't have the key, you can't receive a fax on your computer if you don't have the appropriate permission to receive faxes.

How to fix it

1. Start with the basics. Make sure the phone line works and that it's connected to your modem. If the modem is an external model, make sure that it's correctly connected to your computer and, if it uses external power, that it's plugged in. If you can make outgoing calls—connecting to the Internet, for example—your system passes this check.

2. Now you need to confirm that your computer is set up for faxing. When Windows 2000 is installed, or if a modem is installed later, Windows determines whether the modem has fax capabilities. If it does, Windows installs Fax. If you've already been able to send faxes, Fax is installed. If you haven't been able to send a fax, or if you haven't yet tried, on the Settings submenu of the Start menu, click Printers. In the Printers folder, look for a fax printer. If it's there, Fax is installed. If a fax printer isn't there, you'll need to check the documentation for the modem to see whether it's capable of sending and receiving faxes. If it is, you'll probably need to troubleshoot the modem to see whether it was misidentified or whether a driver is missing or outdated. If the modem isn't capable of sending and receiving faxes, you'll need to replace it. ▶

Tip

If all your settings are correct, and receiving calls hasn't been prohibited by a system policy, first verify that whoever is sending you a fax can send faxes successfully to other people. If the problem does not lie there, your modem could be faulty or might have incorrect settings. For information about troubleshooting modems, see "Modems," starting on page 146.

3. Check to make sure that Fax is set to receive faxes. On the Start menu, point your way through Programs, Accessories, Communications, and Fax, and click Fax Service Management on the submenu. In the left part of the Fax Service Management window, under Fax Service On Local Computer, click Devices.

4. In the right part of the window, double-click the modem you'll be using. In the modem's Properties dialog box, on the General tab, select the Enable Receive check box if it's not already selected. ▶

5. In the Rings Before Answer box, type or use the scroll arrows to specify a low number, such as 1 or 2. If the number of rings is too great, the calling fax might hang up before your computer answers.

6. On the Received Faxes tab, make sure the Save In Folder check box is selected and the destination is correct. Make a note of the full destination so that you can find any received faxes. Click OK, and close the Fax Service Management window. ▶

7. On the Settings submenu of the Start menu, click Control Panel. In the Control Panel, double-click the Fax icon. In the Fax Properties dialog box, on the Status Monitor tab, select both the Display The Status Monitor and the Status Monitor Always On Top check boxes. Unless you use the same phone line for fax and voice calls, and unless you sit in front of the computer whenever a fax arrives, clear the check box to enable manual answering. Click OK.

8. Have someone send you a fax. The Fax Monitor should appear. If you don't see a log of activity, click the Details button. Note the activity recorded. If the fax was cut off before it was completed, if the modem or Fax didn't answer, or if the Fax Monitor window didn't appear, you have a serious problem. If your computer is on a network that uses system policies, check with the administrator to make sure that the policy has not excluded receiving faxes. If there is no such exclusion, you'll need to trouble-shoot the modem. ▶

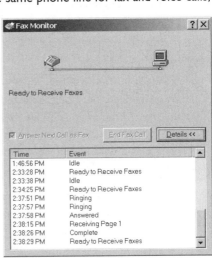

I can't read a fax

Source of the problem

When a fax is received on your computer, it's stored as a graphics file in the TIF (Tagged Image File) format. Windows provides a program called Imaging For Windows, which is designed to view this type of image. This program comes in two versions—one for viewing the fax and printing it, and another that lets you edit the fax by adding annotations. However, a couple of different problems might prevent you from doing either of the above. One is that the file type of the fax isn't associated with the program that is supposed to view it. The other is that a fax from a different source, including a fax from a different version of Microsoft Fax, might be in a format that can't be viewed by the imaging program.

How to fix it

1. Open the folder that contains your received faxes. If you haven't changed the destination for faxes, open the folder by right-clicking the Fax icon on the taskbar and clicking My Faxes on the shortcut menu.

   If the Fax icon isn't displayed on the taskbar, on the Start menu, point your way through Programs, Accessories, Communications, and Fax, and click My Faxes on the submenu. ▶

   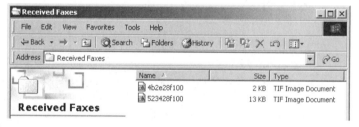

   In the My Faxes folder, double-click the Received Faxes folder.

2. Take a look at the fax file. Use the Views button on the Standard Buttons toolbar of the window to switch to Details view. The file type should be listed as TIF Image Document. If the file is listed as an ASD file or another type of file, the fax was originally received using an incompatible fax program. You'll need that program, or a viewer for it, to view this type of file.

3. If the file is a TIF Image Document, double-click it. If an Imaging Preview window or an Imaging window opens but the entire fax area is gray, you don't have permission to view the fax. You'll need to have an administrator either add you to a group that has permission to access the fax, or change the security setting

Tip

If you open the fax file to read it in Imaging Preview but then decide that you want to annotate it, click the Open Image For Editing button on the Imaging Preview toolbar. You might be asked whether you always want to open all your faxes for editing. If you click Yes, the fax will open in the Imaging window whenever you double-click the fax file.

on the fax or the folder that contains the fax. ▶

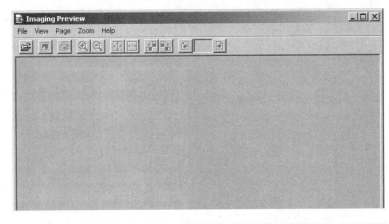

4. If, instead of an Imaging Preview window or an Imaging window, the Open With dialog box appears, it means that this type of file is not correctly registered to work with a specific program. Scroll through the list of programs, and click Imaging Preview. Make sure that the Always Use This Program To Open These Files check box is selected. Click OK, and the fax should open in the Imaging Preview window. ▶

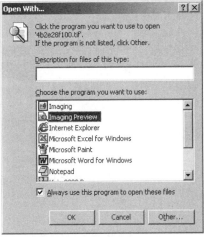

5. If the fax opens in some other program, such as a drawing program or a photo-editing program, it means that that program usurped the association for that type of file. If you're happy with the way the program displays your fax, you can continue using the program to view your faxes. It's possible that this program gives you greater ability to edit your faxes than the Imaging program does. However, if you don't like reading your faxes in that program, you can open them in the Imaging program. Right-click the fax file, and point to Open With on the shortcut menu. If a submenu appears, click any of the following (the submenu might not contain all these choices, and it might contain other programs):

● Imaging to open the fax file in the Imaging window, where you can annotate the fax this time only.

● Imaging Preview to open the fax file in the Imaging Preview window this time only.

● Choose Program to display the Open With dialog box, where you can choose among all the programs that are registered on the computer. If you select the check box to always use this program, whenever you double-click a fax file, the file will open in this program. If you clear the check box, the file will open in this program this time only, but the program will be added to the Open With submenu when you right-click a fax file.

Tip

You can use the Imaging program to add notes to the fax. A couple of useful annotation tools are the Rubber Stamp tool, for stamping the image with items such as the date the fax was received, and the Attach-A-Note tool, for adding text on a little note that can be easily deleted later.

A fax call doesn't wake the computer

Source of the problem

Like most of us, computers like to sleep. And, like many of us, they don't want to be disturbed. Too bad. If you have to get up and go to work, so should your computer! When someone is calling to send you a fax, your computer shouldn't sleep through the call. It should wake up, answer the call, connect to the calling fax, receive the fax, and hang up, and only then should it go back to sleep. Unfortunately, when a computer is asleep in Standby mode, the system sometimes refuses to wake up and simply ignores the prodding of a jangling phone call. To get your system to work properly, you'll need to either reconfigure it to wake up to a call or prevent the system from sleeping while it's waiting for a call.

How to fix it

1. Log on to the computer as an Administrator.

2. Right-click My Computer on the Desktop, and click Manage on the shortcut menu. In the Computer Management window, click Device Manager.

3. In the right part of the window, double-click Modems, and then double-click the modem that is set to receive the call.

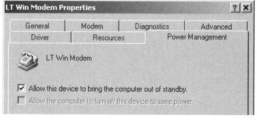

4. On the Power Management tab, click the check box to allow the modem to bring the computer out of Standby, and click OK. ▶

5. If the Power Management tab is absent, either your computer or your modem might not support the ACPI (Advanced Configuration And Power Interface) standard. To check this, in the right part of the Device Manager window, double-click the Computer item in the list, and see whether your computer is listed as an ACPI PC. If it isn't listed but you're sure it has ACPI features, check its documentation to see whether ACPI support has been disabled or hasn't been installed. If your computer does support ACPI, your modem might not support this standard. Check the modem's documentation; if it's supposed to support ACPI, you might need to install an updated driver for the modem.

6. Close the Device Manager and the Computer Management windows when you've finished.

7. Whether or not your modem supports waking up the computer, you need to configure the power management settings correctly. To do so, on the Settings submenu of the Start menu, click Control Panel. In the Control Panel, double-click the Power Options icon.

8. If you were able to set the modem to wake the computer, you'll need to keep the computer from going into hibernation. The modem will wake the computer from Standby mode but not from Hibernate mode. On the General tab, set System Hibernates to Never. Click Save As, and, in the Save As dialog box, type a name for this custom power scheme, and click OK. Click Apply in the Power Options Properties dialog box. If you were unable to set the modem to wake the computer, specify a power scheme that prevents the computer from going into either Standby or Hibernate mode. Click Apply. ▶

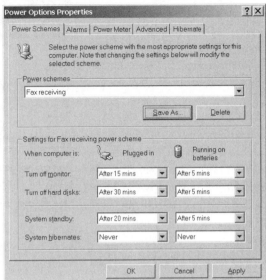

9. On the Advanced tab, select the Always Show Icon On The Taskbar check box. Also, make sure none of the power button settings will place the computer in Hibernate and—if the modem won't wake the computer—Standby modes. Click OK. Your computer should now be able to answer faxes all night—provided, of course, that you have it set to automatically answer incoming faxes.

10. If you know faxes won't be arriving and you want to switch to a more energy-efficient power scheme, right-click the Power Meter icon on the taskbar, and click Adjust Power Properties on the shortcut menu. Specify a different scheme that uses Standby or Hibernate mode, and click OK.

More about power capabilities

Computers are power pigs. To reduce consumption, several power conservation methods have been developed. Normally the system works pretty well—it powers down after a set time, and powers back up when you press a key or push a button. But when the wakeup call is a phone call, the modem must be awake enough to receive the call and wake up the rest of the system. When the computer and the modem have ACPI power management, the computer can talk to devices, and devices can talk back to the computer. Therefore, with ACPI your modem can be running at a low power level when a call comes in but can still wake the system to receive the call and the fax. Without ACPI capabilities, everything remains snoozing in Standby mode. The reason many computers and devices such as modems don't have ACPI power management is that it's a fairly new standard, and older or cheaper systems haven't been equipped with it.

Sending a fax through your computer is a great convenience—provided it works. If it doesn't, there could be several reasons. Your modem might not be set up to send faxes, for example, or there might be a network policy that limits the permission to send faxes to certain groups. Perhaps you're able to send faxes but the information on the fax cover page is incorrect, or your faxes just don't look good. We'll discuss these problems in this chapter.

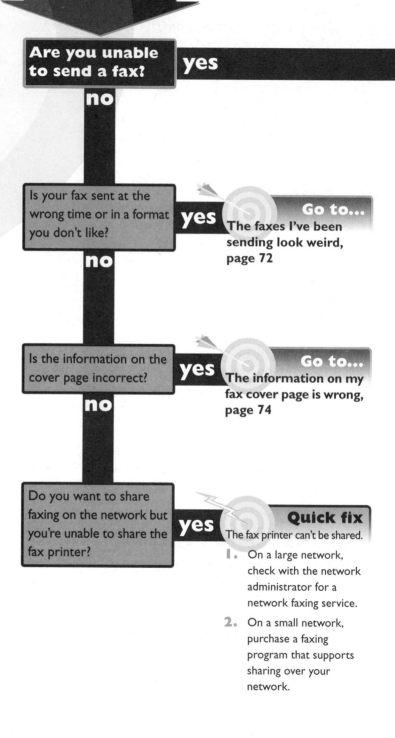

Are you unable to send a fax?

yes

no

Is your fax sent at the wrong time or in a format you don't like?

yes

Go to...
The faxes I've been sending look weird, page 72

no

Is the information on the cover page incorrect?

yes

Go to...
The information on my fax cover page is wrong, page 74

no

Do you want to share faxing on the network but you're unable to share the fax printer?

yes

Quick fix
The fax printer can't be shared.

1. On a large network, check with the network administrator for a network faxing service.

2. On a small network, purchase a faxing program that supports sharing over your network.

Faxes, sending

Is the fax icon displayed in the Control Panel and is the fax printer displayed in the Printers folder?

yes

Is the Print button grayed when you try to print to a fax printer, or do you receive a message that no device is configured?

yes

Go to...
I can't send a fax, page 70

no

Quick fix

If these items are missing, Fax hasn't been installed on the computer.

1. Right-click My Computer, and click Manage on the shortcut menu. Click Device Manager, and confirm that the modem is installed and is working. Close the Computer Management window.

2. If the modem isn't installed, double-click the Add/Remove Hardware icon in the Control Panel, and install the modem.

3. If the modem is installed, check to see whether it's in the Windows 2000 hardware compatibility list and whether it supports faxing. If necessary, replace the modem with one that's designed to send faxes from Windows 2000.

no

Is your fax just sitting in the fax printer and not being sent at its scheduled send time?

yes

Quick fix

The fax printer is paused or is set to work off line.

1. On the Settings submenu of the Start menu, click Printers.

2. Right-click the fax printer.

3. If there's a check mark next to the Use Printer Offline item, clear the item to get the fax printer on line.

4. Right-click the fax printer again.

5. If there's a check mark next to the Pause Printing item, clear the item to resume sending faxes.

If your solution isn't here

Check these related chapters:

Date and time, page 10
Faxes, receiving, page 58
Hardware installation, page 96
Modems, page 146

Or see the general troubleshooting tips on page xiii

I can't send a fax

Source of the problem

When Windows 2000 detects a fax-capable modem, it installs faxing capabilities and a fax printer on your computer. If, however, that modem hasn't been set up to send faxes, Windows will tell you that no device is configured for faxing. In a similar manner, Windows sets up faxing so that just about everyone who uses the computer is allowed to send faxes, but—either because of changes made to the local computer or as the result of a network system policy—the permission to send faxes can be limited to certain groups. If you find that you're unable to send faxes, first you'll need to set up the modem to send faxes, and then, if that doesn't solve the problem, you'll have to negotiate either to have the permission to send faxes changed or to get yourself added to a group that is allowed to send faxes.

How to fix it

1. Make sure that you're using the correct procedure to send a fax. With the document you want to send open in its program, click Print on the program's File menu. In the Print dialog box, click Fax in the Name list, and click OK. If the program doesn't allow you to specify the printer in the Print dialog box, on the Settings submenu of the Start menu, click Printers. In the Printers window, right-click the fax printer, and click Set As Default Printer on the shortcut menu. Return to the program, and print the document. This should start the Send Fax Wizard.

2. If you can't send the fax from the program, try sending a simple text fax. On the Start menu, point your way through Programs, Accessories, Communications, and Fax, and click Send Cover Page Fax. This should start the Send Fax Wizard. If you can send a fax this way but can't send one from a program, check the documentation of the program and find out why you can't print to a different printer. If you still can't send a fax, click Fax Service Management on the Fax submenu of the Start menu. In the Fax Service Management window, under the Fax Service On Local Computer item, click Devices. Right-click the name of the modem. If there's already a check mark next to Send on the shortcut menu, you'll know that the modem is already set

> **Tip**
>
> If you don't see a fax printer in the Name list in the Print dialog box or in the Printers folder, Fax isn't installed on your computer. Windows installs the service only when it detects a fax-enabled modem. If you have a fax modem installed but Fax isn't installed, you'll need to troubleshoot the modem.

> **Tip**
>
> Make sure the problem really is that you can't send faxes, and not that the faxes are simply waiting for the correct time to be sent. To do so, in the Printers window, double-click the fax printer, and make sure there are no documents in the queue just waiting for the specified send time.

to send faxes, so just click outside the shortcut menu without making any changes. Otherwise, click Send. ▶

3. If you're denied permission to make any changes, log off, and then log on again as the Administrator. Open the Fax Service Management window from the Fax submenu of the Start menu if it isn't already open. Right-click Fax Service On Local Computer, and click Properties on the shortcut menu. On the Security tab, click the group that you're a member of and note the permissions that have been granted.

4. If you want to change only the permissions you've been granted, click the Add button, locate your name in the Select Users, Computers, Or Groups dialog box, click Add, and then click OK. Click your name in the Name list, and then select the Allow check boxes to provide the permissions you want.

5. If you want to allow an entire group to send faxes, click the group name, and then select the Allow check box for the Submit Fax Job item. Click OK to close the Properties dialog box. Close the Fax Service Management window. ▶

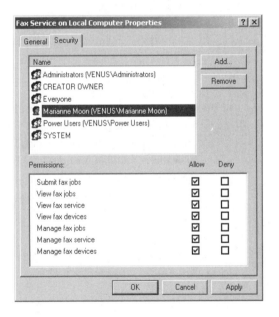

6. Log off, and then log on again using your normal user name and password. On the Fax submenu of the Start menu, click Send Cover Page Fax, and send a fax using the Send Fax Wizard.

7. If you're unable to send a fax, and if your computer is on a network that uses a domain, ask the network administrator whether a system policy is preventing you from sending faxes. If so, request that you be added to those who are authorized to send faxes.

More about Fax

Fax Service is a tool in Windows 2000 that lets you send faxes from your computer and receive faxes on your computer, using a direct phone connection to your computer's modem. Many corporate networks use a more sophisticated type of program that lets you send faxes over the network to a fax server. If this is the way your network is set up, and if you can't send faxes, you'll need to get help so that you can use that specific program.

The faxes I've been sending look weird

Source of the problem

When you send a fax, it's "printed" by the fax printer. Just as you format a document that you print on a traditional printer, you have to set up a fax with the layout you want and with any header and footer information properly completed. If you're not happy with the appearance of your faxes—or if you've been told that the design looks a bit strange—you can adjust the way your faxes are set up on your fax printer. And, at the same time, you can schedule when you want the faxes to be sent. You have to provide most of this information only once. If you need different setups for different types of faxes—one for your regular local clients, for example, and another for potential clients elsewhere in the country or around the world—you can set up more than one fax printer, each with a different layout and sending schedule.

How to fix it

1. If the strange look of your faxes is not an intentional design feature, take a look at one of the faxes you've sent. To do so, on the Start menu, point your way through Programs, Accessories, Communications, and Fax, and click My Faxes on the submenu. In the My Faxes folder, double-click the Sent Faxes folder. Double-click one of the faxes in the folder, and examine it to see what's wrong.

2. If there are no faxes in the folder, click Fax Service Management on the Fax submenu. In the Fax Service Management window, right-click Fax Service On Local Computer, and click Properties on the shortcut menu. On the General tab, click the check box to archive outgoing faxes, and click OK. Leave the Fax Service Management window open, as you'll need to use it again shortly. Send a fax to someone as you normally would, either by "printing" it from a program or by clicking Send Cover Page Fax on the Fax submenu of the Start menu. Examine the sent fax as in step 1.

3. In the Fax Service Management window, once again right-click Fax Service On Local Computer, and click Properties on the shortcut menu. On the General tab of the Fax Service On Local Computer Properties dialog box, select or clear the check boxes to specify the information

you want to be included in your faxes. ▶

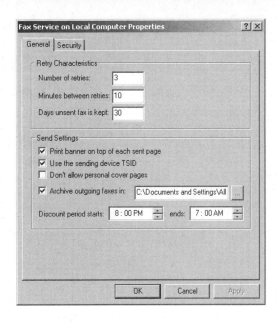

- Banner: Includes the date and time, the TSID or fax number from the user information you supplied, the sender's company, the fax number called, and the page number of the fax.

- TSID: Includes the Transmitting Station Identifier that you've specified in the fax you're sending. If this option isn't selected, the fax number from the user information will be used.

4. Specify the hours that provide discount phone charges, and then click OK to close the Properties dialog box. Although you've specified the discount hours, you don't have to use them when you send the fax.

5. If you clicked the TSID check box, make sure the correct TSID is listed. Click Devices in the left part of the Fax Service Management window. Right-click the fax modem that appears in the right part of the window, and click Properties on the shortcut menu. On the General tab, type

your fax identifying number in the TSID box, and click OK. The TSID is usually your fax number plus any other identifying information, such as the fax identification name or number if there's more than one fax using the same phone number. Close the Fax Service Management window when you've finished.

6. On the Settings submenu of the Start menu, click Printers. Right-click the fax printer, and click Printing Preferences on the shortcut menu. Specify how and when you want the fax to be printed, and click OK. ▶

7. To create a completely different set of printing preferences, on the Settings submenu of the Start menu, click Control Panel. In the Control Panel, double-click Fax. On the Advanced Options tab, click Add A Fax Printer, and wait for the new printer to be created. Close the dialog box and the Control Panel. Repeat step 6 to set up the new printer. Try sending faxes from the different fax printers, and inspect your results.

The information on my fax cover page is wrong

Source of the problem

When you send a cover page with a fax, all you need to do is supply the subject and the text of any note you want to include. Windows 2000 obligingly inserts the rest of the information for you. Windows gathers that information from the user information you provided, along with data it extracts from the document and from the computer's clock. Because you can create and use various customized cover pages, the type of information on the cover page will vary depending on which cover page you're using. If any information is missing or incorrect, you'll need to provide or correct it. And because Windows inserts the information for you, if you want to supply different information on certain faxes, you'll need to set up more than one fax printer and specify different information for each printer.

How to fix it

1. On the Settings submenu of the Start menu, click Printers.

2. Right-click the fax printer, and click Properties on the shortcut menu.

3. On the User Information tab, complete or correct the information. This information will be stored with your personal settings, so if someone else logs on to the computer and sends a fax, his or her settings will be used instead of yours. To make sure the information is stored correctly, log on as you normally do, and not as an Administrator. ▶

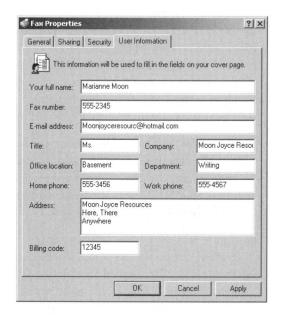

4. If you want to provide different or additional information on the fax cover page, you can create another fax printer that contains different user information. To do so, however, you must have the proper permission. On the Settings submenu of the Start menu, click Control Panel. Hold down the Shift key, right-click the Fax icon in the Control Panel, and click Run As on the shortcut menu. In the Run As Other User box, enter the user name of an account that's a

member of the Administrators group, enter the password, and click OK. If you're already logged on as a member of the Administrators group, double-click the Fax icon.

5. On the Advanced Options tab, click the Add A Fax Printer button, and click OK when you're advised that the new fax printer has been created. ▶

6. On the Settings submenu of the Start menu, click Printers. Right-click the new fax printer, click Rename on the shortcut menu, type a descriptive name for the printer, and press Enter.

7. Right-click the printer again, and click Properties on the shortcut menu. On the User Information tab, modify the information that you want included.

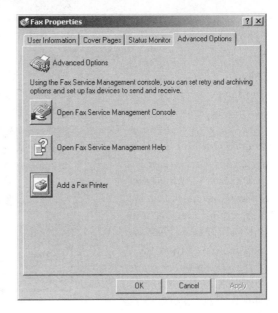

8. On the General tab, click the Printing Preferences button, and, in the Printing Preferences dialog box, specify when and how you want the fax to be sent. Click OK to close the Printing Preferences dialog box, and click OK again to close the Fax Properties dialog box.

9. Using the fax printer you just created and customized, create and "print" a document with a cover page, thus sending the fax. To review the fax you just sent, on the Start menu, point your way through Programs, Accessories, Communications, and Fax, and then click My Faxes. In the My Faxes folder, double-click the Sent Faxes folder. Double-click your fax in the folder, and then check its contents to make sure everything is correct. If not, modify the user information to suit your needs.

Tip
You can use a new fax printer for purposes other than simply changing the user information. You can, for example, set one printer to send faxes immediately and another to send faxes only during discount hours. You can also use a different billing code for each printer.

More about the information on fax cover pages

Fax cover pages use a special code to extract information from the User Information tab and from other sources. Because the content of cover pages can be modified, and because entirely new and differently designed cover pages can be created, you might be able to modify the design of a fax cover page to meet all your needs without relying on two or more fax printers. Bear in mind, however, that a tyrannical local administrator or rigidly enforced system policies can prevent you from creating custom fax cover pages or modifying existing ones. To edit or create a new fax cover page, double-click Fax in the Control Panel, and use the Cover Page tab of the Fax Properties dialog box.

The contents of your folders represent all those hours of inspiration and perspiration that you've poured into your work. But if the folder windows don't tell you anything about the folders stashed away inside them, you might find it difficult and time consuming to locate and access the items you need. To make the folder windows work for you, you can set them to display information about the documents they contain—subject, file size, date the file was last worked on, author's name, and so on. You can even show a picture preview in the window of a folder that contains pictures. And you can open all your files in one folder window or open each file in its own window, whichever you prefer.

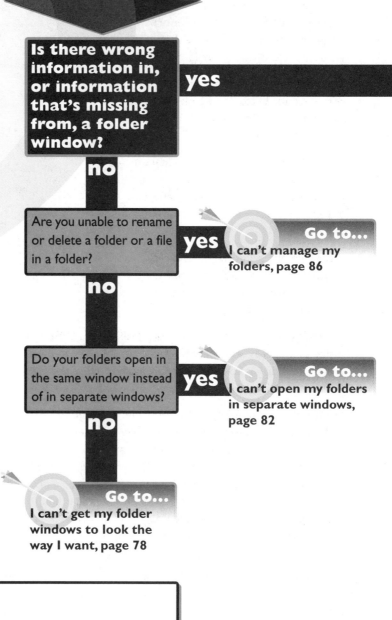

Is there wrong information in, or information that's missing from, a folder window?

yes

no

Are you unable to rename or delete a folder or a file in a folder?

yes

Go to...
I can't manage my folders, page 86

no

Do your folders open in the same window instead of in separate windows?

yes

Go to...
I can't open my folders in separate windows, page 82

no

Go to...
I can't get my folder windows to look the way I want, page 78

If your solution isn't here
Check these related chapters:
- Access to the computer, page 2
- Desktop, page 16
- Disk storage, page 36
- Encryption, page 52
- Toolbars, page 286

Or see the general troubleshooting tips on page xiii

Is the information in a folder window not updated when the contents have changed?

yes

Quick fix

Windows doesn't constantly update the contents of a window. However, when necessary, you can do so manually.

1. Click in the folder window you want to update.

2. Press the F5 key, and wait for the window to be updated.

no

Is the information about a file truncated in, or missing from, a folder window?

yes

Go to...

My folder windows don't display all the information I need, page 80

no

Are thumbnails missing for some file types?

yes

Quick fix

Thumbnail images are displayed only for certain file types for which Windows has special programs, or filters, installed. To display thumbnails for other file types, you must save the file with a preview.

1. For a Microsoft Office document, open the document, click Properties on the File menu, select the Save Preview Picture check box, click OK, and save and close the document.

2. For other types of documents, check the program's documentation to see whether a preview picture can be saved. Note that not all previews will show up as thumbnails.

no

Is information specific to certain file types not displayed in folder windows?

yes

Go to...

My folder windows aren't set up for certain types of files, page 84

I can't get my folder windows to look the way I want

Source of the problem

Folder windows are the gateways to your files and documents. Your folder windows can display all sorts of information that can help simplify your work and shorten the time it takes you to find what you're looking for. However, to make those folder windows work for you, you have to tell Windows what you want displayed and how you want it to look. Unless you know a few tricks, any changes you make to a folder will affect only that folder window and won't be applied to all your other folder windows. Also, if you're not careful, Windows will forget the changes you've made when you log off, and you'll have to make them all over again.

How to fix it

1. If Windows forgets the changes you've made whenever you log off, you'll have to gently remind it to remember your settings. To do so, open the folder window you want to modify if it isn't already open, and click Folder Options on the Tools menu. On the View tab of the Folder Options dialog box, scroll through the Advanced Settings list, and select the Remember Each Folder's View Settings check box if it isn't already selected. With this check box selected, Windows will remember most of your settings. Make any other changes you want in the Advanced Settings list. The changes you make to your settings here will apply to all your folder windows. When you've finished, click OK to close the dialog box. ▶

2. In the folder window, customize the folder so that it looks the way you want:

   ● On the View menu, specify whether you want the status bar displayed at the bottom of the folder window.

> **Tip**
> There are certain settings Windows won't remember, including which Explorer Bars are displayed and the position of the folder window on the Desktop.

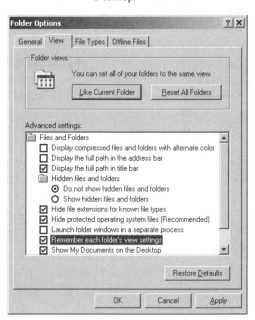

- On the View menu, specify how you want the icons displayed in the folder window.

- On the View menu, specify how you want the icons arranged in the folder window.

- On the View menu, click Customize This Folder, and use the wizard to add a picture or a comment, or to modify the basic structure of the folder window.

- Change the size of the folder window either by dragging one of its sides or by clicking the Maximize button.

3. On the Tools menu, click ▶ Folder Options. On the General tab, in the Web View section, specify whether you want all your folders to use the web-style view to display additional information, or to use the classic Windows style, in which information appears only on the status bar. Click Apply.

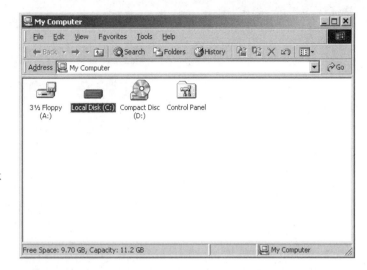

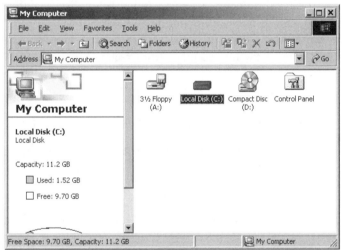

The bottom window is set to display web content, and the top window is set in the classic Windows style.

4. If you want all your folder windows to use the setup you created for this folder, on the View tab, click the Like Current Folder button, and then click OK.

More about customizing a folder window

When you customize a folder window and then click the Like Current Folder button, you're using the current folder as a template for all your other folders. However, if you make changes to the folder after you click the button, those changes won't be made in the other folders unless you click the Like Current Folder button again.

My folder windows don't display all the information I need

Source of the problem

If a folder window is going to help you work efficiently, it must provide all the information you need about the documents or files contained in the folder. For example, if you can see only part of a long file name, you might not be able to determine whether the item is the one you want. Additionally, when you select a document, its folder window often displays information about the author, the subject, and so on. Of course, if the information wasn't properly recorded, it won't be available. Some document types don't support including additional information, so in those cases you'll have to make do with the limited information that's available.

How to fix it

1. Windows offers several views of your files, each with its own pros and cons.

   ● Large Icons view makes the icons easy to see, but long file names are often truncated.

   ● Small Icons view lets you see the entire file name, but the files will probably appear a bit jumbled in the window because they don't line up nicely.

   ● List view is probably the best view to use when you're working with long file names. It displays the entire file name and lines up all the files in neat columns.

   ● Details view provides information about each file—its size and the date it was last modified, for example—but will normally truncate long file names.

   ● Thumbnails view has an alignment that's similar to that of Large Icons view, except that each file takes up a lot more room, and long file names are often truncated.

2. To use Details view, adjust the size of the Name column to show the entire file name. To do so, point to the right border of the Name column, and drag the border to the right. ▶

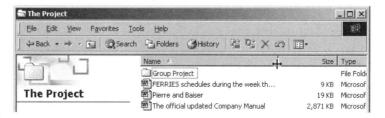

3. When you point to a file, a little window pops up and provides information about the file. When you click a file to select it, some information should appear in the web content area of the window, and more information should appear in the status bar at the bottom of the window.

If you don't see any of this information, you'll need to confirm that the folder is set to show these elements. ▶ To do so, on the folder window's Tools menu, click Folder Options. On the General tab, click the Enable Web Content In Folders option if it isn't already selected. On the View tab, select the Show Pop-Up Description For Folder And Desktop Items check box if it isn't already selected. Click OK. Finally, click Status Bar on the View menu if it isn't already checked.

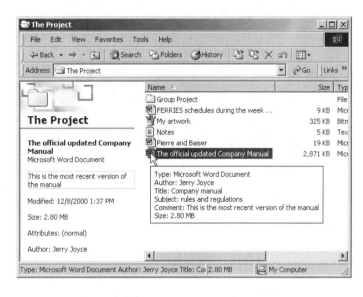

4. If you see only very limited information about the file, you might be able to add more information so that the file is easier to find and use. Some documents, such as Microsoft Office documents, support adding a great deal of information to a file's properties. Some other file types can have information added only if they're stored on a disk that uses the NTFS file system.

To add information to a file's properties, right-click the file, and click Properties on the shortcut menu. On the Summary tab, make your additions and/or changes to the file's properties. Click OK when you've finished. If you don't see a Summary tab, the file isn't stored on a disk that uses the NTFS file system. Note that some files, such as Microsoft Office documents, also have a Custom tab, where you can create and include additional data and data fields. ▶

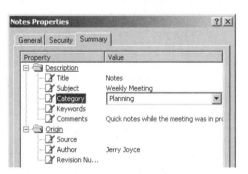

5. If you have recorded information about a file, be careful about moving the file to a location where the NTFS file system isn't in use. Some types of documents, such as Microsoft Office documents, will preserve the information, but many other types will not. Fortunately, you'll be warned if your data will be lost, so click Yes in the Confirm Stream Loss dialog box only if you're willing to lose the information.

I can't open my folders in separate windows

Source of the problem

Are you and Windows having a slight disagreement? Windows has decided that the best way for you to work when you're managing your files and folders is, in most cases, with only one folder window open. So, when you double-click a subfolder, the contents of the parent folder are replaced by the contents of the subfolder. "No, no, no!" you might say, "I can't work like that...I need to see my folders in separate windows." Well, fortunately, Windows 2000 doesn't insist on having its own way, so you can use procedures to open your folders in separate windows when you want, or, if you agree with Windows, you can set your system to always open a folder in a new window.

How to fix it

1. Click the Show Desktop button on the Quick Launch toolbar to start with a clean Desktop. Double-click My Computer, and, in the My Computer window, double-click a disk drive, such as drive C. If the My Computer window is replaced by the contents of the drive you double-clicked, your computer is set to use single windows.

2. If you want to open a second window for a different folder but don't always want a new window to appear for every folder you open, do any of the following: ▶

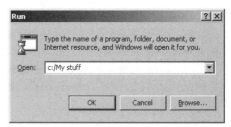

- In My Computer, navigate to a drive or folder. Then double-click My Computer on the Desktop. In the new My Computer window, navigate to the folder you want to display.

- In the Address toolbar on the taskbar, type the path to the folder you want to display. Provided the folder isn't already open in a window, a new window will open.

- On the Start menu, click Run. In the Open box, type the full path to the folder, and click OK. Make sure the folder isn't already open; otherwise, you'll just be switching to the opened folder.

You can open a folder in a new window by typing the full path to the folder in either the Address toolbar or the Run dialog box.

- If you have a window that you opened from My Computer, double-click My Documents or My Network Places on the Desktop. In the new window that appears, navigate to the folder you want to use. If you click the Folders button on the Standard Buttons toolbar to display the Folders Explorer Bar, or if you open the list of addresses in the Address Bar toolbar, you can navigate to any folder on your computer or on the network.

3. Instead of opening only selected folders in new windows, you can tell Windows to always open a folder or a drive in a new window. To do so, on the Tools menu in any folder window, click Folder Options. On the General tab of the Folder Options dialog box, click the option to open each folder in its own window, and then click OK. ▶

4. As you continue to work with the folders, if you find that you have too many windows open on the Desktop, use any of the following techniques to manage the windows:

- Hold down the Shift key and click the Close button in a folder window. This closes not only the folder you clicked, but all the folders on a direct path to the original folder window you opened.

- Right-click the taskbar, and click either Tile Windows Horizontally or Tile Windows Vertically on the shortcut menu to arrange all the open (and non-minimized) windows. ▶

- Click the Show Desktop button on the Quick Launch toolbar to minimize all the

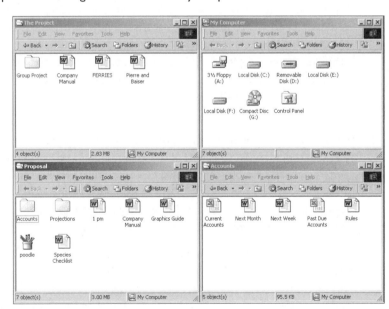

windows. Click the icon on the taskbar for each folder window you want to use, keeping all the other folder windows minimized.

My folder windows aren't set up for certain types of files

Source of the problem

Some folder windows in Windows are already set up to display information for specific types of content. The My Pictures folder, for example, contains a picture viewer that displays previews of the pictures that are stored in the folder. The viewer can show larger previews and can also be used to print the pictures. The My Computer folder window, when viewed in Details view, displays information about disk type and capacity (which is different from the information in most windows). When you create a new folder, its window is generic—that is, it isn't adapted to the specific type of information stored in the folder. However, you can quickly set up the folder window to display the relevant information.

How to fix it

1. If you're starting a new folder to hold specific information, open My Computer on the Desktop, and navigate to where you want to store the new folder. Right-click a blank spot in the window. On the shortcut menu, point to New, and click Folder. Type a name for the new folder. Double-click the new folder to open it. If you want to modify an existing folder rather than create a new one, navigate to its location, and double-click the folder to open it.

2. Decide what type of information you want to be displayed in the folder window. For example, if the folder is going to contain pictures, you'll probably want to include the picture preview tool. If the folder is going to contain all the documents for a specific project, you'll probably want to display the author's name and the subject of the project in the folder window.

3. To redesign the folder to contain a picture preview, on the View menu, click Customize This Folder. Click the Next button to step into the Customize This Folder Wizard. Click the Customize option if it isn't already selected, and select the Choose Or Edit An HTML Template For This Folder check box. Make sure no other check boxes are selected, and click Next.

4. In the Change This Folder page of the wizard, click Image Preview in the Choose A Template list. Make sure the I Want To Edit This Template check box is cleared, click Next, and then

> **Warning**
>
> The Customize This Folder Wizard lets you edit the HTML template for the folder. If you're not familiar with working in HTML, you should probably avoid entering this minefield. If you do edit the template, however, and the results are not to your liking, you can rerun the wizard and remove all your customizations.

click Finish. The folder window is now set up to display your pictures. ▶

5. If, rather than pictures, you're storing other types of files, and you want to display additional information about them in the folder window, you can customize the information that's displayed in Details view. To do so, create a folder (or navigate to the one you want to modify), and open it. On the View menu, click Details to switch to Details view. Open the View menu again, and click Choose Columns.

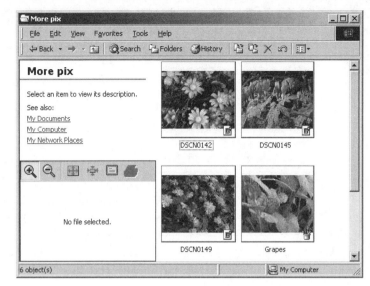

6. In the Column Settings dialog box, select the check boxes for the items you want to be displayed in Details view, and clear the check boxes for the items you don't want displayed. To arrange the order of the columns, select an item, and click the Move Up or Move Down button. The order of items from top to bottom determines the order from left to right in which the items will be displayed in the folder window. To set the width of each column, select an item, and then type the width, in pixels, in the The Selected Column Should Be [ ] Pixels Wide box. Click OK when you've set up all your columns. ▶

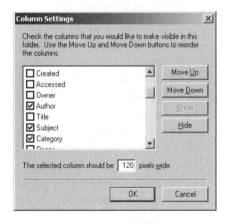

7. Examine the folder window, and add files to it if they're not already there. With the files in place, make sure the columns are arranged as you want them. If they're out of order, if an item is missing, or if you don't want to display a certain column, return to the Column Settings dialog box and make your adjustments. If you want to adjust the widths of the columns, you can do so by dragging the borders between them. ▶

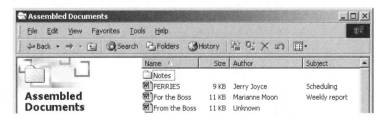

I can't manage my folders

Source of the problem

Your folders are the containers that hold the precious files you need. Like so many other things in life, they sometimes require some cleaning up. A folder can lose some of its usefulness, however, if you're limited as to what cleaning up and organizing you can do. For example, if you want to delete some files but they just won't go away, your file-management scheme can become…well, unmanageable. What causes the interference in your file-management capabilities can be anything from the minor inconvenience of lacking the permission to manage files to the near catastrophe of a hard-disk problem. When you figure out what's causing your headache, you can then go about remedying it.

How to fix it

1. The most likely reason you can't delete or rename a folder or a file in a folder is that you don't have permission to do so. This applies both to folders on your computer and those you access over a network. If the folder is on a network, there's little you can do except ask whoever is sharing the folder to change the way the folder is shared or to change the permission used to access the contents to include Modify or Write permission. ▶

Depending on the type of access restrictions that are in place and the type of computer that contains the shared folder, you'll see different messages explaining why you can't delete or rename a file or folder.

2. If the folder is on your computer, you'll need to have the permission changed on the folder. For information about changing the permission on a folder, see "Other people can access the files on my computer" on page 8. To modify the permission on a folder, you must be either the owner of the folder (usually the person who created it) or an Administrator. Permission settings for individual files and folders are available only on a disk drive that uses the NTFS file system.

3. If the problem isn't about permission, it might be that a system policy prohibits you from modifying or deleting files or folders. To find out whether such a policy exists, contact the person responsible for implementing system policies either on the entire network or on your computer.

4. If the problem isn't a matter of security or policy, there could be something seriously wrong with the file system on your computer. To find out, log off, and then log on again as the Administrator for the computer. Try to rename or delete the file or folder in question. If you're unable to do so, you've got a problem that requires some more detective work.

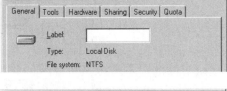

5. Open My Computer, and right-click the drive that contains the folder in question. On the short-cut menu, click Properties. On the General tab, in the File System entry, note the system the disk uses. ▶

6. Now comes the time-consuming work. Click the Tools tab, and click the Backup Now button. Use the Windows 2000 Backup program to back up the entire disk.

On this system, the F drive (top) uses NTFS, and the E drive (bottom) uses FAT32. These are the two most common file systems.

7. After you've backed up the disk to a safe location, click the Check Now button. In the Check Disk dialog box, select both of the check boxes for a comprehensive check and repair, and click Start. Wait for the program to complete the check. Close the Disk Properties dialog box when you've finished. ▶

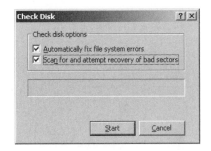

8. Return to the folder that had the problem, and try renaming or deleting the file or folder in question. If you still can't do it, and if the disk uses the NTFS file system, there's almost certainly a problem with the file system itself. A repair of this magnitude usually involves backing up all but the damaged files and folders (the ones you can't rename or delete) and then reformatting the hard disk. Because this is so extreme and can lead to all sorts of additional problems, *don't do it!* Instead, consult with a professional who might provide a simpler remedy using third-party tools or who is familiar with the safeguards involved in reformatting a drive and recovering all the information.

Heed the warning signs

When you encounter an inexplicable file-management problem—you're unable to rename a file, for example—it's a warning sign that something serious might be wrong. As a precaution, back up your disk immediately, making sure you don't overwrite any previous backups. That way, if things get worse, you'll have all your files backed up and ready to be restored. And if you were brave enough to try to fix your problems—and if you made a mess of it—you'll be less embarrassed when you can produce your backed up files and recover from a disaster that's only partly of your own making.

Computer games can be a lot of fun, whether you play by yourself, compete with a few other people over a network, or use the global reach of the Internet to play games with an international group of competitors. However, fun becomes frustration if the game runs too slowly or doesn't run at all, if your mouse doesn't work properly in some games, or if Windows won't let you install a joystick or some other device that you need to in order to play the game. We'll help you troubleshoot these and other problems in this chapter.

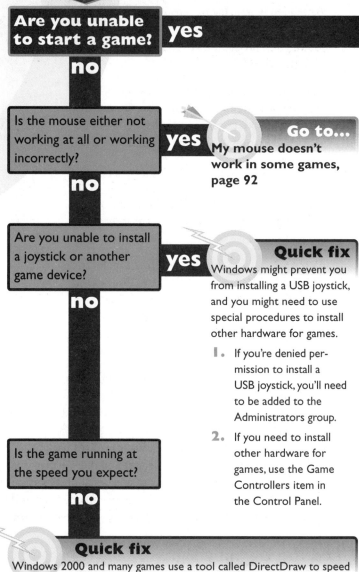

Are you unable to start a game? yes

no

Is the mouse either not working at all or working incorrectly? **yes**

Go to...
My mouse doesn't work in some games, page 92

no

Are you unable to install a joystick or another game device? **yes**

Quick fix
Windows might prevent you from installing a USB joystick, and you might need to use special procedures to install other hardware for games.

1. If you're denied permission to install a USB joystick, you'll need to be added to the Administrators group.

2. If you need to install other hardware for games, use the Game Controllers item in the Control Panel.

no

Is the game running at the speed you expect?

no

Quick fix
Windows 2000 and many games use a tool called DirectDraw to speed up game play. Unfortunately, there's a bug in DirectDraw.

1. Obtain and install a Windows 2000 service pack.

2. Restart Windows, start the game, and see whether it runs faster. If it's still too slow, make sure all your other programs are closed, and try again.

3. If the game is still too slow, check with the manufacturer to make sure you have the proper equipment installed.

Is the game a DVD-based game? → **yes**

Quick fix

Some older games and multi-media programs use an older DVD system that no longer works with Windows 2000.

1. Try starting the game. If you see a message referring to MCI or MCI-DVD drivers, you can't play the game.

2. Contact the manufacturer for an update of the game that uses Direct-Draw or other DirectX tools instead of MCI.

no ↓

Is the game an Internet game that you're trying to play over a shared (ICS) connection? → **yes**

Go to...

I can't play an Internet game over a shared connection, page 94

no ↓

Is the game an MS-DOS game? → **yes**

Quick fix

MS-DOS games often violate the security requirements of Windows 2000. You need to run the game in a different environment.

1. Check with the game manufacturer to verify that the game won't run in Windows 2000. Ask whether there's an available fix.

2. If the game won't run in Windows 2000, install the game on a FAT (also called a FAT16) hard disk on your computer.

3. Using the manufacturer's directions, create an MS-DOS boot disk for the game.

4. Start the computer with the boot disk, and play the game.

no ↓

Go to...

My game won't run, page 90

If your solution isn't here

Check these related chapters:

Hardware installation, page 96

Internet Sharing client, page 112

Modems, page 146

Programs, page 220

Screen, page 230

Sound, page 250

Or see the general troubleshooting tips on page xiii

My game won't run

Source of the problem

A fast-paced game—or even a slow-paced one that uses complex graphics—demands a lot from your computer system. To get your games working at their best, assorted hardware and software support has been developed, but the technology is still evolving, so many of the games, the hardware, and the software support from the operating system aren't always compatible. When everything is working as it should, game performance can be thrilling. When there's a conflict between the game, the hardware, and/or the operating system, game performance decreases, or the game fails to run or stops running in the middle of the game when a particular resource is needed. If a game doesn't work, you can try deactivating some of the support to see whether you can then run the game, albeit a bit more slowly than you'd like.

How to fix it

1. A game is a program, just like a word processor or a spreadsheet (but more fun). As you do with any other misbehaving program, you need to verify that the game is compatible with Windows 2000 and whether any special software updates are needed to make the game run properly. To do so, check with the manufacturer of the game or with Microsoft for a list of tested programs at *http://www.microsoft.com/windows2000/upgrade/compat*.

2. If the game is compatible with Windows 2000, there might be a problem with the way the DirectX software that's used to enhance games is interacting with the computer's hardware. You'll need to do some trial-and-error testing to see whether there's a conflict between the software and the hardware. You must be logged on as an Administrator to make any changes, so log off if necessary, and log on again as the local Administrator.

3. To see whether there's a problem between the DirectX software and your display adapter, on the Settings submenu of the Start menu, click Control Panel. In the Control Panel, double-click the Display icon. On the Settings tab, click the Advanced button. On the Troubleshooting tab, drag the Hardware Acceleration slider to the left, stopping one step before None. Click OK, and then click OK again to close the Display Properties dialog box. Shut down Windows, restart your computer, log on as yourself, and then try playing the game. Log off, log on as the Administrator, and return to the Troubleshooting tab from the Display Properties dialog box. If you were able to play the game, experiment with how much hardware acceleration you can use by dragging the slider to the right one step, restarting, and playing the game. Continue the experimentation until the game fails, and then move the slider one step to the left. If you weren't able to play the game, return the slider to its original position (usually all the way to the right.)

4. If the game still doesn't work, your next step is to see whether there's a problem between the DirectX software and your sound adapter. Again, log on as the local Administrator, and, in the Control Panel, double-click the Sounds And Multimedia icon. On the Audio tab, in the Sound Recording section, click the Advanced button. In the Advanced Audio Properties dialog box, drag the Hardware Acceleration slider to the left, stopping one step before None. Click OK, and then click OK again. Shut down Windows, restart your computer, log on as yourself, and try playing the game. If you can play the game, log on as the Administrator, return to the Advanced Audio Properties dialog box and move the slider one step to the right, restart the computer, log on as yourself, and try the game again. If you can't play the game, repeat the process and reset the slider one step to the left. If you still can't play the game, return to the Advanced Audio Properties dialog box, click the Restore Defaults button, click OK, and then click OK again.

Tip

Sometimes a virus-protection program can interfere with a game. If you're sure the game is safe, disable the virus-protection program, and try playing the game.

5. If you still can't play the game, check to verify that all the DirectX files you need are installed. To do so, on the Start menu, click Run. In the Open box, type **dxdiag**, and click OK. On the DirectX Files tab, look in the Notes section; it should indicate that no problems were found. Check the status on the DX Media Files and DirectX Drivers tabs. If they indicate that no problems were found, you should have all the required DirectX files installed. If there's an error message on any of the tabs, you have a problem with the DirectX files. Visit the Windows Update site to replace and/or update any missing files.

6. If all the DirectX files are present, use the DirectX Diagnostic Tool to see whether any specific part of the DirectX files is causing the problem. Click each of the tabs, and look for a test button. Use the test button to test each feature. If any feature fails, note the part of DirectX that is causing the problem. Close the DirectX Diagnostic Tool when you've finished.

7. If you've identified any area that's causing a problem, contact the manufacturer of your video adapter (for DirectDraw, Direct3D, or hardware acceleration settings in the Advanced dialog box), or the manufacturer of your sound adapter (for DirectSound, DirectMusic, or hardware acceleration settings in the Advanced Audio Properties dialog box), and see whether there's any known solution.

Tip

When you download and install a game from the Internet, the game might be downloaded but either not installed or incorrectly installed because you don't have permission to install a program.

8. If none of the foregoing is the problem, there might be a problem with the installation of the game. The simplest solution is to uninstall the program and then reinstall it. To do so, log on as the local Administrator, and, in the Control Panel, double-click Add/Remove Programs. Click the game, click the Change/Remove button, and follow the directions on the screen. Then restart Windows, log on as the Administrator, reinstall the game as you did previously, and try playing the game again.

My mouse doesn't work in some games

Source of the problem

When your mouse isn't working, or isn't working correctly, it's usually a symptom of a conflict between the mouse and its drivers, and possibly something else—a program or a piece of hardware, for example—that's trying to control the screen or that wants to use the same resources the mouse is using. If you have mouse problems only when you're playing certain Windows games, you can be fairly certain there's a battle going on over control of the screen. If however, the problem occurs only when you're playing an MS-DOS game, you might be able to fix the problem by simply changing a setting.

How to fix it

1. Make sure your nonfunctioning mouse really is a problem, and that what you're experiencing isn't a "feature" of the game. Check the game's documentation for information about using the mouse. Many games don't use the mouse, and they disable the mouse pointer in the game's window. Some games don't respond to mouse clicks at all. Also, try using your mouse in a Windows program when you don't have a game running to see whether there's a system-wide problem with the mouse. If there is, see "Mouse," starting on page 156.

2. By default, Windows sets the mouse to mark content (a simple text-selection method) in a Command Prompt window instead of the mouse's usual click-and-drag features. If you're playing an MS-DOS game that runs in a Command Prompt window, and if the mouse doesn't work with the game, see whether the mouse is set to work in a way that's wrong for the game. To make sure the mouse isn't set only to mark content in the window, right-click the title bar of the window, and click Properties on the shortcut menu. (If the program is running in full-screen mode, right-click the Command Prompt icon on the taskbar, and click Properties on the shortcut menu.) In the Properties dialog box, on the Options tab, clear the QuickEdit Mode check box, and click OK. ▶

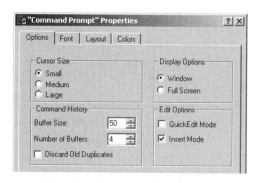

3. When you're prompted to specify the way you want the change to be applied, click the Apply Properties To Current Window option to make the change this time only, or click

the Modify Shortcut That Started This Window option if you want to make the change permanent. Click OK. ▶

4. If the MS-DOS game doesn't start in a Command Prompt window but instead starts in a window of its own, you might still be experiencing similar problems, and you might be able to make the same type of change to this window. Use My Computer to locate the game on your computer. Right-click the program file for the game, and click Properties on the shortcut menu. On the Misc tab, clear the QuickEdit check box if it's selected. Select the Exclusive Mode check box, and click OK. When you run the game using the Exclusive Mode option, you should be able to use the mouse in the game, but it will be disabled for use in any other program or in Windows. Once you've ended the game, you'll be able to use the mouse again. If the Exclusive Mode option doesn't solve the problem, return to the Properties dialog box for the game's program file, and clear the Exclusive Mode check box. (You might not be able to make these changes in all your MS-DOS games; some programmers have disabled these features.)

5. If, instead of not working at all, the mouse acts though a button were being pressed (so that whatever you point to is selected, opened, or run), you've encountered a bug that affects only a few games. To fix the problem, you need to install a Windows 2000 service pack. See Appendix A, "Installing a service pack," on page 295 for information about obtaining and installing a Windows Service Pack.

6. If the mouse seems to work but the mouse pointer isn't displayed correctly—if, for example, it appears as a black square—there's probably a problem with the way your system interacts with the DirectX software that's used to help display games and other graphics-intensive programs. To see whether this is the case, on the Settings submenu of the Start menu, click Control Panel. In the Control Panel, hold down the Shift key and right-click the Display Properties icon. Click Run As, and log on as an Administrator. On the Settings tab of the Display Properties dialog box, click the Advanced button. On the Troubleshooting tab, drag the Hardware Acceleration slider one step to the left. This disables the use of DirectX to speed up the mouse pointer and should eliminate any problems with the pointer. Click OK, and click OK again to close the Display Properties dialog box. Restart your computer and see whether the mouse pointer is working correctly now. ▶

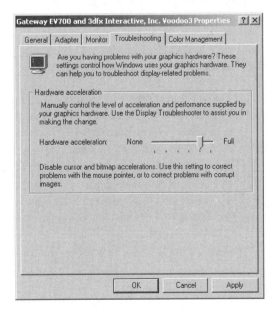

I can't play an Internet game over a shared connection

Source of the problem

If you want to play a game over the Internet, and your computer is on a network, you might encounter problems even though you've configured your computer correctly for playing the game. If your computer is on a large network that uses a proxy server for the connection, there might not be much you can do about it—for some reason, most network administrators are not the least bit sympathetic toward your tragic inability to play games over the Internet. However, if your connection to the Internet uses ICS (Internet connection sharing), you might be able to work out some of your problems and learn to live with the restrictions that go along with this type of Internet access.

How to fix it

1. The primary requirement for playing Internet games is, of course, that you be connected to the Internet. From your computer, use your web browser to go to a couple of locations on the Internet. Click the Refresh button to make sure you're not looking at an offline page instead of one that you're downloading from the Internet. If the pages are up to date, you're properly connected to the Internet using ICS. Try playing your game to see whether it works. If it doesn't, or if you receive an error message, disconnect from the server. ▶

Depending on the game and the way you connect to it, you can receive a variety of error messages that all mean the same thing—you can't play the game.

2. If possible, test the game by connecting directly to the Internet from your computer—by dialing in using the computer's modem, for example. If you can do this, go to the location of the game and play it. If all works well, you'll know the game is properly set up on your computer. If the game doesn't work, however, you might need to reinstall the software. Don't try getting the game to work over a network until you've verified that the game works over the Internet from your computer. Disconnect from the Internet, and restore your settings to connect to the Internet using the ICS connection over your network. For information about changing the way you connect to the Internet, see "My computer uses the wrong connection to connect to the Internet" on page 116.

3. Connect to the Internet using the ICS connection, and try playing the game again. If any tweaking you did to your game's settings still hasn't made it possible for you to play the game using ICS, you might start suspecting your ICS host's ability to translate and send the game to you over the network.

4. Different games have different requirements for being played over a network. In most cases, you won't be able to play the game unless it's installed on the computer that is the ICS host on your network. Go to the ICS host computer and see whether the game is installed. If it isn't installed, install it on the host computer. If the host computer isn't currently connected to the Internet, connect now. Play the game to verify that it works properly on the host computer. If you have any problems, check the game's documentation for the information you need to get the game working correctly.

5. If you were able to play the game from the ICS host computer, go back to your own computer. Make sure you're connected to the Internet, and try playing the game again. If you can play the game from your computer, note what you did on the ICS computer so that you'll be able to make similar changes if you have problems the next time you try to play a different Internet game.

6. If you were able to play the game on your computer when you were using a direct connection, and you could play the game on the ICS host computer, but you're still having problems, you need to see whether anyone else is playing the game on the network. ICS supports playing a game that's hosted on a public computer for only the ICS host computer and one ICS client. If someone else is playing the game over the ICS connection, have them log off, and then try your connection again.

7. If no one else is using the ICS connection, it's likely that the problem can't be solved. Although the ICS host computer usually does a good job of translating the information from the Internet connection to the network and back again, some games simply can't be translated correctly. To play any such game, you'll have to connect your computer directly to the Internet, play the game from the host ICS computer, or decide to play a different game.

Sometimes a game works for a while...

Some games require a fast Internet connection and will fail, or time out, if your connection is too slow. When you're using ICS, you need to worry about the speed of the Internet connection, the speed at which information is translated between the Internet and the network, and the speed of your network. If you can play a game but it frequently times out, try playing a simpler and slower game and see whether it works over your connection. If it does, consider using a faster connection by connecting directly to the Internet, using the ICS connection when the network isn't busy, or getting a faster Internet connection for the ICS computer.

So you installed a piece of hardware, but it doesn't work, or Windows misidentified it or didn't even detect it. What's going on? Don't blame Windows right away—there could be a problem with the hardware. We'll walk through some possible scenarios here.

Did Windows detect and install software for the new hardware you attached?   **yes**

no

Were you denied permission to install new equipment?   **yes**

no

Quick fix

Only members of the Administrators and Power Users groups can install hardware.

1. If you have an Administrators or Power Users account, log on using that account.

2. If you don't have either of these accounts, ask someone who does to install the hardware for you.

Do you have a disk that contains an installation or setup program designed for Windows 2000?   **yes**

no

Go to...
The device wasn't detected, page 98

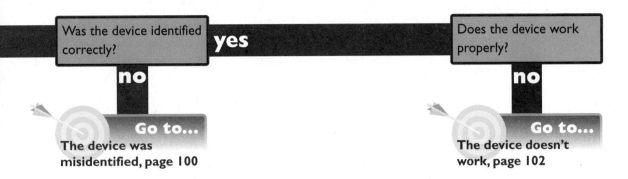

Was the device identified correctly?

yes

Does the device work properly?

no

no

Go to...

The device was misidentified, page 100

Go to...

The device doesn't work, page 102

Quick fix

Many hardware devices contain programs that add functionality to the device.

1. Make sure the program is designed to work with Windows 2000 and that it uses Windows 2000 drivers.

2. Log on to Windows as an Administrator, as a Power User, or as any user with authorization to install a new hardware device.

3. Follow the manufacturer's instructions for installing the software and the hardward device.

> **If your solution isn't here**
> Check these related chapters:
> Access to the computer, page 2
> Modems, page 146
> Mouse, page 156
> Sound, page 252
> Or see the general troubleshooting tips on page xiii

The device wasn't detected

Source of the problem

When you install a piece of hardware on your computer, Windows 2000 usually detects it and installs the correct software support. However, some devices—especially older ones—aren't always detected by Windows. If you're certain the device will run in Windows 2000, you can tell Windows which device you're installing and where it's located so that Windows can install the correct drivers. Before you do too much detective work, though, you should make sure that your computer is using the same connection you're using to communicate with the device.

How to fix it

1. Check that your device is listed in the most recent Windows 2000 hardware compatibility list by visiting the web page *http://www.microsoft.com/hwtest/hcl*. If the device isn't in the list, check with the hardware manufacturer for recent fixes and drivers.

2. With the computer turned off, make sure the device is ready. If the device uses exterior power, make sure it's plugged in and turned on, and that any cables are connected properly. Turn on the computer, and log on as an Administrator.

3. If the device is connected to a parallel (or LPT) port, a serial (or COM) port, or to a USB (universal serial bus) connection, right-click My Computer on the Desktop, and click Manage on the shortcut menu. In the Computer Management window, click Device Manager in the left pane. In the right pane, check under Ports (COM & LPT) to verify that the communications port or printer port you're using is listed, or that the Universal Serial Bus Controllers are listed at or

near the bottom of the list if the device is connected to the USB port. If the connection you're using isn't listed, consult the owner's manual for your computer to learn how to enable the connection in the computer's BIOS (basic input/output system). (When you start the computer, you're usually prompted to press a key to enter a setup screen.) Close the Computer Management window when you've finished. ▶

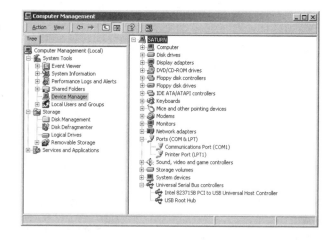

4. On the Settings submenu of the Start menu, click Control Panel. In the Control Panel, double-click the Add/Remove Hardware icon. Click Next in the Add/Remove Hardware Wizard that appears, and step into the wizard.

5. Make sure the Add/Troubleshoot A Device option is selected, and click Next. If Windows finds the device you want to install, click Next, complete the wizard, and kiss your problems goodbye.

6. In the list that appears, double-click Add A New Device. With the option to search for new hardware selected, click Next. If the hardware you want to install is detected, click it, and complete the wizard. If no hardware was detected, click Next in the Detected Hardware page of the wizard.

7. In the Hardware Types list, double-click the type of hardware you want to install.

8. Click the manufacturer's name and the model. Make sure the information is correct, click Next, and complete the wizard. If the manufacturer or model isn't listed, download or obtain a disk from the manufacturer with the correct Windows 2000–compatible drivers, and click Have Disk. ▶

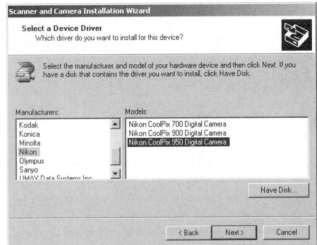

9. In the Install From Disk dialog box, click the Browse button and locate the downloaded files. Windows will look for the appropriate information file (a file with the .inf extension). When the file has been located, click Open, and complete the wizard.

10. Restart the computer when prompted, and verify that the device is working as expected. If the computer doesn't start correctly, see "Windows won't start correctly" on page 262. Check with the manufacturer of the device to figure out what went wrong.

More about detecting devices

Most hardware devices that you add to your computer are Plug And Play devices. A Plug And Play device contains information about itself, and when it's installed, Windows reads the information and understands how to set up the device, provided the correct drivers are available. In non–Plug And Play devices, however, the information either isn't stored in a format Windows can use or isn't stored at all. In these cases, Windows might detect the device and either identify it or label it as an unknown device, or it might not be able to detect the device. It's usually when you attach a device to a serial or parallel port that the device isn't detected.

The device was misidentified

Source of the problem

When you install new hardware on your computer, Windows 2000 attempts to detect it and to determine what type of hardware it is, what supporting software it needs, and what special settings need to be made. Provided Windows can determine all this information, it goes ahead and installs the device. Sometimes, however, the information supplied by the device is ambiguous, and sometimes Windows simply doesn't have the software to support the device. In these situations, you can (or at least you can try to) tell Windows which item you're installing, make any settings you need, and add whatever software Windows needs.

How to fix it

1. Your first step is to confirm that the hardware is compatible with Windows 2000 by checking the Windows 2000 hardware compatibility list at *http://www.microsoft.com/hwtest/hcl*. Use this list rather than any lists you might have on your CD, network, or hard disk, which could be out of date. If your hardware isn't in the list, check with the manufacturer to confirm that the device is fully compatible with Windows 2000. If it isn't certified as compatible, you should consider either installing the device on a computer that isn't running Windows 2000 or replacing the device with one that is compatible.

2. Log on to Windows as an Administrator. Right-click My Computer on the Desktop, and click Manage on the shortcut menu. In the left pane of the Computer Management window, click Device Manager.

3. Double-click the type of device you're installing, and double-click the device to display its Properties dialog box. On the Driver tab of the dialog box, click the Update Driver button.

4. In the Upgrade Device Driver Wizard, click Next to enter the wizard. Click the option to display a list of all the drivers for this device, and click Next.

5. If the device is listed in the Models list, click it, and then click Next. Follow the instructions to complete the wizard.

Tip
If the device isn't listed in the Device Manager, see "The device wasn't detected" on page 98.

Tip
If you're certain that Windows doesn't have the correct driver, and if you have the correct driver on a disk, you can click the option to search for a suitable device instead of displaying a list of known devices. The result will be the same as what you get by using the Have Disk button in step 7.

6. If the device isn't listed, click the option to show all hardware. Click the device's manufacturer and model. Make sure you have the correct information, click Next, and complete the wizard.

7. If the device's manufacturer and/or model aren't listed, download or obtain a disk from the manufacturer that contains the correct Windows 2000–compatible drivers, and click Have Disk. In the Install From Disk dialog box, click the Browse button and locate the downloaded files. Windows will search for the appropriate information file (a file with the *.inf* extension). When Windows has found the file, click Open, and complete the wizard.

8. Restart the computer when prompted. If the computer doesn't start properly, or if there are serious problems after it starts, see "Windows won't start correctly" on page 262 for information about starting up with the Last Known Good Configuration or in Safe Mode. Go back to the Device Manager and install a different driver. If the system still doesn't work properly, click the Uninstall button on the Driver tab, and restart the system. Windows should reinstall the device using the drivers it identifies as being correct. Contact the device manufacturer for updated drivers or for a software or hardware fix.

More about drivers

Drivers are software files that make it possible for hardware devices to work with Windows 2000 and that allow Windows to configure the computer to work with the hardware. By having different drivers for different software, Windows can figure out how to adjust the system to the different configurations of the hardware and what to do with the different features each device offers.

Because Windows 2000 requires hardware devices and drivers to comply with a set of rigorous standards, many drivers for various devices were unavailable when the Windows 2000 CD was created. Instead, drivers are continuously being tested and certified, and many new ones are available from the software vendors. New drivers are also installed when you install a Windows 2000 service pack (see Appendix A, "Installing a service pack," on page 295).

Windows wants to use only the drivers that were designed for Windows 2000. However, if a driver isn't available for a device that you absolutely must have on your computer, check with the manufacturer to see whether the device will work correctly with Windows 2000 if you use a Windows NT 4 driver for the device. Don't, however, try to use a driver designed for Windows 95, Windows 98, or Windows Millennium Edition.

Tip
If Windows shuts down or otherwise crashes when you try to update a driver, uninstall a driver, or uninstall a device using the Add/Remove Hardware Wizard, and you can't seem to do anything with the device, there's probably a serious error on the hard disk or in the Registry. Try using the Windows maintenance tools to repair the disk. If this doesn't help, you can try to repair the Windows installation and restore the Registry. For information about repairing Windows and restoring the Registry, see "Windows won't start correctly" on page 262.

The device doesn't work

Source of the problem

When you hook up a piece of hardware to your computer, and you watch as Windows 2000 recognizes it and goes through the motions of setting it up, you expect the device to work properly. If it doesn't, your first reaction is probably to blame Windows, and you could be right. Quite often, however, the problem lies elsewhere. Sometimes it's caused by poor engineering by the hardware manufacturer, sometimes the required support software is missing, and sometimes it might be because someone (surely not you!) did a poor job of setting up your computer. Regardless of who or what is the source of the problem, you need to figure out how you can get that piece of hardware working.

How to fix it

1. You can be sure that a piece of hardware will work with Windows 2000 only if you can find it in the hardware compatibility list, which is located at *http://www.microsoft.com/hwtest/hcl*. Check this site for the most recent list of hardware that has proved to be compatible with Windows 2000. If your device isn't in the list, check with the hardware manufacturer for recent fixes and drivers.

2. Make sure the device is installed according to the manufacturer's instructions and that its exterior power source, if it has one, is turned on. To make any changes to the system, you must be logged on as a member of the Administrators group.

3. Right-click My Computer on the Desktop, and click Manage on the shortcut menu. In the left pane of the Computer Management window that appears, click Device Manager.

4. Double-click the type of device you've installed if the listing isn't expanded to show all devices of that type. Note whether there's a yellow exclamation-mark icon, an X icon, or an I icon next to the device. The exclamation-mark icon means that the device isn't functioning (often referred to as being *banged out*—in the old days of typography, an exclamation mark was called a *bang*); the X icon indicates that the device has been disabled; and the I icon means there's some information available about possible settings problems.

5. Double-click the device to display its Properties dialog box. On the General tab, note any specific problems for the device. If the device is listed as disabled, ask around to make sure it wasn't

> **Warning**
>
> Modifying system settings can cause substantial problems with your computer system. Don't make changes recklessly, hoping that things will somehow work out. If you do decide to make system changes, make sure that you have an updated ERD (Emergency Recovery Disk) on hand. Use the Windows Backup program on the System Tools submenu of the Start menu to create your ERD.

intentionally disabled for a good reason. Otherwise, click the Enable Device button, and step through the Device Troubleshooting Wizard to enable the device. Click Close to close the Properties dialog box. Try using this device and your other devices to make sure they're all working properly. ▶

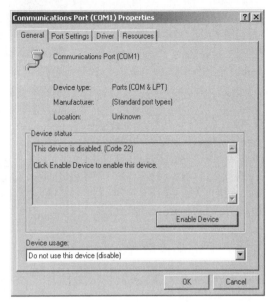

6. If the device isn't disabled but the Device Status indicates that the driver isn't installed, click the Reinstall Driver button, and step through the Upgrade Device Driver Wizard to install the correct driver. The Reinstall Driver button will appear on the General tab if Windows detects a problem with the driver. If you don't have the correct driver, contact the manufacturer.

7. If the driver isn't the problem, click the Resources tab, and verify that the listed Input/Output Range and Interrupt Request match those listed in the device's documentation. If they don't match, check the documentation for information about changing the device's settings to match those values. If you can't make the hardware match the settings, try changing the settings. To do so, clear the check box for using automatic settings, double-click the item you want to change, and make the changes in the dialog box that

appears. If you can't clear the check box, or if you get a message telling you that you can't change the settings, your only recourse is to consult with the device's manufacturer. ▶

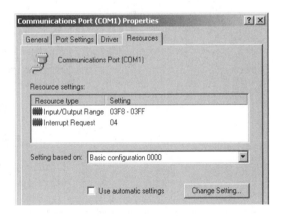

8. If the problem isn't with the Input/Output Range or the Interrupt Request, click the Troubleshooter button on the General tab, if there is one. If not, search Help for the correct troubleshooter. Work your way through the troubleshooter to figure out the steps for the specific type of hardware you're trying to use.

9. After you've made your changes, restart the computer. If either the device or the entire computer doesn't work properly, open the Properties dialog box for the device as you did in steps 3 and 4, disable the device, and close the dialog box. Contact the device manufacturer for updated drivers or for a software or hardware fix.

The Internet puts a dizzying array of news and knowledge at your fingertips, and Microsoft Internet Explorer is your window on that wide world of information. In this chapter, we'll discuss some of the problems you might encounter while you're using Internet Explorer (a slow connection to the Internet, the wrong home page, a changed default browser), as well as some of the choices you can make (installing language packs, changing the font and font size in web pages) so that Internet Explorer looks and works the way you want it to.

Does Internet Explorer connect properly?

yes

no

Does a program other than Internet Explorer open?

yes

no

Quick fix

Installing some software packages can switch your default web browser. You can easily switch back to use Internet Explorer as your default browser.

1. In the Control Panel, double-click Internet Options.
2. On the Programs tab, click the Reset Web Settings button, click Yes, and then click OK. Click the program you want to use.

Does Internet Explorer start up with the wrong home page?

yes

no

Go to...

Dial-up connection, starting on page 28

If your solution isn't here

Check these related chapters:

Internet Sharing client, page 112

Modems, page 146

Outlook Express, page 178

Or see the general troubleshooting tips on page xiii

Internet Explorer

When you open a web page that's in another language, does Internet Explorer display the correct characters?

yes → Are you unable to change the font or the font size on a web page?

yes →
Go to...
I don't like the font or the font size on some web pages, page 108

no ↓

Go to...
Web pages in other languages are unreadable, page 110

Is Internet Explorer really slow?

yes →
Go to...
It takes so long to download web pages, page 106

no ↓

Does Internet Explorer use the wrong program to send e-mail or to view newsgroups?

yes →
Quick fix

If you have more than one program installed on your computer that can do the task, you need to tell Windows which program to use.

1. In Internet Explorer, click Internet Options on the Tools menu.

2. On the Programs tab, click the program you want to use for each task.

3. If you don't see the program you want to use, click the Reset Web Settings button, click Yes, and then click OK. Then repeat step 2.

Quick fix

If you installed software that caused your home page to change, or if you want a different home page, you can specify the one you want.

1. Start Internet Explorer if it isn't already running. Use whatever tools you normally use to display the web page you want to use as your home page.

2. On the Tools menu, click Internet Options. On the General tab, click the Use Current button. Click OK.

It takes so long to download web pages

Source of the problem

Many web designers live in a world slightly apart from the one most of us live in. With fast computers and very fast Internet connections, they rarely encounter the frustration of waiting…and waiting…and waiting…for a page to download. The web designer's quest is to create the ultimate web page, which means using extensive formatting, creating detailed graphics, and adding more and more features. Your quest is to get the web page downloaded before you lose interest or fall asleep! You can speed up the downloads by tweaking your system a bit, and by sacrificing a few of the features the web designer toiled so hard to include.

How to fix it

1. The first step is to tune up your computer and make sure it's working efficiently. If you're dialing in to a service provider, make sure your modem is working at or near its connection speed. A modem that isn't fully compatible with Windows 2000 might work, but not at its fastest speed. To see the speed at which the modem is connecting, connect to the Internet as you normally would. If the Dial-Up Connection icon is displayed on the taskbar, either note the connection speed when the pop-up message appears, or point to the icon and wait for a pop-up message showing the connection speed to appear. If the icon isn't displayed, or if the pop-up message doesn't appear, right-click My Network Places on the Desktop, and click Properties on the shortcut menu. In the Network And Dial-Up Connections window, right-click the connection you're using to connect to your service provider, and click Status. The speed of the connection will be shown. If it's far below your modem's capabilities, you'll need to troubleshoot the modem. For more information about modems, see "Modems," starting on page 146. ▶

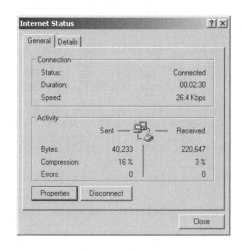

2. The next step is to take out the garbage—that is, the old Internet files—so that you can free up some space for new files and then store the new files with the new settings you'll be making. (This should speed up your downloads in the long run, although it might lengthen the time it takes you the first time you return to a site, because the files that were stored on your computer for that site will need to be downloaded again.) On the

System Tools submenu of the Start menu, click Disk Cleanup. Specify the drive you want to clean up if you have more than one, click OK, select the Temporary Internet Files check box, and click OK. ▶

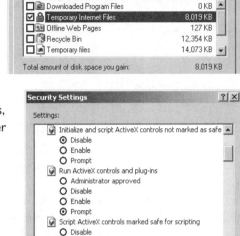

3. Now you must decide which parts of the web pages you can live without. Many web pages contain little programs that you must download if you want to see the special effects or other features they provide. To have Internet Explorer ask you if you want to download any of these programs, as well as any additional fonts the web page designer thinks you should use, in Internet Explorer, click Internet Options on the Tools menu. On the Security tab, click the Custom Level button. In the Security Settings dialog box, click the Prompt option for any or all of the following items: ▶

- Download Signed ActiveX Controls

- Run ActiveX Controls And Plug-Ins

- Script ActiveX Controls Marked Safe For Scripting

- Font Download

- Scripting Of Java Applets

When you've finished, click OK, and confirm that you want to change the security settings. Click OK again to close the Internet Options dialog box.

4. Explore some different web pages. When prompted, click Yes to include the element listed on the web page and wait while it's being downloaded, or click No to skip the item. ▶

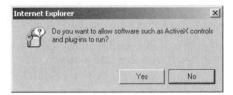

More about slow downloads

Other factors that affect how long it takes to download web pages might be that the web site is busy, is experiencing problems, or is poorly designed. Sometimes the problem is with your service provider, or, if you're connected to the Internet using Internet connection sharing on your network, your network might be too busy to support fast downloads. And don't expect a 56 Kbps modem to actually connect at 56 Kbps—unfortunately, few phone lines will support that speed.

I don't like the font or the font size on some web pages

Source of the problem

A web page often contains hidden information that specifies the font and font size in which the page is laid out. Internet Explorer and Windows then use the font—or, if it isn't available, a similar font—at the specified size to display the text of the web page. Although the specifications assure the designer of the web page that we'll see the page as it was meant to be seen, they can sometimes make the page difficult to read. Fortunately, you can tell Internet Explorer to ignore the designer's settings and to use the font and font size you want. Don't be too eager to make substantial changes, though. Many web pages use specific fonts and font sizes to present the page layout correctly. Changing these defaults can ruin the design and render the page jumbled and unreadable.

How to fix it

1. Not all web pages dictate the font and font size to be used, and some pages control only some of the text. Open Internet Explorer if it isn't already open, and go to the web page you want to view. To see whether you can adjust the font size, on the View menu of Internet Explorer, point to Text Size, and click a different text size on the submenu.

2. If only some or none of the text changes size, you need to tell Internet Explorer to ignore the information about fonts that's included with the web page. You should also do this if you always want to use your own font and font size settings on all the web pages you visit. To do so, click Internet Options on the Tools menu. On the General tab, click the Accessibility button. In the Accessibility dialog box, select the Ignore Font Styles Specified On Web Pages check box, and click OK. Click OK to close the Internet Options dialog box. ▶

3. Now test the web page. On the View menu, point to Text Size, and click a different text size. The size of the text on the web page should change.

> **Tip**
>
> Don't be fooled by what looks like text but is really a picture. Many of the elements you see on a web page—buttons, bullets, fancy formatted text—are actually pictures. These elements won't change when you change the font or the font size.

4. You can also change which fonts are used if you want to enhance the readability or the appearance of the web page. The fonts you specify will apply to the text of all web pages that don't specify a font—and to all those that do—if, in step 2, you told Internet Explorer to ignore font styles. To change the font, on the Tools menu, click Internet Options. On the General tab, click the Fonts button.

5. In the Fonts dialog box, make sure the correct language group is shown in the Language Script list. (The language group you normally use should be listed and usually won't need to be changed.) ▶

6. In the Web Page Font list, click the font you want to use for all the text that's usually formatted on a web page. (Formatted text is generally the text that makes up the main body of the web page.)

7. In the Plain Text Font list, click the font you want to use for all the other text on the web page. Plain text is often used for titles and other headings. Examine the samples of the selected text below each font list to make sure you've chosen appropriate fonts. Click OK when you've finished. Click OK to close the Internet Options dialog box.

8. Examine the web page now that it shows the different fonts. On the View menu, point to Text Size, and click a different text size on the submenu. See whether you like the changes you've made to the web page. If you don't, return to the Internet Options dialog box, and click either the Fonts button to specify different fonts or the Accessibility button to restore the ability of the web pages to designate which fonts to use. ▲

Tip

If you're using a mouse with a wheel, hold down the Ctrl key on your keyboard and rotate the mouse wheel to quickly change the font size on your web page.

Web pages in other languages are unreadable

Source of the problem

The Internet is your window on a world that speaks many different languages. When you access web pages that are written in a different language, what you see on your screen might be a bewildering display of unreadable symbol characters. To see those same web pages with the proper characters used, you'll need to install the correct language files from the Internet Explorer language pack. When you install these elements, you're also modifying Windows 2000 so that it can operate in that language.

How to fix it

1. If you're not logged on as an Administrator, log off, and then log on again as an Administrator. (When you add languages to Internet Explorer, you're also adding those languages to Windows 2000. These are system changes that require Administrator permission.)

2. Open Internet ▶ Explorer and connect to the web page you want to read. Examine the page. If you can connect to the page but all or part of it is unreadable, you'll need to add the language pack files.

3. If, when you connect to the web page, you see a dialog box asking you whether you want to install the language for the web page, click Install. ▶

---

4. If you go to the page but aren't prompted to install the required files, you'll need to install them yourself. On the Tools menu in Internet Explorer, click Internet Options, and, on the General tab, click the Languages button. In the Language Preference dialog box, click Add. In the Add Language dialog box, click the language you want, and click OK. Click OK to close the Language Preference dialog box, and click OK again to close the Internet Options dialog box. ▶

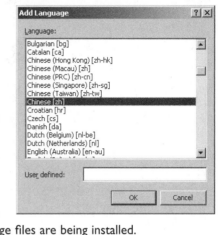

5. Whichever method you used to indicate that you want to install a language, you'll need either the Windows 2000 Professional CD or network access to the installation files to complete the process. Wait while the language files are being installed.

6. Click OK when you're notified that the installation is complete, and then review the web page. If the characters aren't correct, click the Update button on the Standard Buttons toolbar. If the characters are still incorrect, restart your computer. (When you install the language, Internet Explorer uses it right away. However, although Windows has also installed the language, it isn't using it correctly until the computer has been restarted.) The web page should now display the text in the correct characters. ▶

7. If the characters are still incorrect after you've restarted the computer, you can try forcing the page to use a specific language. To do so, point to Encoding on the View menu, and click Auto-Select on the Encoding submenu. If this doesn't cause the correct characters to be displayed, try selecting a specific language or language group from the Encoding submenu. Click the Refresh button on the Standard Buttons toolbar to force the page to be updated.

8. If you still can't get the web page to be displayed correctly, you might need to add a different language, as you did in steps 4 and 5.

When one computer on a network (the host) is set up with a connection to the Internet, other computers on the network (the clients) can use ICS (Internet connection sharing) to use the host computer's connection to connect to the Internet. This type of connection-sharing can be a bit tricky, though, and can even disrupt the network. If you do run into problems with the network, there are diagnostic tools you can use to figure out what's wrong, and you can probably make changes to a few settings to get the connection working properly.

Can you connect to the Internet through the ICS host when the host computer is connected to the Internet?

yes

no

Are you unable to use My Network Places to browse the computer that is hosting ICS?

yes

Go to...
My network connection to the ICS host computer is broken, page 114

no

Does your computer try to dial up directly instead of connecting through the ICS host?

yes

Go to...
My computer uses the wrong connection to connect to the Internet, page 116

If your solution isn't here
Check these related chapters:
Dial-up connection, page 28
Games, page 88
Internet Explorer, page 104
Internet Sharing host, page 118
Or see the general troubleshooting tips on page xiii

Can you connect if the host computer isn't connected?

yes

Are you unable to play games over the Internet?

yes

Go to...
I can't play an Internet game over a shared connection, page 94

no

no

Quick fix

If the host computer is using a dial-up connection, you can ask to have it set for dialing up whenever anyone on the network wants to connect. Someone will have to log on to the host computer as an Administrator and do the following:

1. Right-click the shared connection, and click Properties on the shortcut menu.

2. On the Sharing tab, select the Enable On-Demand Dialing check box.

3. Click OK.

Is your connection really slow?

yes

Quick fix

The time it takes information to pass through a shared connection depends on the number of people using the connection; how much information you're downloading; and the speed of the connection, the web site, your ISP, and the Internet.

1. Ask whoever is using the host computer to test and remedy connection-speed problems when the connection isn't being used by others.

2. Try using the connection when few people are connected through the host computer.

3. See "It takes so long to download web pages" on page 106 for information about speeding up the viewing of web pages.

My network connection to the ICS host computer is broken

Source of the problem

When ICS (Internet connection sharing) is set up on your network, the computer that's sharing its Internet connection becomes a local server on the network, and it tells each "client" computer on the network how to connect to and communicate with the other computers. If either the network or your computer isn't set up properly, your computer might be receiving contradictory information—or no information at all.

How to fix it

1. Before you get deeply involved in diagnosing problems, check to see whether ICS should be set up on your network. If your network is set up with a domain, there could be serious problems with using ICS. If your network uses a domain, consult with whoever set up the system to make sure it's configured correctly.

2. If ICS was set up recently and you haven't restarted your client computer, make sure the host computer is running, and then, on your computer, shut down Windows and restart the computer. See whether you can connect to the host computer after your computer starts.

3. If you still can't connect, on the Accessories submenu of the Start menu, click Command Prompt. In the Command Prompt window, at the command prompt, type **ipconfig /all**, and press Enter. The resulting list provides information about your network configuration. Under the Local Area Connection section, the Internet Protocol (IP) address should be in the form ▶ 192.168.0.*xxx*, where *xxx* is any number. It should also list the Default Gateway, DHCP Server, and DNS Servers as 192.168.0.1.

4. If you see these numbers, ICS is installed and should be working correctly. To make sure that you're looking for the correct computer, double-click My Computer on the Desktop, and, in the box

on the Address toolbar, type \\192.168.0.1, and press Enter. If the window displays the contents of the computer, make sure the shared folders you see are the ones you'd expect to see on the computer that you believe is the host computer. If the folders aren't what you're expecting, a different computer is hosting the Internet connection sharing. If, after you've typed its address, the host computer can't be found, and if you're certain that the host computer is turned on, you'll need to check the network connections on both your own and the host computer.

5. If you saw different numbers from those in step 3, either ICS isn't working properly or your computer isn't configured correctly. If other computers can't connect to the host computer, the person running it will need to do additional trouble-shooting. If, however, other computers can connect to the host computer, your computer is the leading suspect.

6. To reconfigure your settings, you'll need to be signed on as an Administrator, so log off if you need to, and use an Administrators account to log on again.

7. Right-click My Network Places on the Desktop, and click Properties on the short-cut menu. In the Network And Dial-Up Connections window, right-click Local Area Connection, and click Properties. In the Local Area Connection Properties dialog box, click Internet Protocol (TCP/IP), select the check box if it isn't already selected, and click the Properties button. Both the Obtain An IP Address Automatically and the Obtain DNS Server Address Automatically options should be selected. If either or both are not selected, click one or both options, click OK, and then click OK to close the Local Area Connection Properties dialog box. ▶

8. Shut down Windows and, after making sure the ICS host computer is running, restart your computer, logging on as yourself instead of as an Administrator. You should now be able to connect to the host computer.

Tip

If, in the Local Area Connection Properties dialog box, you don't see Internet Protocol (TCP/IP) in the list, this critical network compo-nent is missing and you can expect major network prob-lems. TCP/IP is installed by default when Windows 2000 Professional is installed, so someone must have modified this setting. Use the Install button in the Local Area Connection Properties dialog box to reinstall TCP/IP. If the component is present in the list but its check box is not selected, select it to use the TCP/IP protocol.

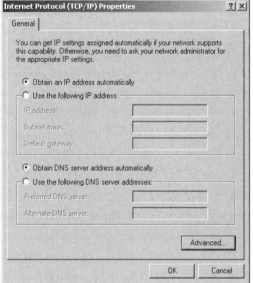

My computer uses the wrong connection to connect to the Internet

Source of the problem

When your computer is connected to a network that uses ICS (Internet connection sharing), but you also have a dial-up connection, your computer might use the wrong connection to connect to the Internet. This can become even more confusing if there are times when your computer isn't connected to your network, or if for some other reason you want to use the dial-up connection instead of the network connection.

How to fix it

1. Several programs use the same settings, so you can change your settings at a single location to have them changed for any programs to which they apply. Right-click the Internet Explorer icon on the Desktop, and click Properties on the shortcut menu. (If the Internet Explorer icon isn't displayed on your Desktop, open the Control Panel from the Settings submenu of the Start menu, and double-click the Internet Options icon to reach the same dialog box.)

2. On the Connections tab of the Internet Properties dialog box, click the connection option you want: ▶

   ● Never Dial A Connection if you know you'll always use the connection on the network

   ● Dial Whenever A Network Connection Is Not Present if your computer won't always be connected to the network and you'll want to use the dial-up connection at that point

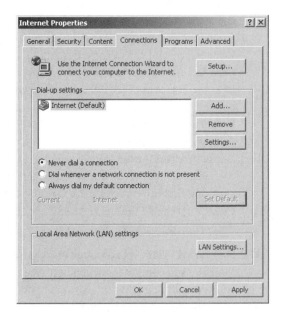

3. Click the LAN Settings button. Make sure that the Automatically Detect Settings check box is selected. The Use A Proxy Server check box should be cleared if you're using Internet

connection sharing. (This option is used if your system employs a different method of connecting to the Internet, whereby a proxy server is used on the network to prevent unauthorized access through the Internet connection. The ICS system provides similar security.) Click OK, and then click OK to close the Internet Properties dialog box. ▶

4. You have now configured the connection for Internet Explorer and any other program—Outlook Express, for example—that uses these same settings. You do, however, need to configure any other programs that connect to the Internet using their own settings. For example, if you use Microsoft Outlook instead of Outlook Express, you might need to configure the connection. To do so, in Outlook, click Services on the Tools menu, and, on the Services tab, click the service that connects, and then click Properties. On the Connection tab of the Properties dialog box, click the option to connect using your ▶ local network, and click OK. Close the Services dialog box, log off from Outlook to save the changes, and then log on again. For other programs, consult the program's documentation or Help for information about specifying the way you connect.

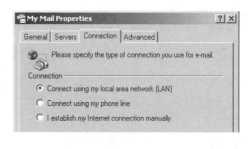

5. If for some reason—such as the network being really slow at the moment—you want to connect to the Internet using your modem while you're still connected to the network, you can manually establish the connection. To do so, right-click My Network Places on the Desktop, and click Properties on the shortcut menu. In the Network And Dial-Up Connections window, double-click the connection, and, in the Connect dialog box, click ▶ the Dial button. Once you're connected, most of your programs should use this connection. If a program hangs up this connection and tries to establish a different connection, you'll need to adjust that program's settings.

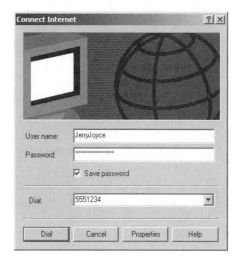

Provided your computer has a good connection to the Internet, you can use ICS (Internet connection sharing) to share your connection with other computers on your network. To do so, you turn your computer (the host) into a server that manages the connections (the clients) on the network. As the network administrator, you'll need to configure the system so that it works smoothly with the other computers that are using the connection. You might even have to run some network tools from the command prompt to figure out why the network isn't working. We'll walk you painlessly through the process.

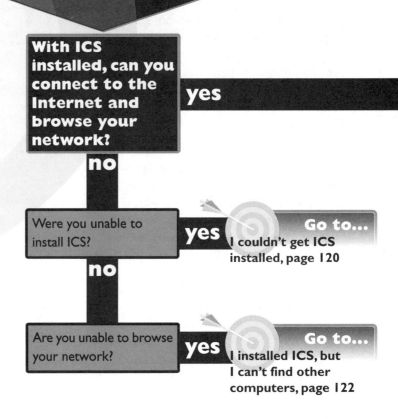

With ICS installed, can you connect to the Internet and browse your network?

yes

no

Were you unable to install ICS?

yes

Go to...
I couldn't get ICS installed, page 120

no

Are you unable to browse your network?

yes

Go to...
I installed ICS, but I can't find other computers, page 122

If your solution isn't here
Check these related chapters:
Dial-up connection, page 28
Games, page 88
Internet Sharing client, page 112
Or see the general troubleshooting tips on page xiii

Do you get disconnected soon after you've connected?

yes

no

If you're using a dial-up connection, can the ICS clients connect if you're not already connected?

no

Quick fix

If you set the connection to dial up when requested, the ICS clients can connect when you're not connected.

1. Right-click My Network Places, and click Properties on the shortcut menu. In the Network And Dial-Up Connections window, right-click the connection to your service provider, and click Properties on the shortcut menu.

2. On the Sharing tab, select the Enable On-Demand Dialing check box.

3. On the Options tab, set the amount of time the connection must be idle before disconnecting.

4. Click OK.

Quick fix

This is probably because the ICS host is running software that isn't completely compatible with Windows 2000 when certain security settings are in effect. You need to burrow deeply to get to this setting, and you must be logged on as an Administrator.

1. Right-click My Network Places, and then click Properties on the shortcut menu. In the Network And Dial-Up Connections window, right-click the connection to your service provider, and click Properties on the shortcut menu.

2. On the Networking tab, click Internet Protocol (TCP/IP) in the list, and click Properties. On the General tab, click Advanced.

3. On the Options tab of the Advanced TCP/IP Settings dialog box, click IP Security in the list, and click Properties.

4. Click either the Do Not Use IPSEC option or the option to use it with the Client (Respond Only) item selected. Click OK, and then close all the open dialog boxes.

I couldn't get ICS installed

Source of the problem

ICS (Internet connection sharing) is an extremely powerful tool. When you set it up on the computer that will host the sharing, that computer becomes a server that takes control of many aspects of your network. This control can cause conflicts with other computers that control other aspects of the network. If you've tried to install ICS without success, you need to diagnose the problem on the network, and, if possible, make some changes that will allow you to install ICS successfully.

How to fix it

1. If you're trying to set up an ICS host computer on a network that has at least one server and is set up with a domain, here's some simple advice—*don't do it!* The ICS host computer will be in direct conflict with the network server, and you could make quite a mess of the network. However, ICS can be set up on the network server, or a different program (a proxy server) can be set up on a network server to provide shared Internet access.

2. If your network is set up as a workgroup rather than as a domain, you'll probably be able to set up ICS. Setting up to host ICS is going to make substantial changes to your computer and to the way the network is running, so you'll need to be able to log on as the Administrator for this computer. Also, make sure you can connect to the Internet from this computer and that you have the correct hardware—that is, a network card that connects the computer to your network, and a modem or a network card that connects you to the Internet.

> **Tip**
> When you set up an ICS host, it will assign the new Internet Protocol (IP) addresses to itself and to the other computers on your network. If there's a good reason for an individual computer to have a specific IP address (if you're not sure about this, check with whoever set up your computer system), you shouldn't set up ICS. With IP, each computer is assigned a unique series of numbers that identify the computer to the other computers on the network.

3. When you install the ICS host, you'll almost certainly disrupt the network and disconnect anyone who's working on network documents. So, before you start, make sure that everyone, on every computer on the network, has closed any document that's open on the network and saved all the other documents they're using. You might also need the password for the Administrators account for each computer on the network.

4. Before you set up ICS, you need to check a couple of settings. To verify that all the computers on the network that will be ICS clients are using the correct networking protocols, right-click My Network Places on each client computer, and click Properties on the shortcut menu. In the

Network And Dial-Up Connections window, right-click the Local Area Connection icon, and click Properties on the shortcut menu. In the Local Area Connection Properties dialog box, make sure Internet Protocol (TCP/IP) is listed, and that its check box is selected. If this protocol isn't present or selected, someone has removed or disabled it. Find out why before continuing. If there's no valid reason, click the Install button to add the protocol, or, if it is present, select it, and click OK. You'll then need to restart the computer and resume this procedure. If the protocol is present and selected, click the Properties button. ▶

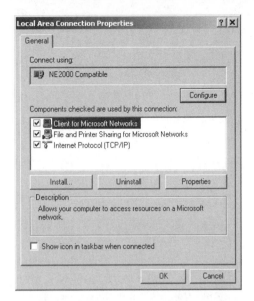

5. In the Internet Protocol (TCP/IP) Properties dialog box, verify that both the Obtain An IP Address Automatically and the Obtain DNS Server Addresses Automatically check boxes are selected. Click OK, and then click OK again to close the Local Area Connection Properties dialog box.

6. On your host computer, in the Network And Dial-Up Connections window, right-click the Internet connection you're going to share, and click Properties on the shortcut menu. On the Sharing tab, select the check box to enable ICS. ▶

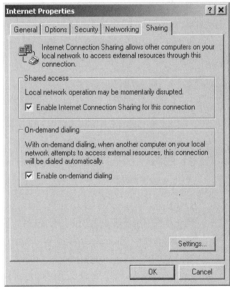

7. If you're using a dial-up connection to the Internet, select the Enable On-Demand Dialing check box so that the connection will be made whenever it's needed by a client computer. Clear the check box if you want others to use the connection only when you have manually connected your computer to the Internet.

8. Click OK, and restart your computer when prompted to do so.

More about IP addresses

When you set up the ICS host, it is automatically assigned an IP address of 192.168.0.1. It then gets busy providing the other computers on your network with addresses such as 192.168.0.110 or 192.168.0.32. These cryptic numbers are the way computers identify each other.

I installed ICS, but I can't find other computers

Source of the problem

When you install ICS (Internet connection sharing) on a computer, that computer becomes a server that provides all the computers on the network with the addresses they need to communicate with each other. Unfortunately, as you know, things don't always go smoothly—conflicts can occur among the addresses assigned to the computers, sometimes a computer won't accept the new address assigned to it, and sometimes you just have to be patient and wait for everything to start working. The following procedure assumes that the network was working before you installed ICS, that the network failure occurred immediately after you installed ICS, that you made no other changes to the network configuration, and that there's no physical reason for the network failure. This approach also assumes that you aren't scared about running a couple of network tools from the command prompt.

How to fix it

1. If you haven't already done so, after you've installed ICS on your computer and with your computer running, restart all the other computers on the network. This will force them to get their new ICS addresses from your computer. If your My Network Places window is open, press the F5 key to refresh the contents, and check to see whether the other computers are listed in your workgroup.

2. If this doesn't solve the problem, you'll need to check out and possibly adjust your system. To do so, log on to your computer as the local Administrator. On your computer, right-click My Network Places on the Desktop, and click Properties on the shortcut menu. In the Network And Dial-Up Connections window, right-click your connection to the Internet, and click Properties on the shortcut menu. On the Sharing tab, verify that the check box to enable ICS is selected. Close the dialog box.

3. Next, make sure the correct address has been assigned to your computer. On the Accessories submenu of the Start menu, click Command Prompt. At the command prompt, type **ipconfig**, ▶ and press Enter. You should see your network card listed with an address of 192.168.0.1.

```
Command Prompt                                                    _ □ ×
Microsoft Windows 2000 [Version 5.00.2195]
(C) Copyright 1985-1999 Microsoft Corp.

C:\>ipconfig

Windows 2000 IP Configuration

Ethernet adapter Local Area Connection:

        Connection-specific DNS Suffix  . :
        IP Address. . . . . . . . . . . . : 192.168.0.1
        Subnet Mask . . . . . . . . . . . : 255.255.255.0
        Default Gateway . . . . . . . . . :

C:\>
```

4. If you see a different address, or if the command doesn't produce any results, you'll need to rerun your setup for ICS. To do so, in the Network And Dial-Up Connections window, right-click the Internet connection you're sharing, click Properties on the shortcut menu, and, on the Sharing tab, clear the check box to share your connection. Click OK, restart your computer, and then follow the procedure in "I couldn't get ICS installed" on page 120.

5. If you see the correct IP (Internet Protocol) address, run the *ipconfig* command on all the computers on your network. If their IP addresses are not in the form 192.168.0.*xxx*, where *xxx* is any number, or if the command returns no results, you'll also need to follow the procedure in "I couldn't get ICS installed." If, however, you do get the correct result, write down the IP address of one of the computers.

6. On your own computer, in the Command Prompt window, at the command prompt, type **ping** and a space, and then the IP address of one of the computers. Press Enter, and wait for a response. ▶

```
Command Prompt                                            _ □ x
C:\>ping 192.168.0.110

Pinging 192.168.0.110 with 32 bytes of data:

Reply from 192.168.0.110: bytes=32 time<10ms TTL=128
Reply from 192.168.0.110: bytes=32 time<10ms TTL=128
Reply from 192.168.0.110: bytes=32 time<10ms TTL=128
Reply from 192.168.0.110: bytes=32 time<10ms TTL=128

Ping statistics for 192.168.0.110:
    Packets: Sent = 4, Received = 4, Lost = 0 (0% loss),
Approximate round trip times in milli-seconds:
    Minimum = 0ms, Maximum =  0ms, Average = 0ms

C:\>_
```

7. If the response indicates that none of the test packets was received, there could be something wrong with your network card, with your connection to the network, or with the network itself. Uninstall ICS as described in step 4, and then try diagnosing the problem with the network, including the possibility of having to replace the network card.

8. If the response shows that all the test packets were received, try to reach one of the computers on the network. Make sure the computer you're trying to reach had been available on the network and did have shared folders before ICS was installed. In the Address toolbar in any folder window, type the name of the computer, in the form **computername**, and press Enter. If the shared folders of that computer are displayed, you should be able to access the computer when you reopen the My Network Places window. If you can't find the computer in your workgroup, press the F5 key to refresh the connection.

9. If the shared files don't appear, in the Address toolbar, type the IP address of the computer in the form **192.168.0.xxx**, and press Enter. If the window now shows the shared folders of the computer, it's likely there's a problem with the DNS (Domain Name System) that maps IP addresses with computer names. Try restarting your computer to see whether this restarts the DNS and lets you find the computer by its name. If this doesn't solve the problem, you might have manually specified a DNS server when you set up the ICS. If you did, uninstall and then reinstall the ICS as in step 4, making sure that you delete any reference to a specific DNS and letting ICS set up the DNS on the host computer.

If your keyboard and your computer aren't talking to each other, you're in trouble! We'll come up with some answers as to why they aren't getting along and what you can do about it. We'll also show you how to insert into your documents special characters such as ® and £ that don't exist on your keyboard, how to prevent characters from repeating, what to do if you get strange and unexpected characters that you know you didn't type on your screen, and how to navigate your way around Windows using the keyboard instead of the mouse.

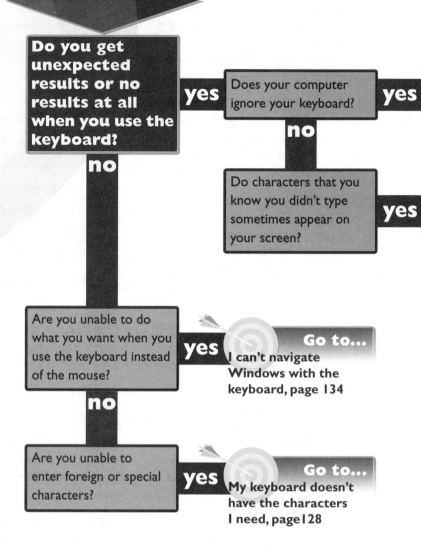

Do you get unexpected results or no results at all when you use the keyboard?

yes → **Does your computer ignore your keyboard?** → yes

no

Do characters that you know you didn't type sometimes appear on your screen? → yes

no

Are you unable to do what you want when you use the keyboard instead of the mouse? → yes

Go to...
I can't navigate Windows with the keyboard, page 134

no

Are you unable to enter foreign or special characters? → yes

Go to...
My keyboard doesn't have the characters I need, page 128

If your solution isn't here
Check these related chapters:
    Internet Explorer, page 104
    Mouse, page 156
Or see the general troubleshooting tips on page xiii

Keyboard

Go to...
My keyboard doesn't work, page 126

Does the Caps Lock or the Num Lock key accidentally get turned on or off?

yes

Quick fix

If your flying fingers on the keyboard sometimes accidentally hit the Caps Lock key so that most of your characters are uppercased, or you hit the Num Lock key so that you get numbers when you don't want them—or don't get numbers when you do want them—you can activate an alarm that beeps whenever you press these keys or the Scroll Lock key.

1. On the Settings submenu of the Start menu, click Control Panel.

2. In the Control Panel, double-click Accessibility Options.

3. On the Keyboard tab of the Accessibility Options dialog box, select the Use ToggleKeys check box.

4. Click OK.

5. To manually turn the feature on or off, hold down the Num Lock key for five seconds.

no

Are you having a problem with repeating characters?

yes

Go to...
Characters are repeated when I don't want them to be, page 130

no

Go to...
I get characters I don't expect on the screen, page 132

My keyboard doesn't work

Source of the problem

If your keyboard doesn't work, your computer becomes a useless object that sits on your desk and does nothing, and your work comes to an abrupt standstill. And doesn't something like this always happen at the worst possible time? In order to get back to work, you're going to have to try to be patient and do some digging around to figure out why your computer and your keyboard aren't getting along with each other. The possibilities can range from the keyboard not being plugged in to your using software that's causing a conflict with the keyboard and the software drivers that control the keyboard.

How to fix it

1. Start with the basics. Turn off your computer and work through the following tests to see whether anything listed here is causing the problem.

   - Check to make sure the keyboard is firmly plugged in to the computer; if any extension cables are used for the keyboard, that they're properly connected; and if there's a connector for the cable in the keyboard, that the cable is firmly in place.

   - If the keyboard is plugged into a USB (universal serial bus) hub, try connecting the keyboard directly to the computer. If you want to continue using the hub, make sure it's properly connected to the computer, that the power is turned on if the hub is externally powered, and that the hub is compatible with Windows 2000.

   - If a mouse is connected through the keyboard, disconnect the mouse and connect it directly to the computer.

   - If the keyboard is wireless, verify that there are no items interfering in the transmission between the computer and the keyboard.

   - If the keyboard is connected through a switchbox, connect it directly to the computer.

Warning

If you want to change the connection of a USB keyboard from a hub to a direct connection to the computer, don't disconnect the hub while Windows is running. A sudden disconnection can cause the computer to crash.

Tip

If the keyboard was working while you were in Windows, and it suddenly stopped working and just beeped when you pressed a key, the problem might be that the system has crashed. For information about recovering from a system crash, see "I can't shut down Windows" on page 244.

- If possible, install a different keyboard to make sure there isn't something physically wrong with the keyboard or the connections.

2. Start your computer and Windows after you're sure the keyboard is installed correctly. When Windows starts, it redetects the devices attached to your computer and configures their interactions. If a PS/2-type keyboard is attached to the computer while it's running, the keyboard might not be detected and, depending on the computer, could damage either itself or the system.

Tip

It's possible that software drivers or software programs other than those for the mouse or keyboard are causing the keyboard to stop working. Contact the manufacturer of any software that you installed recently to see whether there are any reported problems. Be particularly suspicious if you installed software to support removable disks.

3. If none of the foregoing problems is the cause of your keyboard's problem, you could be in a bit of trouble because you might have difficulty accessing the system to fix problems. Before you start panicking, though, you can try to force the system to work. To do so, restart Windows and, when you see the "Starting Windows" message, press the F8 key. If the computer doesn't respond to the key, you'll know there's probably something physically wrong with the computer or the keyboard rather than with Windows. If the Windows 2000 Advanced Options menu appears, use the Down arrow key to select Last Known Good Configuration, and press Enter. If your computer starts but you still can't use the keyboard, restart the computer, and press F8 when you see the "Restarting Windows" message. With Safe Mode selected, press Enter.

4. If Windows starts and you can use the keyboard, log on as an Administrator. If you recently loaded software or installed a software upgrade for your mouse or your keyboard, you'll need to remove it. To do so, on the Settings submenu of the Start menu, click Control Panel, and, in the Control Panel, double-click the Add/Remove Programs icon. Use the Add/Remove Programs window to remove the programs. When you've finished, restart Windows, and let it start up normally. If the keyboard works properly, contact the manufacturer of the software and/or the hardware driver for an update that's compatible with Windows 2000.

Tip

If you were able to get your keyboard working in Safe Mode, but your mouse isn't working, see "My mouse doesn't work" on page 158 for information about fixing problems without using the mouse.

5. If you couldn't get the keyboard to work in Safe Mode, you'll need to get professional help. If your computer is attached to a network, you might be able to log on to your computer from another computer on the network, and possibly diagnose and fix the problem. This process, of course, is well beyond the scope of this book, and might be a bit beyond the ability of some network administrators.

My keyboard doesn't have the characters I need

Source of the problem

We're fortunate to live in a time of instant worldwide communications—but unfortunate to live in a time of regional keyboards. You can search in vain on a U.S. keyboard—you won't find the ê, ñ, ¥, €, £, # or any other commonly used international characters. Regional keyboards in other countries are similarly lacking. To get around this limitation, you can use a tool to insert a special character you use only rarely, you can use a keyboard shortcut to insert a character you use frequently, or you can switch your keyboard layout to match that of the country and language in which you need to work.

How to fix it

1. To insert a rarely used character or group of characters, on the System Tools submenu of the Start menu, click Character Map. Click the font you want to use in the Font list, and then scroll through the display of characters until you find the one you need. Click it, and use the enlarged view of the character and the description at the bottom of the dialog box to confirm that it's the

   one you want. Click Select. To insert additional characters at the same location in your document, click each character, and then click Select. When you've selected all the characters you want, click Copy to copy the characters to the Windows Clipboard. Switch to the document that is to include the characters, and click the spot where you want to insert them. Use the Paste button or the Paste command on the Edit menu to insert the characters. ▶

   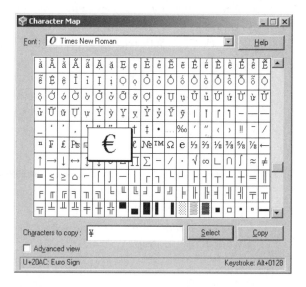

2. If you use a few characters frequently, write down the keyboard shortcut for each character. To find the keyboard shortcut, in the Font list in the Character Map dialog box, click the font you'll be using in the document, and click the character you want to insert. Note the Keystroke item at the bottom right of the dialog box. Write this

key combination down, and then repeat the process for the other characters you use frequently. Close the Character Map dialog box.

Tip

When you use a different keyboard layout, you can use the appropriate keyboard, or you can use your existing keyboard and try to remember the differences in the keyboard keys and the layout.

3. In the document into which you're going to insert the characters, first make sure you're using the correct font. (Not all fonts include the same special characters; other fonts assign different characters to the keyboard shortcuts.) To insert a character, turn on the Num Lock key if it isn't already turned on, hold down the Alt key, and type the numeric code on the numeric keypad. When you release the Alt key, the special character should appear in the document. For example, to insert the Euro symbol (€) that's shown in the Character Map dialog box, with the Num Lock key turned on, hold down the Alt key, type **0128** on the numeric keypad, and then release the Alt key.

4. If you're working in a language other than the one set for your computer and keyboard, and if there are too many special characters to insert one at a time, you can set your keyboard to a different language. To do so, in the Control Panel, double-click the Regional Options icon. On the Input Locales tab, click Add, and, in the Input Locale list, click the location you need. Make sure the correct keyboard layout is selected in the Keyboard Layout/IME list. Click OK. ▶

5. In the Regional Options dialog box, make sure the Enable Indicator On Taskbar check box is selected, and click OK. To install a different keyboard, shut down Windows and your computer, install the keyboard, and then restart the computer and Windows. On the taskbar, click the Indicator, click your new locale, and start typing.

6. If you selected a different locale but didn't install a different keyboard, on the Accessibility submenu of the Start menu, click On-Screen Keyboard. Note the positions of the keys. Click the Shift key on the On-Screen Keyboard, and note the positions of those keys. Close the On-Screen Keyboard, and use your own keyboard, substituting the key locations you noted from the On-Screen Keyboard. ▶

More about locales and characters

When you switch to a different locale and keyboard layout, Windows uses the same fonts but associates different keys on the keyboard with different characters in the fonts. Because not all fonts supply all the different characters, you might need to use different fonts to get all the characters you need. Also, be careful about changing your user name or password when using a different keyboard layout. If you do, you might not be able to enter the same characters you used in your user name or password when you return to your regular keyboard.

Characters are repeated when I don't want them to be

Source of the problem

When you're involved in your work, it can be extremely annoying to look up at the screen and see that characters you've typed have been repeated two, three, or more times. Of course, if you hold down a key to repeat a character intentionally and the result is a single character only, or if it takes forever for each character to be inserted, those are problems too. You can adjust the way Windows interprets your typing to control when a character is repeated and when it is not. If you have a larger problem with repetitive keystrokes, you can use an additional tool that prevents characters from being repeated.

How to fix it

1. On the Settings submenu of the Start menu, click Control Panel. In the Control Panel, double-click the Keyboard icon.

2. On the Speed tab of the Keyboard Properties dialog box, adjust the settings for repeating characters. To change how long a key is held down before the characters start repeating, drag the Repeat Delay slider to the left (toward Long) to increase the time a key is held down before the character is repeated, or drag the slider to the right (toward Short) to decrease the time before the character is repeated. ▶

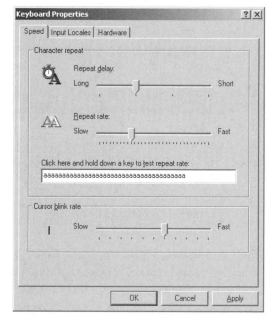

3. To adjust how fast characters are repeated once they start repeating, drag the Repeat Rate slider to the left (toward Slow) to increase the time between character repeats, or drag the slider to the right (toward Fast) to decrease the time between character repeats.

4. Click in the text box to test the repeat delay and the repeat rate. Hold down a key and see how long you need to hold it before the letter is repeated for the first time, and then notice how

quickly the additional characters appear. If the rate seems reasonable, open or switch to a document, and try typing with these settings. Return to the Keyboard Properties dialog box, and either change the settings and try them again, or click OK to keep the settings.

5. If reducing the repeat delay and the repeat rate doesn't solve the problem, you can exert a greater degree of control over repeating characters. To do so, double-click Accessibility Options in the Control Panel. On the Keyboard tab of the Accessibility Options dialog box, in the FilterKeys section, select the Use FilterKeys check box, and then click the Settings button.

6. In the Settings For FilterKeys dialog box, under Filter Options, click either the option to ignore all repeated keystrokes or the option to ignore quick keystrokes. Click the Settings button for the option you chose.

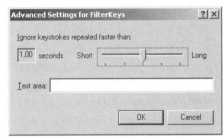

7. If you chose to ignore all repeated keystrokes, set the time that must elapse before pressing the same key again will cause the character to be repeated. ▶ Test the rate, and then click OK if you want to keep the setting.

8. If you chose to ignore quick keystrokes, set the options. If you want no repetition of characters when a key is held down, click No Keyboard Repeat. Click Slow Down Keyboard Repeat Rates if you want to modify the repeat delay and repeat rate to values greater than those you were able to set in the Keyboard Properties dialog box (steps 2 and 3). Use the Test Area to see whether the settings are correct, and, when they are, click OK. Click OK twice to close the other dialog boxes. ▶

More about setting the repeat rate

Changing the repeat rate can create some unexpected consequences. If you often hold down one of the arrow keys on your keyboard to move the cursor in a document, a slow repeat rate can slow the movement of the cursor to a maddening snail's pace. If you use the Tab key to navigate in Windows, you might find that its movement has also slowed to an unacceptable crawl. As you work, you'll probably find other actions that have slowed down. You might have to reach a compromise between limiting those unwanted repetitive characters and maintaining efficiency when you're using navigational keys. You can do this by setting the repeat delay to a longer time and setting the repeat rate to a faster speed.

I get characters I don't expect on the screen

Source of the problem

Windows 2000 can display a variety of languages in a wide range of different fonts. You can run into problems with unexpected characters on your screen if, for example, Windows is set to work in one language when you're set to work in another. You can also get unexpected results if you're working with a font that doesn't support some of the characters you want to use, whether they're symbol characters or characters from another language. If you're surprised by characters that you don't think you typed, you'll need to figure out which of several possibilities is causing the problem.

How to fix it

1. Open a WordPad document and type some characters. If it's obvious that what you're typing are characters from another language, you probably have the wrong regional setup for your computer. ▶

2. To make sure your computer is using the proper keyboard for your region, on the Settings submenu of the Start menu, click Control Panel. In the Control Panel, double-click Regional Options. Click the Input Locales tab. If there's more than one language listed, click your location, and click the Set As Default button. Click OK. ▶

3. Try typing some characters again. If your text is correct now, your problem was with the keyboard layout. If what you see is still indecipherable to you, there might be a problem with your selection of the font or with the font file itself. If you see several instances of characters that don't make any sense—boxes, bars, or exclamation marks, for example—the problem might be that the font you're using doesn't support the characters you're trying to enter. Select the text, and try another font. If the characters change to the ones you expected, either the font you were using doesn't include those characters or there's a problem with the font file.

---

4. To see which characters are available in the font you want to use, on the System Tools submenu of the Start menu, click Character Map. In the Font list, click the font, and scroll through the display of characters. Close the Character Map dialog box when you've finished. ▶

5. If a font you want isn't listed or properly displayed in the Character Map, it might be a font that's available only from your printer, a font that can't be used by Windows, or a font whose file is corrupted. If, when you open the Font list in WordPad, the font you're using has a printer icon next to it, it's probably a printer font. Use the instructions from the printer to print characters in that font. If the font is associated with a specific program or type manager, use that program to view or print characters in that font.

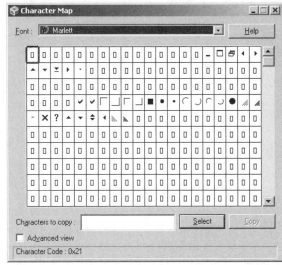

A font that displays few characters and many boxes isn't intended for standard text. The boxes are place-holders for missing or indecipherable characters.

6. If you can't display a font—and especially if your computer has been mysteriously locking up— you might have a bad font file. Most fonts are stored in the system's Fonts folder. To access this folder, on the Settings submenu of the Start menu, click Control Panel. In the Control Panel, double-click the Fonts icon. In the Fonts folder, double-click the font to see whether it's displayed properly. Close the window when you've finished. ▶

7. If the font isn't displayed correctly—or isn't displayed at all—or if you have problems whenever you use the font, check with the provider of the font (if it didn't come with Windows). If the font came with Windows, delete it and reinstall a new copy. To delete a font, click its name in the Fonts folder, and press the Delete key. To install a new font, on the File menu of the Fonts folder, click Install New Font. You'll need access to the Windows 2000 CD or installation files.

I can't navigate Windows with the keyboard

Source of the problem

Getting around in Windows 2000 is very mouse-centric. Toolbars, scroll bars, menus, icons, and so on are all designed to be used by clicking and/or dragging with the mouse. Because of this, the procedures and instructions in most books (yes, even in this book) depend on using the mouse to accomplish almost everything. But there are some very legitimate reasons to use the keyboard instead of the mouse—sometimes it's faster, sometimes it's difficult or inconvenient to use the mouse, and sometimes it's just a personal preference. When your decision to use the keyboard instead of the mouse collides with the design of Windows, here's how to make Windows respond to your keyboard actions.

How to fix it

1. The preeminent sign that Windows 2000 is totally mouse-oriented is that, unlike in previous versions of Windows, the keys you use to access menus and commands are no longer under-lined in menu and command names. You can, however, display the underlines either when you need them or all the time. To display them only when you need them, press and release the Alt key. To access an item, press the underlined letter.

> **Tip**
> When you display the under-lines by pressing the Alt key, the menu items and any Windows dialog boxes should also display the underlines. The underlines appear in dialog boxes that are opened by using the mouse only if you've set the underlines to always be displayed.

2. To display the underlines at all times, press Ctrl+Esc to open the Start menu, use the Up arrow key to select Settings and the Right arrow key to select Control Panel, and press Enter. Use an arrow key to select the Display icon, and press Enter. In the Display Properties dialog box, press Shift+Tab to move to the tab names, and use an arrow key to move to the Effects tab. Use the Tab key to select the Hide Keyboard Navigation Indicators Until I Use The Alt Key item, and press the Spacebar to clear the check box. Press Enter. (This lengthy process makes a good case for using the mouse, doesn't it?) Menu names, menu items, and dialog-box buttons and options will all display an underline beneath the key you use to access that item. To access a menu, press the Alt key and then the underlined letter. ▶

3. To move through the menus once they're open, press the underlined letter of the command you want, or use the Up or Down arrow key to move up or down the menu, and the Right arrow key to open a submenu. Press Enter when you've selected the command you want.

4. To control Windows from the keyboard without using menus, use these key combinations. ▶

5. If you want, you can control the mouse using the numeric keypad keys. To do so, you activate the Windows MouseKeys feature. In the Control Panel, use an arrow key to select the Accessibility Options icon, and press Enter. In the Accessibility Options dialog box, press Shift+Tab to move to the tab names, and use an arrow key to move to the Mouse tab. Press Tab to select the Use MouseKeys item, and press the Spacebar to select the check box. Press Tab to select the Settings button, and press Enter to open the Settings For MouseKeys dialog box. Make your settings to customize the way you want to use MouseKeys. To adjust the pointer speed, press the Tab key to select the slider, and then use the Left or Right arrow key to move the slider. When you've finished, press Enter. In the Accessibility Options dialog box, press Tab to select the OK button, and then press Enter.

Key	What it does
F1	Shows Help.
F2	Renames an item.
F3	Searches for a file or folder.
F4	Opens the Address Bar toolbar in a folder window.
Alt+F4	Closes a window, dialog box, or program.
F5	Refreshes the contents of a window.
F6	Cycles through items that can be selected on the Desktop or in a window.
Shift+F10	Opens the shortcut menu for an item.
Alt+Tab	Cycles through open windows, programs, or dialog boxes.
Alt+Esc	Switches to the next open item.
Alt+Spacebar	Opens the System menu to move or resize a window.
Ctrl+A	Select All
Ctrl+C	Copy
Ctrl+V	Paste
Ctrl+X	Cut
Ctrl+Z	Undo
Esc	Cancel

6. To use MouseKeys, simply press the keys on the numeric keypad. If the mouse doesn't move, turn the Num Lock key on or off to match the settings you made in the Settings For MouseKeys dialog box. Note that if you press a numeric key at the corner of the keypad, the mouse moves diagonally. Press the 5 key to click, and press the plus (+) key to double-click. To right-click, press the minus (–) key and then the 5 key.

More about keyboard shortcuts

There are many more keyboard shortcuts than the ones listed here. See Windows Help for other useful shortcuts, as well as those you can use if your keyboard has a Windows key. You can also define your own shortcut keys by modifying the properties of a shortcut. A shortcut you define lets you quickly switch to that particular program (but the program must already be running).

What can you do when your computer won't let you log on? First, put that hammer down! Then read this chapter to find out about the three main reasons for a failed logon and what you can do to fix the problem and get back to work. Perhaps you can log on to your computer but not to the network. We'll help you solve that problem too. We'll also discuss why it's important to keep your computer secure with a password, even if you aren't required to use one to log on. If you have to delete the names of other people who use your computer before you can log on, you might—depending on local policies—be able to tell Windows not to display their names.

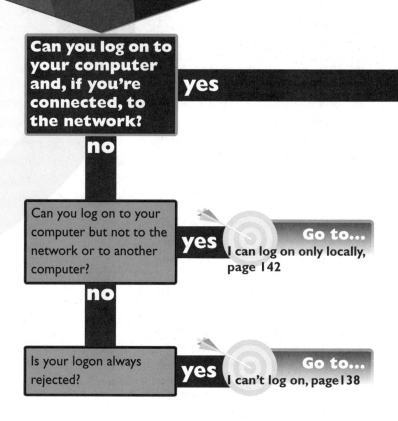

Can you log on to your computer and, if you're connected, to the network?

yes

no

Can you log on to your computer but not to the network or to another computer?

yes

Go to...
I can log on only locally, page 142

no

Is your logon always rejected?

yes

Go to...
I can't log on, page 138

If your solution isn't here

Check these related chapters:

Access to the computer, page 2

Dial-up connection, page 28

Keyboard, page 124

Power options, page 188

Starting up, page 260

Or see the general troubleshooting tips on page xiii

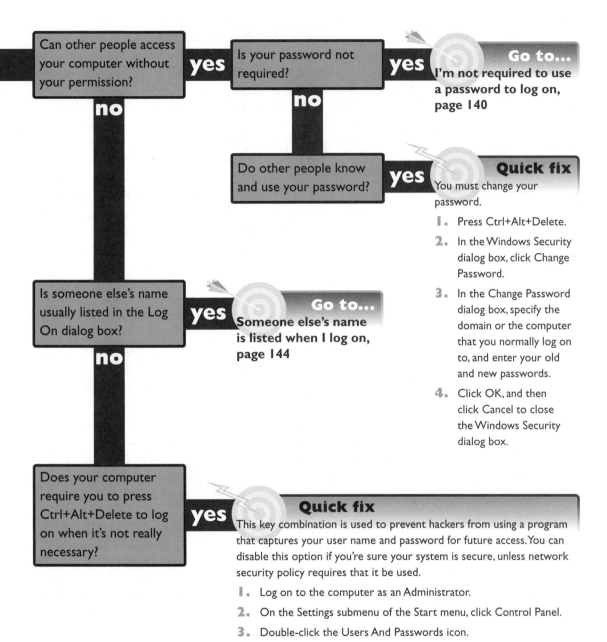

Can other people access your computer without your permission?

yes → Is your password not required?

yes → **Go to...** **I'm not required to use a password to log on,** page 140

no

Do other people know and use your password?

yes → **Quick fix** You must change your password.

1. Press Ctrl+Alt+Delete.
2. In the Windows Security dialog box, click Change Password.
3. In the Change Password dialog box, specify the domain or the computer that you normally log on to, and enter your old and new passwords.
4. Click OK, and then click Cancel to close the Windows Security dialog box.

no

Is someone else's name usually listed in the Log On dialog box?

yes → **Go to...** **Someone else's name is listed when I log on,** page 144

no

Does your computer require you to press Ctrl+Alt+Delete to log on when it's not really necessary?

yes → **Quick fix** This key combination is used to prevent hackers from using a program that captures your user name and password for future access. You can disable this option if you're sure your system is secure, unless network security policy requires that it be used.

1. Log on to the computer as an Administrator.
2. On the Settings submenu of the Start menu, click Control Panel.
3. Double-click the Users And Passwords icon.
4. On the Advanced tab, under Secure Boot Settings, clear the check box to require pressing the key combination. Click OK, and log on as yourself.

I can't log on

Source of the problem

Of the many mysteries you can encounter in your relation-ship with a computer, being unable to log on is one of the most frustrating. What can you do when, no matter how hard you try, the computer refuses to let you log on? Stay calm. There can be a variety of reasons for this major nuisance, but it usually comes down to one of three: you're entering the wrong user name or password; you're logging on to a computer for the first time and the network is down, so your logon can't be verified; or your account is inactive. You can remedy some of these problems, but if you're working on a corporate network that uses a domain, you'll probably need to get help from the network administrator. But don't go crying to him or her just yet. Try a couple of the following suggestions to see whether you can solve the problem on your own.

How to fix it

1. Make sure you're correctly entering your user name, password, and—if necessary—domain. In the Log On To Windows dialog box, use the mouse to drag over any existing user name to select it. Now type your own user name exactly as it was assigned to you, using the same spacing, if any, and the correct characters—for example, if your assigned user name contains an underscore, be sure to type an underscore, not a hyphen.

2. Press the Tab key to move to the Password box. Type the password exactly as it was given to you. Many passwords have a mix of upper- and lowercase characters, plus numbers. Make sure you type the password using the same capitalization. Click the Options >> button if the Log On Using Dial-Up Connection check box isn't visible. If there's a Log On To box, verify that the correct domain is listed. Unless you're logging on through a dial-up connection, make sure the check box for a dial-up connection is cleared. Click OK.

3. If your password is rejected again, press the Caps Lock key once, reenter your password, and press OK. If you can log on now, note the state of the Caps Lock key, and use it that way whenever you log on.

4. If this is the first time you've logged on to this computer, and if the computer is connected to a domain, check to see whether the network is down. The easiest way to do this is to see whether any coworkers on other computers are having network problems. If they aren't, it still doesn't mean there are no network problems. If possible, have

> **Tip**
>
> If you logged on to the net-work previously using this computer, you should be able to log on locally, even if the network is down. Windows stores the network logon to authorize local logon in case of network problems.

someone who logs on to the same domain as yours log on to the computer. If either result indicates that the network is down, let someone in authority know about it, and do something else until the network gets going again.

5. If the problem isn't with the network, two possibilities remain: either you're using the wrong user name and/or password, or your account is inactive. If your computer is on a network with a domain, it's time to seek help. Check with the network administrator (or whoever in your group is authorized to modify user accounts) to see whether your account is active; whether you're authorized to connect at this particular time; and, if you're connecting by dialing up, whether you're authorized to do so. If your account is in good standing, you should be provided with a new password.

6. If your computer isn't on a network with a domain, it's time to do some administration of your own. To do so, log on to the computer using an Administrators account, right-click My Computer on the Desktop, and click Manage on the shortcut menu. In the Computer Management window, double-click the Local Users And Groups item to expand it, and click the Users folder. In the right part of the window, double-click the account that's unable to log on. Make sure the account hasn't been disabled or locked out. If it has, clear the check box for the appropriate option. Click OK. ▶

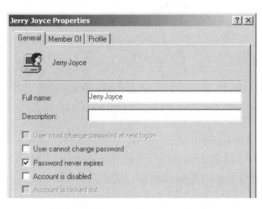

7. If the account is active, change the password to make sure you haven't been entering the wrong one. To do so, in the Computer Management window, right-click the account, and click Set Password on the shortcut menu. In the Set Password dialog box, enter the new password twice, and click OK. Make sure you can remember the password, including its capitalization. Click OK when you're notified that the password has been changed. ▶

8. If there's no account listed for you, you'll have to create one. To log on to a stand-alone computer or one that's connected to a workgroup, you must have an account on each computer you use. To create an account, right-click a blank spot in the right part of the Computer Management window, and click New User on the shortcut menu. In the New User dialog box, enter the user name and password, and indicate whether the password must be changed. Click Create, and then click Close.

9. Close the Computer Management window, log off as the Administrator, and log on as yourself.

I'm not required to use a password to log on

Source of the problem

If your computer isn't connected to a network, or is connected to a network that doesn't use a domain, the requirement to enter your user name and password can be disabled. In most cases this isn't a good idea, because it circumvents much of the security built into Windows 2000. Without being required to enter a password, anyone who can gain physical access to your computer not only can access the contents of your computer but can use your stored connections, passwords, encryption keys, and security certificates to wreak havoc in your name—with or without malicious intent. Depending on how your system is set up, access to your unattended computer isn't always prevented by requiring a logon in the Log On To Windows dialog box. If you often leave the unattended computer with a screen saver running, or if the computer is set to go into Standby or Hibernate mode, you need to make sure that your user name and password are required whenever anyone tries to access your computer.

How to fix it

1. On the Settings submenu of the Start menu, click Control Panel. In the Control Panel, double-click the Users And Passwords icon. If you're not a member of the Administrators group, you'll be prompted to log on as the Administrator. Enter the Administrator's password (or the user name and password of a member of the Administrators group), and click OK. ▶

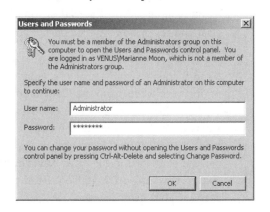

2. In the Users And Passwords dialog box, select the check box that requires the entry of a user name and password. When the check box is selected, a list of users becomes available. If you don't remember your user name, examine the list until you find it. If you want to change your password (especially if you don't remember your old one), click your name, click Set Password, type the password twice, and click OK. When you've finished, click OK to close the Users And Passwords dialog box. ▶

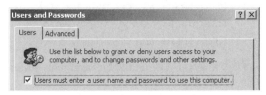

3. On the Start menu, click Shut Down, click Log Off in the Shut Down Windows dialog box, and click OK. When the Log On To Windows dialog box appears, enter your user name if it isn't already displayed, and your password. If you can't log on because you can't remember your user name or password, see "I can't log on" on page 138.

4. Now that a logon is required for your computer, you must also make sure the computer requires your password when it comes out of Standby or Hibernate mode. This is an area of great vulnerability—many people set the computer to hibernate or go on standby so that they don't have to shut down Windows. To require a password every time the computer wakes up, double-click the Power Options icon in the Control Panel. On the Advanced tab, select the check box to prompt for a password. Don't worry that the check box mentions Standby only—a password is required for the computer to come out of Hibernate mode, and if your computer supports Standby mode, it also requires a password to come out of Standby mode. Click OK. ▶

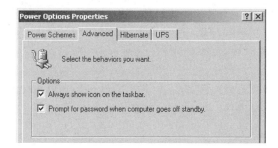

5. Another area of vulnerability is the screen saver that's in place when your computer is unattended. To require a user name and password when you end the screen saver so that you can get back to work, double-click Display in the Control Panel, and, in the Display Properties dialog box, click the Screen Saver tab. Select the Password Protected check box, and click OK. If the Password Protected check box is grayed (unavailable), click a screen saver in the Screen Saver list, and then select the check box. ▶

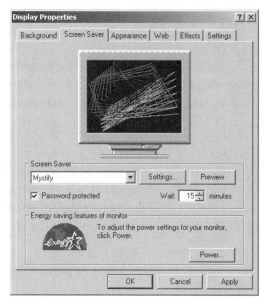

6. Now you should test your settings. On the Start menu, click Shut Down, click either Hibernate or Standby in the list, and click OK. Give the computer enough time go into Hibernate or Standby mode, and then wake up the computer. You should see the Computer Locked dialog box. Log on, and wait for your computer to start the screen saver. Let it run for a minute or two, press any key, and you should see the Computer Locked dialog box again. Note that the screen saver will not require a password if you start it manually by using the Preview button, by double-clicking the screen-saver file, or by using a program or a toolbar to start the screen saver.

I can log on only locally

Source of the problem

Windows 2000 requires that you have a user name and a password in order to log on. These two elements are the credentials that certify you as being authorized to access the system. Even if Windows is set not to display the Log On To Windows dialog box, Windows uses the information you entered at a previous time to provide this certification. However, when your certification works only on your local computer account and not on the network or on another computer, you might be asked again for your user name and password, or for a user name and password that has authorized access—or you might simply be denied access. These situations can be caused by a variety of circumstances, including poor connections, network administration shortcomings, and working with computers that are using different operating systems.

How to fix it

1. Make sure you're trying to log on to the proper location. In the Log On To Windows dialog box, click the Options >> button to expand the dialog box and display all the different options. (If the button reads Options <<, and you can see the Log On Using Dial-Up Connection check box, the dialog box is already expanded.) If there's a Log On To box, click the down arrow next to it, and then click the domain you're supposed to log on to. If there's no domain listed, type the domain name. (Make sure it exactly matches the one that was provided to you with your user name and password.) If there is no Log On To box, the computer is not a member of a domain and you can log on only to your local computer or workgroup. Complete the User Name and Password boxes, and click OK. ▶

> **Tip**
>
> The user name and password you use to log on to the network can be different from those you use to log on to your computer. If you can't log on to the network, make sure you have the correct user name and password, and that they're spelled properly and have the correct capitalization. If you're not sure of either, ask the network administrator to verify your user name and provide you with a new password.

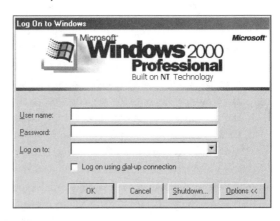

2. If you're trying to log on to a domain and your logon is rejected, there might be a problem with your network account. The account might not have been established or activated properly, the computer might not have been added to the network, or your account might have been disabled. You can't fix any of those problems from your computer, so contact the network administrator and ask for some maintenance on your account. If, however, you're advised by Windows that your account couldn't be verified and/or that some network services aren't available, there could be a problem with the network itself or with your connection to it. Check the cables to verify that you're properly connected to the network, give the network some time to start working again, and then log off and log on again to see whether the network is working properly.

3. If you're working on a network that uses a workgroup instead of a domain, and you try to access another computer in the workgroup, you might be denied permission and asked to log on using a different name. In a workgroup, all accounts are stored on individual computers, so, if you want to access another computer, you should have yourself added to the list of users on that computer, or use the account of an authorized user each time you connect. ▶

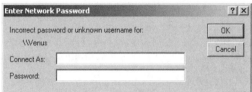

4. To create a user account for yourself on another computer, log on to the computer as the local Administrator. Right-click My Computer on the Desktop, and click Manage on the shortcut menu. In the Computer Management window, double-click Local Users And Groups to expand it, right-click Users, and click New User on the shortcut menu. In the User Name and Password boxes, enter your user name and password exactly as you do to log on to your own computer. Clear the check box that requires the user to change the password, and select the Password Never Expires check box. Click Create, and then click Close. Close the Computer Management window. ▶

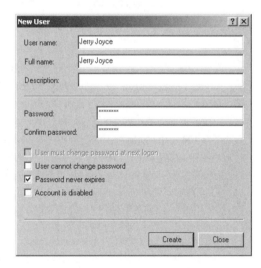

5. Return to your computer and connect to a shared folder on the other computer. If you see the Enter Network Password dialog box, you probably didn't enter the same user name and/or password that you use to log on to your own computer. You can either return to the other computer and correct the error, or you can enter the user name and password you created on the other computer whenever you want to access it. The problem could also be caused by your trying to connect to a Windows95/98/Me computer that has restricted access to shared folders. Check with the user of that computer about gaining access.

Someone else's name is listed when I log on

Source of the problem

When you log on to Windows, the Log On To Windows dialog box usually displays the name of the last person who logged on to the computer. This is convenient when you're the primary person using the computer—you don't need to enter your user name each time you log on, and you don't have to worry that mistyping your name will cause your logon to fail. However, if several people use your computer and you're tired of having to delete the previous user's name before you can enter your own, you might be able to tell Windows not to display the unwanted name. We say "might," because if you do this, you'll be editing a local security policy, and local policies are often overridden by the policies that are implemented over the entire network. Because policies are hugely powerful, interfering with them can cause major problems, so if you can make changes to the policies on your computer, make sure you understand the potential repercussions of any change. However, if having to delete someone else's name before you can log on is aggravating enough, it's worth a try.

How to fix it

1. You're going to be making substantial changes that require full authority, and you'll need to log off and log on again later anyway, so log off from the computer and log on again as the Administrator. If you're on a network with a domain, make sure that when you log on, you're logging on locally instead of logging on to the network. To do so, in the Log On To Windows dialog box, if the Log On To box isn't displayed, click the Options >> button. In the Log On To box, click the item that's listed as This Computer. If the Log On To box isn't present, it means that you're always logging on to the local computer. ▶

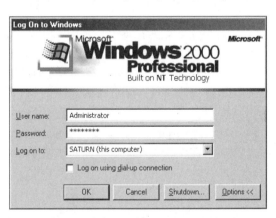

2. When you're logged on, on the Settings submenu of the Start menu, click Control Panel. In the Control Panel, double-click Administrative Tools. In the Administrative Tools window, double-click Local Security Policy. If you don't see the Administrative Tools icon in the Control Panel, this feature of Windows has either been omitted or deleted from the Windows installation. If that's the case, it's unlikely you'll be able to implement local policy settings, so you'll either have

to learn to live with the settings you have or ask the network administrator to change the system-wide policy.

3. In the Local Security Settings window, double-click the Local Policies item in the left part of the window. This expands the listing so that you can see the various types of policies. Click the Security Options item. In the right part of the window, look for the Do Not Display Last User Name In Logon Screen item. If you can't see the whole name, point to it, and the full name should appear in a pop-up window. If it doesn't, drag the border between the Policy and Local

Setting items at the top of the list to widen the Policy column. If the Local Setting for the item is listed as Enabled but the Effective Setting is listed as Disabled, there's nothing you can do—the network policy has taken control of this option, and you can't change the way it works. ▶

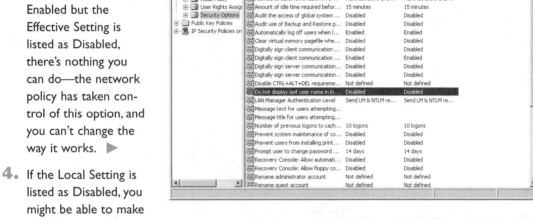

4. If the Local Setting is listed as Disabled, you might be able to make a change. Double-click the Do Not Display Last User Name In Logon Screen item. In the Local Security Policy Setting dialog box, click the Enabled option, and then click OK. Note that in the Local Security Settings window, the Do Not Display Last User Name In Logon Screen item is now listed as Enabled for the Local Setting but is still Disabled for the Effective setting. That's okay at this point. ▶

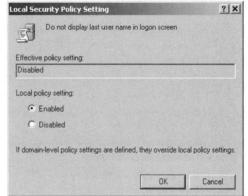

5. Close the Local Security Settings window, the Administrative Tools window, and the Control Panel, and log off as the Administrator. When you log on again, if there's no name in the User Name box of the Log On To Windows dialog box, you'll know you were successful. If the unwanted name is still there, the network settings have taken effect, and you can't change this feature.

The litany of complaints involving modems is a long one: the modem is too slow, it's too noisy, it won't connect, it won't dial a phone number, it won't answer incoming calls, Windows didn't detect it.... You can go a long way toward solving many—but not all—modem problems by making sure your modem is compatible with Windows 2000 and by verifying that the modem is correctly connected to the phone line. But there's more—the following pages will help you figure out how to make that modem do its job.

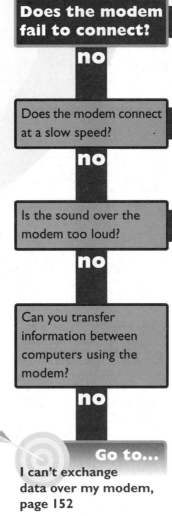

Does the modem fail to connect?

yes

no

Does the modem connect at a slow speed?

yes

no

Go to...
My modem is really slow, page 154

Is the sound over the modem too loud?

yes

no

Quick fix

The modem has its own speaker. You can set the volume or turn the sound off completely for most modem models.

Can you transfer information between computers using the modem?

no

1. On the Settings submenu of the Start menu, click Control Panel.

2. Hold down the Shift key and right-click Phone And Modem Options. Click Run As on the shortcut menu, and log on as the Administrator.

Go to...
I can't exchange data over my modem, page 152

3. On the Modems tab, click your modem if it isn't already selected, and click the Properties button.

4. On the General tab, drag the Speaker Volume slider to adjust the volume.

5. Click OK, and then click OK again.

If your solution isn't here
Check these related chapters:
Dial-up connection, page 28
Faxes, receiving, page 58
Faxes, sending, page 68
Hardware installation, page 96
Internet Sharing host, page 118
Or see the general troubleshooting tips on page xiii

Modems

Is the modem listed as being installed on your computer?

yes →

Does the modem fail to dial out?

yes →

Go to...
My modem can't dial a phone number, page 150

no

Go to...
My modem isn't detected, page 148

no

Does the modem fail to connect?

yes →

Quick fix

If the computer tries to send information to the modem too quickly, the modem connection can fail.

1. On the Settings submenu of the Start menu, click Control Panel.

2. Hold down the Shift key and right-click Phone And Modem Options. Click Run As on the shortcut menu, and log on as the Administrator.

3. On the Modems tab, click your modem if it isn't already selected, and click the Properties button.

4. On the General tab, change the Maximum Port Speed to 9600. Click OK twice, and then try reconnecting.

5. If the modem connects, repeat steps 2 through 4, but specify a higher speed. Continue experimenting with the speed to find the highest speed that works.

no

Are you able to receive incoming calls?

no

Quick fix

Windows uses specific tools and settings to allow calls to be answered. Use the index in this book to locate information about these tools and settings.

1. To answer a fax call, use Fax Service Management.

2. To answer a call and grant network access, create an incoming connection in the Network And Dial-Up Connections window.

3. To answer a call and transfer data manually, use HyperTerminal.

My modem isn't detected

Source of the problem

A modem can be a real pain in the…computer. Windows normally detects any modem that's connected to your computer and, if it hasn't done so already, installs whatever software Windows needs to be able to work with the modem. Sometimes, however, Windows ignores a modem and pretends it doesn't exist. Why? Most problems occur either because the modem isn't fully compatible with Windows 2000 or because the modem is an external one that isn't configured correctly or wasn't functioning properly when you started Windows. If you have an external modem, you can solve the problem—provided it isn't hardware related—by having the modem fully functional when you start Windows, or by manually forcing Windows to detect the modem after Windows has started. If your modem isn't fully compatible with Windows 2000, there's a simple solution—*get one that is!* However, if you're not willing to replace your current modem, you might be able to get it installed and working, although it might lack the speed and features you expect.

How to fix it

1. Before you immerse yourself in the murky world of modems, make sure your modem really is undetected. Right-click My Computer on the Desktop, and click Manage on the shortcut menu. If you receive a message telling you that you don't have the necessary permission to make changes, ignore it and click OK—you're just looking, not making changes. In the Computer Management window, double-click the Modems item if it isn't already expanded. If the Modems item is missing, or if your modem isn't listed under it, you'll know that your modem hasn't been detected. If the modem is listed, double-click it, examine its Properties dialog box, and note any problems. Click OK. If the modem has been disabled or if there's a conflict with other hardware, you'll need to log off and then log on as the Administrator and try to remedy those specific problems. For information about fixing problems of this nature, see "The device doesn't work" on page 102.

    > **Tip**
    >
    > If you upgraded to Windows 2000 from an earlier version of Windows, don't expect your modem to work as well—or even to work at all—simply because it functioned flawlessly before you upgraded. Windows 2000 has much stiffer requirements for modem compatibility than do most other versions of Windows.

2. If you have an external modem, make sure it's turned on and connected to the correct port on your computer. In the Computer Management window, at the top of the right pane, right-click the computer, and click Scan For Hardware Changes on the shortcut menu. This should force Windows to detect and install the modem.

3. If your modem still isn't detected, you need to verify that Windows can use the modem. Check the Windows 2000 hardware compatibility list at *http://www.microsoft.com/hwtest/hcl*. If your modem isn't listed or is listed but requires additional software, contact the modem's manufacturer to see whether there's a software patch or any updated software to make the modem compatible with Windows 2000. If so, obtain the software, and install it as specified by the manufacturer.

4. If your modem isn't compatible with Windows 2000, you can try to make it work, but you do so at your own risk. By forcing Windows to use incompatible hardware, and by specifying a modem that Windows can't verify as the correct modem, you can make the system unstable. However, if you decide to take this risk, in the Control Panel, hold down the Shift key, right-click Add/Remove Hardware, and log on as the Administrator. In the Add/Remove Hardware Wizard, click the Add/Troubleshoot A Device option if it isn't already selected, and click Next. On the Choose A Hardware Device page, double-click Add A New Device. On the Find New Hardware page, click No, and then click Next. On the Hardware Type page, double-click Modems. On the first Install New Modem page, select the check box to not detect the modem, and click Next. On the second Install New Modem page, click the manufacturer of your modem in the Manufacturers list. In the Models list, click a model that's similar to the one you have installed, and click Next. Complete the wizard, and, after restarting your computer, repeat step 1 to see whether the modem is now installed and functional. If it isn't functioning, you'll need to log on as the Administrator again and use the Add/Remove Hardware item in the Control Panel to remove the modem.

5. If you really want to get the modem working in even the most minimal way, and if you're willing to have it connect at a very slow speed, repeat step 4, with the following differences: in the Manufacturers list, click Hayes; in the Models list, click Hayes Compatible 9600; and then complete the wizard. This installs a basic generic modem, running at a slow speed of 9600 bps.

6. If you can no longer stand the lack of features and the dreadfully slow data transfer that result from using an incompatible modem, buy and install a new Windows 2000–compatible modem. Use it once or twice, and you'll know the money was well spent.

More about modem compatibility

A modem can cause all sorts of problems in Windows 2000, violating security and working in ways Windows strictly prohibits. This is because much of the software the modem needs is built right into the modem card, so the software can't be updated to become compatible with Windows 2000. Windows avoids problems by not supporting a modem that doesn't comply with its rigid requirements. However, if you're lucky, Windows will use a generic modem driver that supports the modem but disables incompatible features.

My modem can't dial a phone number

Source of the problem

What could be simpler than dialing a phone number? You've been able to do it since childhood—yet your big, expensive computer system can't do it! Well, don't feel too smug just yet. The problem could be that the modem was incorrectly connected to the phone line (you *did* plug the phone line into the right hole, didn't you?) or it could be that you failed to supply the computer system with the proper codes to dial out of your office's phone system or to dial a number outside your area code. So wipe that smirk off your face, and give the modem the information it needs. Then, if it fails, you can demonstrate your superiority by dialing the number yourself and then letting the modem take over and do its work.

How to fix it

1. If, when you try to get the modem to dial, you receive a message that the dialing failed because there's no dial tone, you need to verify that the modem is correctly connected to the phone line. Inspect the connections on the modem, and make sure you've plugged the phone line into the correct connection. If you're using an external modem, make sure it's turned on. If the modem wasn't turned on when you started Windows, Windows probably didn't detect it.

> **Tip**
> If your modem was working fine and then suddenly stopped working, check to verify that the phone line is working by picking up an extension or plugging a phone into the wall jack that the modem uses.

2. Now it's time to play detective and gather some information. On the Settings submenu of the Start menu, click Control Panel. In the Control Panel, hold down the Shift key, right-click the Phone And Modem Options icon, click Run As on the shortcut menu, and log on as the Administrator. On the Modems tab, verify that your modem is correctly identified, and, if it is, double-click it. On the Diagnostics tab, click the Query Modem button. Wait for the results to be returned. If you don't get any results, or if only error messages appear, either the modem is incorrectly installed or there's a hardware problem, and you'll need to do some troubleshooting. You can also click the View Log button to see a record of the communication commands that are sent and received by the modem. These

> **Tip**
> If your modem hasn't been detected and properly installed, or if you think there's a hardware problem, see "My modem isn't detected" on page 148. If your modem has been misidentified, see "My modem is really slow" on page 154.

commands are difficult to interpret, though, and at best all you'll probably be able to deduce is that your call didn't successfully complete a connection—something you already know.

3. On the General tab of the Phone and Modem Options dialog box, verify that the Wait For Dial Tone Before Dialing check box is selected. This causes the modem to suspend dialing until there's a dial tone—a useful feature if your phone system is slow. Click OK, and then click OK again to close the Phone And Modem Options dialog box.

4. Try making your modem connection again. If it fails, double-click the Phone And Modem Options icon in the Control Panel again. (You don't need to log on as the Administrator this time.) On the Dialing Rules tab, click the location you use to dial out (the default location is often listed as *New Location*), and click Edit. On the General tab, complete any of the required information, such as the access numbers for an outside line or for long-distance calls. Also make sure that the Dialing Using option matches the way your phone works.

5. If your modem dials incorrectly—for example, it dials a number, including the area code, but doesn't dial 1 before the number—click the Area Code Rules tab, click New, and specify the special dialing rules you need. Click OK when you've finished. Use the Calling Card tab if you want to use a credit card for your calls. Click OK to close the Phone And Modem Options dialog box.

6. Now that you've set up the dialing options, you need to make sure the connection observes the rules. In the Control Panel, double-click the Network And Dial-Up Connections icon. In the Network And Dial-Up Connections window, right-click the connection you're using, and click Properties on the shortcut menu. If you're denied permission to view the properties, you'll need to log off and log on again, either as the Administrator or as the person who created the connection. On the General tab of the Properties dialog box, select the Use Dialing Rules check box if it isn't already selected, and click OK. Double-click the connection, and click Dial to see whether your connection works now.

7. If all else fails, you can make the call manually if you have a phone connected to the same line the modem is connected to. If you're not already logged on as the Administrator, log off and log on again as the Administrator. In the Network And Dial-Up Connections window, click Operator-Assisted Dialing. If you want, log off as the Administrator and log on as yourself.

8. In the Network And Dial-Up Connections window, double-click the connection, and click Dial. When the Operator Assisted Or Manual Dial dialog box appears, pick up the phone, dial the number (or have an operator dial it for you), and click OK. Hang up the phone and wait for the modem to connect. ▶

I can't exchange data over my modem

Source of the problem

Windows 2000 provides many resources for transferring data, including Microsoft NetMeeting or a VPN (virtual private network) connection for transferring data over the Internet, and dial-up connections for transferring data over remote networks. However, you could run into some problems if you want to use your modem to transfer data between your computer and another computer, especially if the two computers are running different operating systems and have different network protocols. Fortunately, Windows provides a program that allows direct transfer between similar, and even dissimilar, computers. Because this is a basic program that can work with other types of data-communications programs, and because you can choose to use different protocols to transfer information, you might need to troubleshoot the settings to tailor the program to your exact requirements.

How to fix it

1. When you're connecting, you'll need to set one computer to make the call and the other computer to receive it. On the Communications submenu of the Start menu, click HyperTerminal. In the Connection Description dialog box, type an identifying name for the connection, click an icon, and click OK. In the Connect To dialog box, type the phone number of the computer you're going to connect to. If you'll be receiving calls only, type your own phone number. (You can enter any number, but if you use your own number, and if you accidentally use this terminal to make a call, you'll get a busy signal and can hang up immediately.) Click OK. In the Connect dialog box, click Cancel. Click Save on the File menu to save your terminal. ▶

2. Notify the operator of the other computer when you're going to call, and have him or her set the program to wait for the call. Click the Call button on the toolbar of your terminal, and, in the Connect dialog box—provided the dialing location is correct—click Dial. If you need different dialing rules to make your call, click a different location in the Your Location list. To create a new location and dialing rules, click the Dialing Properties button, and, in the Phone And Modem Options dialog box, create your new

location. For information about creating a new location, see "My modem can't dial a phone number" on page 150. To receive a call instead of making one, click Wait For A Call on the Call menu, and wait for the other computer to call and connect.

3. Use the terminal screen to send messages back and forth in preparation for any data transfer. To send a file to the other computer, have the operator set the program to receive a file. Click the Send button on the toolbar, and, in the Send File dialog box, use the Browse button to locate the file, and then click Send. To receive a file, click the Receive button on the toolbar, and, in the Receive File dialog box, use the Browse button to specify the folder in which you want the file to be stored. Click Receive, and wait for the file to be transferred.

4. Several things can go wrong with your connection because of incompatible settings. If your connection fails, check with the operator of the other computer to see what type of terminal is being used. Then click the Properties button on the toolbar, and, on the Settings tab of the Properties dialog box, click the same type of terminal in the Emulation list. Click the Terminal Setup button, and make any available settings identical to those of the other computer. Click OK, and try the connection again.

5. If you can connect but you have problems with the text you type in the terminal, click the Properties button on the toolbar, and, on the Settings tab, click the ASCII Setup button. Change the settings as shown in the table. Click OK, and then click OK again. Try typing another message. If you can't send or receive a file, contact the operator of the other computer, and try to find a transfer protocol that both terminals can use. Then, in the Send File dialog box, click that protocol in the Protocol list before sending the file.

6. Click Save on the File menu so that your settings, as well as your message, are saved for future reference.

For this problem	Make this setting
The text you send is in one long line.	Select the Send Line Ends With Line Feeds check box.
You don't see what you send.	Select the Echo Typed Characters Locally check box.
Some of the text you send isn't received.	Enter 1 for Line Delay. Increase the value if necessary.
Some of the characters you send drop out.	Enter 1 for Character Delay. Increase the value if necessary.
The text you receive is in one long line.	Select the Append Line Feeds To Incoming Line Ends check box.
The text you receive is garbled.	Select the Force Incoming Data To 7-Bit ASCII check box.
The ends of lines aren't visible.	Select the Wrap Lines That Exceed Terminal Width check box.

My modem is really slow

Source of the problem

When you use a modem to connect to the Internet or to a network, the connection can sometimes be excruciatingly slow. Many of us have come to expect this, and we use the delay as an opportunity to grab another cup of coffee or exchange a few words with a coworker. However, if your modem consistently underperforms, you might be able to improve its performance. The problem isn't always caused by your computer—it can be caused by the phone wiring you're using in your office or home; the lines and switches used by the phone company; the network or ISP (Internet service provider) you're connecting to; or, if you're connecting to the Internet, problems on the Internet or with the web site you're visiting.

How to fix it

1. Let's see whether the problem is fixable. Connect to the Internet or your network using your dial-up connection. If a connection icon is displayed on the taskbar, point to it with your mouse, and wait for a pop-up window to display your connection speed. If a connection icon isn't displayed, right-click My Network Places, and click Properties on the shortcut menu. In the

   Network And Dial-Up Connections window, double-click the connection. Note the speed that's shown. Do this each time you connect. If you're connecting with a 56 Kbps modem, don't expect the connection speed to be 56 Kbps. Phone systems aren't capable of supporting that rate of data transfer. If your connection is fairly fast sometimes but slow at other times, the problem is probably because some part of the connection is overtaxed—for example, the network is slow, or your ISP is running at near capacity. If you're consistently connecting at a much slower speed than your computer is capable of, you might have a larger problem. ▶

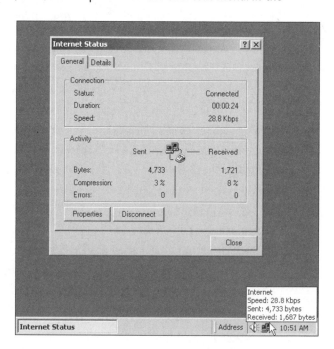

2. The next time you connect, write down the number your modem is calling. Check with whomever you're connecting to (your ISP, for example) to see whether you can use a different phone number to try connecting at a faster speed. Some ISPs and networks support fast connections using specific phone numbers; some experience slowdowns when too many people use the same access phone number.

3. If you can't solve the problem by switching phone numbers, make sure your modem is correctly set up on the computer. If your modem isn't fully compatible with Windows 2000, it might have been set up as a generic modem, which would cause it to lose some of its features, including speed. For example, a 56 Kbps modem that isn't fully compatible with Windows 2000 and has been set up as a generic modem might connect at 28.8 Kbps or less. To see whether your modem is compatible with Windows 2000, gather all the information you can about manufacturer and model from the modem's documentation, and then check the Windows 2000 hardware compatibility list at *http://www.microsoft.com/hwtest/hcl*. If the modem is in the list, make a note of any files you need to download and install to get the modem to work correctly, and/or contact the manufacturer to see whether a fix or any updated files are available for the modem. If the modem isn't in the hardware compatibility list and the manufacturer doesn't have a fix, you'll have to live with the slow connection speed until a fix is created or until you go out and buy a fully compatible modem.

4. If you were able to obtain a fix for the modem, you'll need to install it. The fix should include an information file (a file with an *.inf* extension) that tells Windows what drivers are required, plus any additional files that are needed to support specific features of, or correct problems with, the modem. To install the files, on the Settings submenu of the Start menu, click Control Panel. Hold down the Shift key, right-click the System icon, click Run As on the shortcut menu, and log on as the Administrator. On the Hardware tab of the System Properties dialog box, click Device Manager. In the Device Manager window, double-click the Modems item to expand it, and then double-click your modem. On the Driver tab, click Update Driver. In the Upgrade Device Driver Wizard, click Next to enter the wizard, and click Next again. In the Locate Driver Files page of the wizard, select the check box that indicates where you've stored the downloaded *.inf* and associated files. If you specified a location, click the Browse button in the Upgrade Device Driver Wizard dialog box, locate the file, click Open, and then click OK to close the dialog box. Click Next, and complete the wizard. Restart the computer, and connect using your modem. You should find that your connection speed has increased and that all the features of your modem are working.

Warning
If you download files from the manufacturer, make sure they're the correct files for your modem. Using the wrong files can make your system unstable. If you're not sure which modem model you have, contact the manufacturer to learn how you can determine the exact model number. As you should whenever you're troubleshooting, make sure you've saved and closed all your documents, and that you have a recent backup of your work in case something tragic and unexpected occurs.

It's easy to take your hard-working and reliable little mouse for granted, but when it doesn't work properly—or doesn't work at all—you realize how much you rely on it. There are some simple things you can do to revive a mouse that moves erratically or hardly moves at all, or that appears on the screen in an unfamiliar guise—as a black square, for example. You can also customize the way your mouse works—you can configure it for left- or right-handed use, set it to open items with one click or two, adjust the double-click speed, and change the pointer's color and increase its size if you have difficulty finding or following it on the screen.

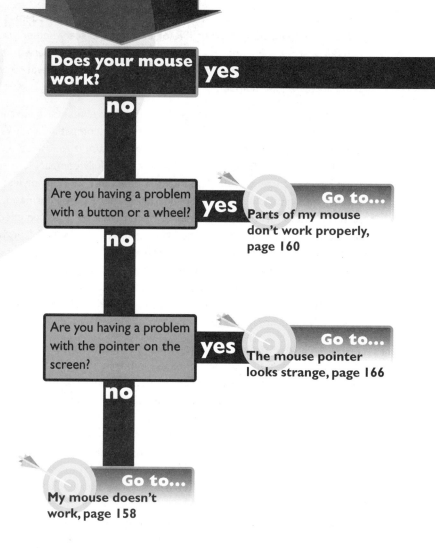

Does your mouse work?   yes

no

Are you having a problem with a button or a wheel?   **yes**

no

Go to...
Parts of my mouse don't work properly, page 160

Are you having a problem with the pointer on the screen?   **yes**

no

Go to...
The mouse pointer looks strange, page 166

Go to...
My mouse doesn't work, page 158

Mouse

Can you control the mouse pointer's movements?

yes → **Is it difficult to see the mouse pointer?**

yes →

Go to...
I can't find or follow the mouse pointer, page 164

no ↓

Do items in Windows respond incorrectly when you use a single- or a double-click?

yes →

Quick fix

Windows can respond to your mouse clicks when you use the traditional double-click to open or start an item or, if you prefer, you can change to the single-click method popular in web pages.

1. Open My Computer from the Desktop, using a single- or a double-click, depending on your settings.

2. On the Tools menu, click Folder Options.

3. On the General tab, click the single-click or the double-click option.

4. If you chose the single-click option, click either the option to use your browser settings for underlining or the option to underline icons only when you point to them.

5. Click OK.

no ↓

Go to...
I can't control my mouse, page 162

If your solution isn't here
Check these related chapters:
Games, page 88
Keyboard, page 124
Or see the general troubleshooting tips on page xiii

My mouse doesn't work

Source of the problem

There are all sorts of reasons your mouse won't work, and the troubleshooting challenge here is primarily to identify the cause. Once you've found the cause, the solution is usually pretty inexpensive. In other words, a new mouse might be the answer! In this situation, we're going assume that using the mouse makes your system lock up or crash, or that you can move your mouse around all over the place but there's no mouse pointer on the screen—or that if there is, it doesn't move at all.

How to fix it

1. Never overlook the obvious! Make sure the mouse is plugged in to the computer. If it isn't, shut down the computer, plug in the mouse, and restart the computer. Don't you wish you could solve every problem this easily?

2. If that didn't fix it, it's time for some serious troubleshooting. Let's start with the most critical problem: the mouse is making your system unstable. Try to identify any mouse action that's associated with the problem. For example, on some computers, if you move the mouse while the computer is going into Standby mode, the computer can lock up or have other problems. In cases like this, the problem is usually associated with the computer's internal system—the BIOS (basic input/output system)—and you'll need to check with the computer manufacturer for a fix or an update of the BIOS. Or, of course, you could simply not repeat that action!

> **Tip**
> For information about how to check for hardware and software compatibility, see "The mouse pointer looks strange" on page 166.

3. If you can't associate a specific action with the problem, it could be caused by extra software you installed to enhance the mouse or the keyboard, or by some other software. For example, Microsoft IntelliPoint software versions 2.2 and earlier can cause Windows to stop responding. Although versions of IntelliPoint prior to version 3.1a aren't compatible with Windows 2000 and probably couldn't be installed directly onto your Windows system, the software might continue to be in use if you upgraded from an earlier version of Windows that did use that software. If you do have any software programs to enhance the mouse or keyboard, or if you installed software just before your mouse expired, make sure the software is compatible with Windows 2000. If it's not, check with the manufacturer for a fix. If there's no fix, uninstall the software, using Safe Mode if necessary. For information about upgrading IntelliPoint software, go to the web site http://www.microsoft.com/products/hardware/mouse/driver.

4. Perhaps there's no software conflict at all, and Windows simply isn't detecting your mouse. To see whether the mouse has been detected, do the following (without using the mouse): Press

Ctlr+Esc to open the Start menu. Use the Up arrow key to move to Settings, and the Right arrow key to open the Settings submenu. With Control Panel selected, press Enter. In the Control Panel, use the arrow keys to move through the Control Panel until the Mouse icon is selected, and then press Enter. In the Mouse Properties dialog box, press Shift+Tab to select the Buttons tab, and use the Right arrow key to select the Hardware tab. ▶

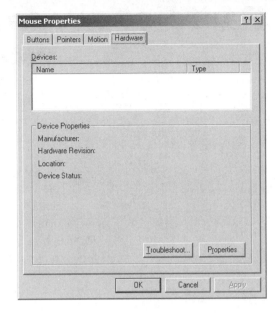

5. If nothing is listed on the tab, Windows didn't find the mouse. The mouse is normally detected automatically (you can't add it using the Add/Remove Hardware item in the Control Panel), so there's probably something wrong with the connection or with the mouse itself. Windows 2000 does not fully support some types of connections, and even if the mouse worked before you upgraded to Windows 2000, it might not work now. Check for the following types of connections:

● A bus or an InPort connection. These types of connections aren't supported. For information about the type of connection your mouse uses, check the documentation that came with either the mouse or the computer. See whether an adapter is available, or replace the mouse with one that uses a PS/2 or serial connection.

● A connection through a port on the keyboard. Depending on the hardware, this might or might not work. Try connecting the mouse directly to the computer.

● A connection through a manual switch box. Again, this might or might not work, depending on the hardware.

● A USB (universal serial bus) connection through a hub. Some USB hubs aren't fully compatible with Windows 2000, so consult the hardware compatibility list.

6. If the mouse is listed in the dialog box, there might be a problem with its settings or its drive. Press the Tab key until the Properties button is selected, and then press Enter. In the Mouse Properties dialog box, inspect the status. If the device is listed as disabled, click the Enable button. If there's a resource conflict, adjust the resources on the Resources tab. If there's a driver problem, download and install an updated driver. (To make these changes, you must be logged on as an Administrator.) After you make the changes, press the Tab key until the OK button is selected, and press Enter. If you made no changes, press the Esc key twice to close the two dialog boxes. If all else fails, install a new mouse and see whether the problem was caused by a bad mouse.

Parts of my mouse don't work properly

Source of the problem

What can you do when your mouse-clicks don't accomplish anything, or when the wheel on your mouse doesn't make anything happen on the screen even though you keep spinning the wheel over and over again? There could be a couple of simple solutions, such as making a few adjustments to the mouse's settings or forcing Windows to use a particular feature, such as the wheel. Sometimes, alas, the problem can be a bit more serious—anything from a software bug to a very sick little mouse.

How to fix it

1. If the mouse buttons don't behave as you expect them to, make sure they've been set for the way you want to use them. On the Settings submenu of the Start menu, click Control Panel. In the Control Panel, double-click the Mouse icon. On the Buttons tab, set the mouse configuration for right-handed or left-handed use. ▶

2. In the Files And Folders section of the dialog box, specify whether you want to open an item with one click or two.

3. In the Double-Click Speed section, double-click the box in the Test Area. If the jack-in-the-box doesn't pop out of the box (or doesn't go back into the box if it's already out), you need to reset the speed with which you double-click. Drag the slider to the right if you're a very speedy double-clicker, or drag it to the left if you double-click at a more leisurely rate. Double-click the box in the Test Area again. Continue adjusting the double-click speed and testing it until the jack-in-the-box opens or closes with each double-click.

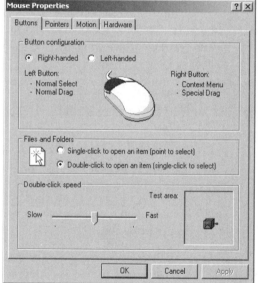

> **Tip**
> For information about fine-tuning the use of a single- or a double-click, see the quick fix on page 157.

4. If your computer has additional software installed, such as Microsoft IntelliPoint software, explore the various tabs in the dialog box to see whether one of the special features, such as

ClickLock, is in effect. If so, and if you think that might be the feature that's affecting the way your mouse is acting, clear the check box for that feature. Click OK, and then check to see whether the mouse is now performing correctly.

5. If you have a mouse with a wheel, and if Windows doesn't do anything when you use the wheel, you need to get Windows to look for the wheel. To do this, however, you must be logged on as an Administrator. In the Control Panel, right-click the Mouse icon, and click Run As on the shortcut menu. Log on as the Administrator.

6. In the Mouse Properties dialog box, click the Hardware tab, click the name of your mouse if it's not already selected in the list, and click the Properties button.

7. On the Advanced Settings tab of the Mouse Properties dialog box, if the Wheel Detection setting is anything but Assume Wheel Is Present, click that setting. If the setting is already set at Assume Wheel Is Present, click Look For Wheel in the Wheel Detection list. Click OK, and restart the computer when prompted. Some mouse devices with a wheel can cause a problem in Windows. If your computer doesn't detect or use the wheel, make sure you're using the mouse that came with the computer (and was tested for compatibility by the manufacturer), or that you're using a Microsoft mouse with a wheel that was designed to be used with Windows 2000. ▶

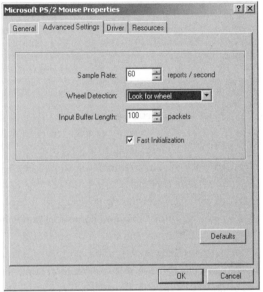

8. If, while you're playing a game, the mouse acts though one of its buttons is being held down, you might have encountered a bug. Make sure you're not holding down a button, or that the mouse isn't wedged against something that is pushing the button down. If you can't figure out what's causing this action, you'll need to get the Windows 2000 service pack, which fixes this problem. For information about Windows 2000 service packs, see Appendix A, "Installing a service pack," on page 295.

9. If none of the above remedies has fixed your mouse problems, it might be time to try some alternative approaches. See "I can't control my mouse" on page 162 for information about cleaning a dirty mouse, and—sad to say—for information about testing to see whether it's time to send your mouse out to mouse pasture.

I can't control my mouse

Source of the problem

Your mouse is an intelligent and hardworking little device. It uses sophisticated software that makes it do exactly what you want it to do—usually, that is. If your mouse pointer is careening out of control, barely moving on the screen, or otherwise behaving erratically, there could be several reasons. These might include settings that you didn't know existed and possibly conflicting software packages. However, the most common reason for bad mouse behavior lies not with the mouse itself but with a mouse wrangler who doesn't pay attention to the mouse's *toilette*.

How to fix it

1. Most mouse problems are caused by lint, hair, oil, dust, and various other substances that can accumulate inside the mouse. (This, of course, applies only to the type of mouse that uses a ball to track your movements on the screen.) If, when you move the mouse or trackball, the mouse pointer is hesitant to move or doesn't move in the right direction, it probably needs a bit of refreshing. Turn off your computer, and carefully open up the mouse. Remove the ball, and look inside. You'll see some little rollers and, probably, some clumps of nasty-looking stuff. Carefully remove this stuff from around the rollers, using your fingers or a swab. Be careful not to pull out any parts that belong inside—some mice have little springs and levers. If you can, use some compressed air to blow out what remains. Then put a little rubbing alcohol on a swab, clean the rollers and the contact areas, and use some more compressed air to leave everything clean and dry. Finally, clean the ball you removed, and reassemble the mouse. If your computer uses a mouse without a ball (such as a touchpad), carefully clean the surface to remove oil and dust. Turn on the computer, and you'll probably see a sprightly, re-energized mouse pointer.

2. If proper hygiene doesn't cure your mouse, see whether there's a pattern to the problem. For example, if the mouse pointer jumps to a different location when you open a dialog box, it might have been set to do exactly that. To change this behavior, on the Settings submenu of the Start menu, click Control Panel. In the Control Panel, double-click the Mouse icon. In the Mouse Properties dialog box, click the Motion tab, and clear the Move Pointer To The Default Button In Dialog Boxes check box. Click Apply, but leave the dialog box open—you can use it to try

> **Warning**
> Don't try to disassemble a mouse that isn't meant to be taken apart. If you have any doubts as to whether or not you should try to clean your mouse, consult the documentation that came with your mouse or with your computer.

> **Tip**
> Don't overlook the basics! If your mouse is connected to your computer, make sure the cable is tightly connected. If you're using a cordless mouse, make sure that nothing is interfering with the transmission between the mouse and the computer.

to fix other problems. (If the Mouse
Properties dialog box looks different from
the one shown here, it's because your computer is using additional software for the
mouse. You should, however, still see these
four basic tabs.) ▶

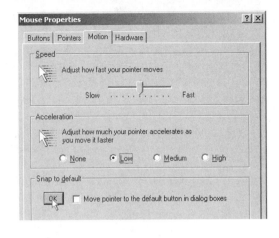

3. If the mouse pointer is moving too fast
for you, experiment with the settings on
the Motion tab. Try different settings for
Acceleration or Speed, and move the mouse
around quickly to see how the changes affect
the pointer's movements. When the speed is
right for you, click OK.

4. If your mouse still isn't working right, and before you go any further, make sure there's nothing
physically wrong with the mouse. Turn off the computer, remove the mouse, borrow a similar
mouse from another computer, and install that mouse to see whether it works properly. If your
mouse is connected to the USB (universal serial bus) port, you don't need to turn off the
computer when you're switching mice, but *don't* forget to use the Unplug Or Eject hardware
command before you remove the mouse.

5. If the mouse pointer's movements are erratic, and the previous steps haven't helped, you need
to get a little more technical. In the Control Panel, hold down the Shift key, right-click the Mouse
icon, and click Run As on the shortcut menu. Log on as an Administrator. On the Hardware tab,
click your mouse's name if it isn't already selected, and click the Properties button.

6. In the Mouse Properties dialog box, click the Advanced Settings tab. Increase the Sample Rate to
100 and the Input Buffer Length to 300, and clear the Fast Initialization check box. Click OK, and

then click OK again to close the dialog box.
Restart Windows to implement the changes,
and see whether this has helped. If it has,
return to the Advanced Settings dialog box,
and experiment to find the settings closest
to the original settings that work. ▶

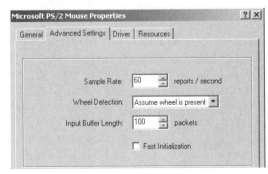

7. If there's no improvement, repeat step 5 and,
on the Advanced Settings tab of the Mouse
Properties dialog box, click the Default button to restore the original settings. Click the
Driver tab, and note the information about the provider, date, version, and digital signer. Click OK,
and then click OK again. If the driver is not a recent one from Microsoft, check with the driver
provider, or with the manufacturer of your mouse or your computer, for an updated driver. For
information about installing updated drivers, see "The device was misidentified" on page 100.

I can't find or follow the mouse pointer

Source of the problem

It's extremely irritating when you can't easily find or follow the mouse pointer on your screen. Depending on the type of screen you're using (and on your visual acuity, of course), spotting the mouse pointer can be a real challenge. To make the pointer easier to see, you can make quite a few adjustments to it. You can change its color, increase its size, and even make it a different shape. And if you don't have problems seeing the pointer, you can change its appearance just for fun. Who wouldn't want a cute little yellow dinosaur pointer with a purple bow on its head?

How to fix it

1. Windows provides a variety of predesigned mouse pointer schemes in various sizes and colors. To change to a different pointer scheme, on the Settings submenu of the Start menu, click Control Panel. In the Control Panel, double-click the Mouse icon.

2. On the Pointers tab of the Mouse Properties dialog box, click a mouse pointer scheme in the Scheme list. The pointers that are included in the selected scheme are shown in the area below the Scheme list. If you think you like the pointer scheme, click Apply. Your mouse pointer will now use the selected scheme. Do some work in Windows, moving the pointer around. If you're not sure the pointer scheme you chose is the best one for you, return to the Mouse Properties dialog box, click a different pointer scheme, and click Apply. When you've found the scheme you want, click OK to close the Mouse Properties dialog box. ▶

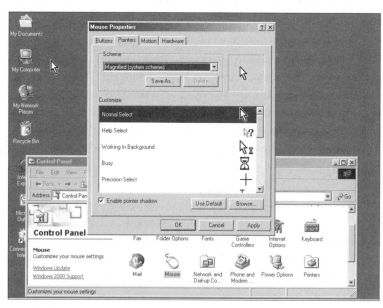

3. If you like the pointer scheme but it doesn't provide the contrast you need to see it clearly, you can change the entire color scheme of Windows. To do so, double-click the Display icon in the

Control Panel. On the Appearance tab, click a different color scheme in the Scheme list. If you like the look of it in the pre-view, click Apply, and wait for the scheme to be applied to all your screen elements. Move the mouse pointer around on the screen. Can you see it more easily now? If not, click another scheme in the Scheme list. When you've found the scheme that's right for you, click OK to close the Display Properties dialog box. ▶

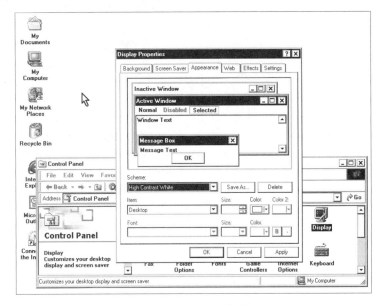

4. If your difficulty is not with the visibility of the stationary mouse pointer but with following it as it moves around the screen, you might need to slow its movements down a bit. Double-click the Mouse icon in the Control Panel, and, on the Motion tab, set Acceleration to None. Move the

mouse around and see whether you can follow the pointer more easily on the screen. If not, drag the slider in the Speed section to the left. Try moving the mouse again, and, if neces-sary, keep adjusting the speed with the slider. Click OK to close the dialog box when you've set the pointer's movements to the speed that works best for you.

> **Tip**
>
> If you have difficulty seeing the small details of many items, not just the mouse pointer, try running the Accessibility Wizard on the Accessibility submenu of the Start menu. In the wizard, you'll be able to reset many Windows elements for easier viewing.

5. If you're still having problems, your screen area's resolution might be set too high, thus making everything, including the mouse pointer, too small. To fix this, double-click the Display icon in the Control Panel. On the Settings tab, drag the slider in the Screen

Area to the left to decrease the screen area and enlarge everything on the screen. Click OK, and then click OK again when you're notified that the changes will take place. When you're asked whether you want to keep the settings, click Yes.

6. You've now adjusted just about every Windows setting available to improve your mouse pointer's visibility. However, many varieties of mice come with enhanced tools that are available when you double-click the Mouse icon in the Control Panel. Explore the different tabs and experiment with the various options that are available.

The mouse pointer looks strange

Source of the problem

Your mouse uses different pointers for different purposes: an arrow for selecting an item, a vertical bar for inserting text, an hourglass telling you to wait, and so on. When you expect to see this type of mouse pointer but instead see something very different, it can be a bit disconcerting. If the pointers are merely different—you see a cute little yellow dinosaur instead of an hourglass, for example—you'll know that someone has changed the pointer scheme, and you can switch it back to whichever scheme you want. If, however, the pointers in question don't look at all like mouse pointers—if, for example, they're small black squares—your computer system needs some remedial help.

How to fix it

1. If the mouse pointers have been changed and you don't like them, you can set them back to the default style, or you can specify the pointer scheme you prefer. On the Settings submenu of the Start menu, click Control Panel. In the Control Panel, double-click the Mouse icon. In the Mouse Properties dialog box, click the Pointers tab. Click None in the Scheme list to return to the default settings, or click a different scheme in the list. If you like the little shadow that's added to the pointer, make sure the Enable Pointer Shadow check box is selected. Click OK.

2. If, rather than a changed pointer scheme, the problem is a mouse pointer that has turned into an unusual image, such as a black square, you might have to do quite a bit of detective work to figure out what's going on. Before you get too deeply into troubleshooting, it's worth testing to see whether this is just a little glitch that you'll never need to deal with again. The tried-and-true way to do this is to shut down your programs, shut down Windows, and restart your computer. If the problem doesn't reappear, you might have fixed it. However, be alert; if the problem recurs, note what you did just before it came back to haunt you.

3. If the problem reappears immediately after you restart the computer, check to see whether the cause could be related to the DirectX technology that Windows uses to speed up displays,

> **Tip**
>
> If you're using more than one monitor on your computer, the pointer shadow might not appear on any of your screens, even though the Enable Pointer Shadow check box is selected in the Mouse Properties dialog box. This can occur when one of the monitors is set to display 256 colors. To solve this problem, make sure the monitors are set to display at least High Color—or learn to live without the shadow.

game-playing, and other features. To check this, you'll need to open the Display Properties dialog box as an Administrator. To do so, in the Control Panel, hold down the Shift key and right-click the Display icon. On the shortcut menu, click Run As, and log on as the Administrator.

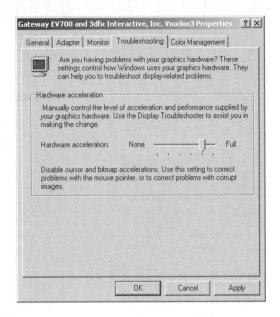

4. On the Settings tab of the Display Adapters dialog box, click the Advanced button. On the Troubleshooting tab of the dialog box that appears, if the Hardware Acceleration slider is set to Full, drag it one step to the left to disable the use of DirectX to draw the pointer. Click OK, and click OK again. If the mouse pointer doesn't revert to its proper setting, shut down Windows and restart your computer. ▶

5. If the problem still exists, it could be caused by a program or device driver. You'll need to check the compatibility of these items. If you installed a program recently—and especially if it was a game—you should make sure there are no known problems. To do so, on the Start menu, click Help. At the top of the window, click the Web Help button. In the right part of the Help window, click Search For Windows 2000-Compatible Software. Connect to the Internet if necessary, and use the Windows 2000 web page to search for the software you installed. Repeat the process

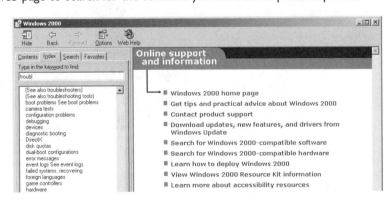

to check on your hardware, particularly your display adapter, and also your mouse if you're not using a Microsoft mouse or the mouse that came with your computer. ▶

6. If there are updates for your programs or device drivers, download and install them as described. If you don't find the items listed, contact their manufacturers to see whether any updates are available. If you can't update a program, consider uninstalling it and seeing whether this remedies the mouse pointer problem. If it does, you might have to live without that program until an update becomes available. For information about uninstalling programs, see "Programs," starting on page 220. For information about updating device drivers, see "The device was misidentified" on page 100.

If your Desktop isn't big enough for you, you can literally spread it out over two or more monitors (but if you want to work on more than ten monitors at once, you're out of luck—ten's the limit). You'll need either a video adapter card for each monitor or an adapter card that supports multiple monitors. When everything is installed and the monitors are arranged as you want them—and you've possibly had to settle a little squabble between Windows and your computer as to which monitor is the primary monitor and which is the secondary one— you can set each monitor to its own color and screen-area settings and spread your work out over a really big Desktop.

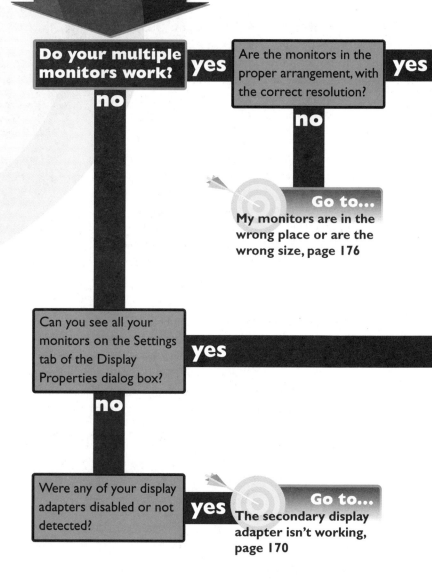

Do your multiple monitors work? **yes**

Are the monitors in the proper arrangement, with the correct resolution? **yes**

no

no

Go to...
My monitors are in the wrong place or are the wrong size, page 176

Can you see all your monitors on the Settings tab of the Display Properties dialog box? **yes**

no

Were any of your display adapters disabled or not detected? **yes**

Go to...
The secondary display adapter isn't working, page 170

If your solution isn't here
Check these related chapters:
  Hardware installation, page 96
  Screen, page 230
Or see the general troubleshooting tips on page xiii

Multiple monitors

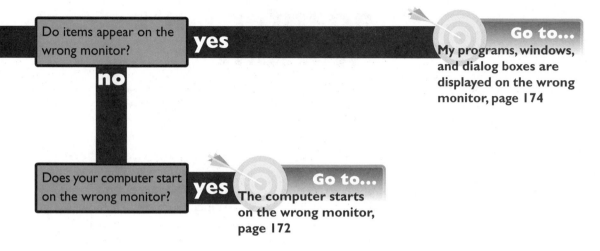

Do items appear on the wrong monitor?

yes → **Go to...**
My programs, windows, and dialog boxes are displayed on the wrong monitor, page 174

no

Does your computer start on the wrong monitor?

yes → **Go to...**
The computer starts on the wrong monitor, page 172

Quick fix

After the equipment has been installed and configured, you still need to specify whether you want to spread your Desktop over the other monitors, or which specific monitors you want to use.

1. Make sure all your monitors are turned on and attached to the computer.

2. Right-click the Desktop, and click Properties on the shortcut menu.

3. On the Settings tab of the Display Properties dialog box, click the secondary monitor.

4. Select the Extend My Windows Desktop Onto This Monitor check box.

5. Repeat steps 2 and 3 for any other monitors you want to use.

6. Click OK.

The secondary display adapter isn't working

Source of the problem

Although you've installed a second display adapter to create a multiple monitors setup on your computer, Windows might not recognize the adapter, or might even disable it. Another possibility is that the new adapter will be set up and recognized as your primary adapter but, alas, your original adapter will be disabled. Windows is very demanding, and it can be a bit quirky when certain display adapters are used as secondary adapters. The majority of such problems, however, are specific to individual makes and models of display adapters.

How to fix it

1. Make sure the secondary monitor is turned on. Right-click the Desktop, and click Properties on the shortcut menu. On the Settings tab, see whether more than one monitor icon is displayed. If so, click the grayed (unavailable) icon that represents your secondary monitor, and select the Extend My Windows Desktop Onto This Monitor check box. Click Apply, and then click the Identify button. You should see a large numeral on each monitor. Click OK.

2. If you don't see a monitor icon for each adapter card that's installed, you need to determine whether the secondary display adapter wasn't detected or was detected but was disabled. Right-click My Computer, and click Manage on the shortcut menu. In the Computer Management window, click Device Manager. Click OK to ignore any message that tells you that you don't have sufficient rights. In the right part of ▶ the window, double-click Display Adapters, and note whether all your adapters are listed and whether any are disabled. Close the Computer Management window when you've finished.

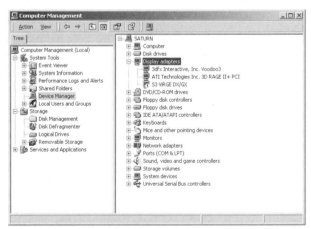

In this situation, three adapters are installed but two of them can work only as primary adapters. One adapter won't work.

3. If your new adapters are disabled, and if you installed more than one new adapter at one time, remove all but one of them, and then restart Windows. If Windows finds the new adapter and the adapter isn't disabled, continue installing the additional adapters one at a time. You can have no more than 10 monitors installed on your system, however.

4. If your new adapter remains undetected, or if either the new adapter or the original one is disabled, check the Windows 2000 hardware compatibility list at *http://www.microsoft.com/hwtest/hcl* to see whether one or both of your adapters can be secondary adapters. If you find your adapters in the list, be sure to read any notes about settings and whether updated drivers need to be downloaded and installed. Download and install any updated drivers you need.

5. Figure out which adapter to use as your primary adapter and which to use as your secondary adapter.

- To be the primary adapter, your adapter must be able to function in VGA mode. Unless VGA mode has been intentionally disabled, all adapters should support this mode.

- To be a secondary adapter, your adapter must be able to have VGA mode disabled. Disabling VGA mode can be done by Windows using the adapter's device driver, or by you—either by changing settings on the adapter card or by running a specific setup program for the adapter.

6. If only one adapter can have VGA mode disabled, you'll need to make this your secondary adapter. Remove this adapter, and, with the other adapter in your computer, start the computer and start Windows. In the Display Properties dialog box, configure this adapter as you want, making sure the color is set at or above 256 colors. When you've finished, shut down Windows and shut down your computer.

7. If you need to manually disable VGA mode, use the documentation that came with the adapter and/or the information you gathered at the Microsoft web site to do so. Install the adapter in your computer, restart the computer and Windows, and wait for the adapter card to be detected. Return to the Settings tab of the Display Properties dialog box and set up the secondary monitor.

Tip

Working in the belly of your computer and switching adapter cards isn't a simple process. See the warnings and information in "The computer starts on the wrong monitor" on page 172. That section also contains information about the types of adapters that can't be switched from primary to secondary adapters.

Tip

Before you order or install a new display adapter, check the Windows 2000 hardware compatibility list to see whether your adapter is in the list of adapters that can be used as secondary display adapters. Use only an adapter that is fully compatible. Instead of using multiple adapter cards, you might consider the possibility of using an adapter that supports more than one monitor.

The computer starts on the wrong monitor

Source of the problem

When you work with multiple monitors, one monitor is always the primary monitor and any others are secondary monitors. There are, however, two ways in which monitors are designated as primary or secondary. The first is by the computer when it starts up—the system detects the display adapters and assigns each of them a priority. The second way is when you tell Windows which adapter—and thereby which monitor—you want to designate as the primary one.

Ah, but here's the rub. Your computer will jump in and use whichever monitor it has decided is the primary monitor—that is, until Windows starts. At that point, Windows is in control and it designates which monitor is the primary monitor. The result of this duel is that your computer might show the "Starting Windows" screen on one monitor and the Log On To Windows dialog box on another monitor. To make things even worse, some items—DVD movies and full-screen MS-DOS games, for example—will run only on the monitor your computer acknowledges as the primary monitor, regardless of which monitor Windows says is the primary monitor.

How to fix it

1. There are a couple of approaches you can take here, depending on how you've set up your computer and the connections you have. The simplest way to solve the problem is to turn off the computer and the monitors, and switch the cables that run from each monitor to a different adapter. Let's say you have monitor 1 and monitor 2. First, take the cable that's attached to monitor 1, and detach it from its display adapter in the computer. Then take the cable from monitor 2, detach it from its display adapter, and attach it to the display adapter that monitor 1 had been using. Finally, attach the cable from monitor 1 to the display adapter that monitor 2 had been using. Turn both monitors on again, restart the computer, and see whether the computer starts on the correct monitor.

> **Warning**
>
> Don't try switching the monitor cables while your computer is running and the monitors are on! Not only could you damage the equipment, but Windows will now have the wrong information about the capabilities of each monitor.

2. If you did change the connections between monitors, right-click the Desktop after Windows starts, and click Properties on the shortcut menu. On the Settings tab, change the arrangement of the monitor icons to match the physical arrangement of your monitors, and designate which monitor is to be the primary monitor in Windows.

For information about designating a monitor as the primary monitor, see "My programs, windows, and dialog boxes are displayed on the wrong monitor" on page 174.

3. If you don't want to switch the monitors because you need specific features of a display adapter to be used with a specific monitor, you might be able to change which display adapter—and thereby which monitor—your computer recognizes as the primary display adapter. Check your computer's documentation to see whether there are settings in the computer's setup program (the BIOS, or basic input/output system) that let you designate which display adapter is used as the primary adapter. If you can make the BIOS changes, follow the computer's documentation carefully.

4. If there's no way to change the BIOS settings, you might be able to physically switch the location of the display adapters to change which one is the primary adapter. However, before proceeding, check the type of display adapter you have; some adapters can't be switched. You won't be able to do this if:

● Your computer uses an integrated display adapter, also called an onboard display adapter. This type of adapter is built right into the computer's motherboard. If you're not sure about it, check the computer's documentation. Any monitor that's attached to an integrated display adapter will be the primary adapter.

● One display adapter doesn't have the features that allow it to be a secondary display adapter. For more information about this problem, see "The secondary display adapter isn't working" on page 170.

5. Turn off your computer and monitors and disconnect their power cords. Disconnect the cables from the monitors at their display adapters, and open up the computer. Making sure that you aren't all charged up with static electricity, switch the positions of the display adapter cards if you can. Reassemble your computer and attach all the cables. Be sure to attach the monitors to the same display adapters they were attached to before, keeping in mind that the adapters are in new positions. Turn your computer and monitors back on, and see which monitor shows the startup information. If the computer hasn't changed which display adapter—and therefore which monitor—is the primary one, you can experiment by going back into the computer (after shutting everything down, of course) and experimenting with using different positions for the display adapter cards.

Warning

Step 5 requires that you open up your computer and work with its innards. Before you do this, make sure you won't get fired for opening the case, and/or that you won't be voiding any warranties or service agreements. If you're not familiar with working inside a computer and taking the standard precautions to avoid damaging yourself or the computer, get someone who's comfortable working with the computer's guts to do this for you.

Tip

If you have two different types of adapters—that is, their cards fit into different types of slots—you'll just have to give up. One of the adapters is an AGP adapter and the other is a PCI adapter, and they can't be switched.

My programs, windows, and dialog boxes are displayed on the wrong monitor

Source of the problem

When you start programs and open windows and dialog boxes, they usually appear on the monitor that you consider to be your primary monitor. However, what Windows 2000 considers to be the primary monitor might not be the one on which you want to do most of your work. So who's the boss here? You are—at least most of the time! You can designate which monitor you want these items to start on, and then you can move items from one monitor to another as it suits your purposes. You can even stretch a window so that it extends onto both monitors. Certain items, however—DVD movies and full-screen MS-DOS games, for example—will appear only on one specific monitor.

How to fix it

1. If most of your Windows 2000 programs are starting on the wrong monitor, you need to take command of which monitor is designated as your primary monitor. Right-click the Desktop, and click Properties on the shortcut menu. On the Settings tab, click the monitor on which you want to have your programs appear by default. Click the Identify button to verify that you've selected the monitor you want. If it's the correct monitor, select the Use This Device As The Primary Monitor check box, and then click OK. If the option is grayed (unavailable), this monitor is already designated as your primary monitor in Windows. ▶

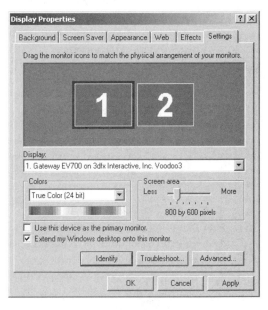

2. To test which is your primary monitor, right-click the Desktop, and click Properties on the shortcut menu. The Display Properties dialog box appears on the default (primary) monitor. Close the dialog box after you've verified that this monitor is the primary monitor.

3. Now that you've designated which is your primary monitor, you're expecting all your programs, dialog boxes, and so on to start on it, aren't you? Ah, if only it were so simple! Some items—most Windows dialog boxes, for example—will open on the primary monitor. Where some other items will open might require a bit of experimentation, not to mention patience. In most cases, a window or a program will open on the same monitor on which you closed it the last time you used it. That is, if you start a program on your primary monitor, move it to the secondary monitor, and then close the program, the next time the program starts it's likely to be on the secondary monitor. However, this doesn't happen in all cases, so you'll need to observe and become familiar with the behavior of the programs you use.

4. If you want to move a window onto a different monitor, click the Restore Down button on a window (if the window is maximized), and then drag the window by its title bar onto the other monitor. If you want the window to extend across two or more monitors, resize the window by dragging its borders so that it's big enough to be seen on the multiple monitors. If you maximize the window, it will fill only one monitor. ▶

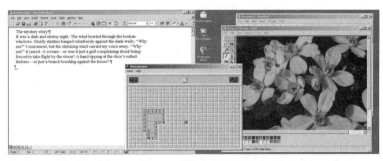

In these side-by-side monitors, a Word document has been moved onto the secondary monitor and has been maximized. Other windows can easily be moved between the monitors. The Minesweeper game is spread across the two monitors.

5. Despite your setting one monitor to be the primary monitor and trying to move items around between monitors, some items—DVD movies or full-screen MS-DOS games—will appear only on the monitor on which your computer starts. If your DVD movies or MS-DOS games are playing on the wrong monitor, you'll need to change which monitor is the system default monitor. For information about how to do this, see "The computer starts on the wrong monitor" on page 172.

A program's quirk can help your work

Although it seems unnecessarily confusing for your programs to keep you in suspense as to which of your monitors they'll start on, you'll get used to their idiosyncrasies—and you might even be able to benefit from them. Let's say you plan to use a second monitor to display the ongoing results of your work—a web page as it's being developed, for example, or a document that displays linked graphics as you're modifying them. Whenever you start up, your working tools will be ready for you on the primary monitor, and your work in progress will always appear on the secondary monitor. Sometimes your computer can surprise you by actually making your work easier—or at least, less predictable.

My monitors are in the wrong place or are the wrong size

Source of the problem

When Windows sets up your computer with two monitors, it does so in the simplest way—that is, it puts the monitors next to each other, and it uses the original settings for the first monitor and simple default settings for the second monitor. You might find, however, that you'll need to move your mouse to the left to get to the monitor on the right or that your Desktop would serve your purposes better if it were stretched vertically rather than horizontally. You might also find that the color settings or the screen area of the second monitor are completely wrong for the work you want to do.

How to fix it

1. Verify that both monitors are turned on and that both are activated. The master control for your multiple monitors is in the Display Properties dialog box. Right-click the Desktop, click Properties on the shortcut menu, and click the Settings tab. If you don't see two or more monitors in the display area, you don't have the multiple monitors configured correctly. Turn to "The secondary display adapter isn't working" on page 170, and figure out why the monitors aren't set up correctly.

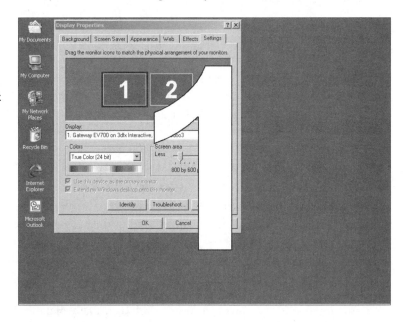

2. Click the Identify button. A large numeral appears on each monitor for a few seconds. This tells you which of your physical monitors corresponds to the monitor icons you see in the Display Properties dialog box. ▲

3. In the Display Properties dialog box, drag the monitor icons to create the arrangement you want. For example, if your physical number 2 monitor is at the left of your physical number 1 monitor, drag a monitor icon so that the number 2 monitor icon is at the left of the number 1 monitor icon. Similarly, if one physical monitor is on top of the other, drag the appropriate icon to place it above the other monitor icon. If you're working with more than two monitors, continue arranging the monitor icons until they match the arrangement of your physical monitors. When you've finished—or if you get confused—click the Apply button to put the changed positions into effect, and click the Identify button to see whether the monitors are arranged correctly.

Warning

Don't just switch cables to rearrange your monitors. See "The computer starts on the wrong monitor" on page 172 for information about physically rearranging the monitors.

4. If the settings for each monitor aren't what you need, you can adjust the individual settings. Click the monitor icon for the screen display you want to change. In the Display list below the monitors, verify that you've selected the correct monitor and adapter.

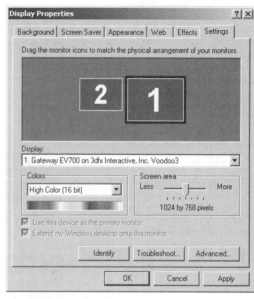

5. For the selected monitor, click a different color level in the Colors list and/or change the size of the display by dragging the slider in the Screen Area section. Note that as you modify the screen area, the monitor icons change in size to represent the difference in their settings. Click Apply to put the settings into effect. ▶

6. Repeat step 5 for any other monitors whose settings you want to change. Click OK to close the Display Properties dialog box.

7. If a monitor flickers or is distorted, move the monitors apart a bit. Some monitors generate enough of an electrical field to cause interference on another monitor. If the flicker continues, right-click the Desktop, and click Properties on the shortcut menu. On the Settings tab, click the Advanced button, and click a different Refresh Frequency on the Monitor tab. If Windows has correctly identified your monitor, only valid frequencies should be displayed. However, check the documentation for your monitor to make sure you choose a valid frequency—one that's too high could damage the monitor. Click Apply, and see whether the flicker has diminished. Continue experimenting with the refresh frequency to reduce or eliminate the flicker. Click OK, and click OK again to close the dialog boxes.

Tip

It's easy to be confused by the size of the monitor icons. Their size doesn't represent the physical size of your monitors. And because the physical size of a monitor doesn't change when you set the display for a larger screen area, items on the screen will actually be smaller, not larger.

Who doesn't love e-mail? It's one of a computer's most used and most valued features. Outlook Express, which comes with Windows 2000, works with three different types of mail servers, so you can connect to most e-mail systems. You can create an individual identity to protect your privacy if several people use Outlook Express on your computer and if your messages and theirs get mixed up in the same folders. If you're spending too much time and money on line, you can tweak a few settings that will allow you to work off line and to connect only when you're ready to send or receive messages. And, because your messages are vulnerable out there in the world, we'll show you how to encrypt them to keep them safe from prying eyes.

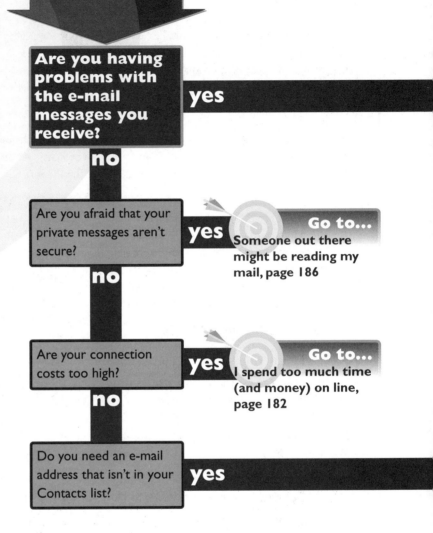

Are you having problems with the e-mail messages you receive?

yes

no

Are you afraid that your private messages aren't secure?

yes

Go to...
Someone out there might be reading my mail, page 186

no

Are your connection costs too high?

yes

Go to...
I spend too much time (and money) on line, page 182

no

Do you need an e-mail address that isn't in your Contacts list?

yes

If your solution isn't here
Check these related chapters:
Dial-up connection, page 28
Internet Explorer, page 104
Modems, page 146
Or see the general troubleshooting tips on page xiii

Outlook Express

Are your messages mixed up with those of other users?

yes →

Go to...
My e-mail messages are mixed up with other people's mail, page 184

no

Are your messages not marked as having been read?

yes →

Quick fix

Outlook Express normally marks a message as having been read after it's been displayed for at least five seconds. If you've upgraded Outlook Express, this setting might not be correct.

1. On the Tools menu, click Options, and, on the Read tab, select the Mark Message Read After Displaying For [ ] Second(s) check box.

2. In the box, specify how many seconds you want Outlook Express to wait while the message is displayed before marking it as having been read.

3. Click OK.

no

Have your messages been deleted from the mail server?

yes →

Go to...
I can't manage my messages on the mail server, page 180

Quick fix

There are several sources of e-mail addresses.

1. When you receive an e-mail message to which you want to respond, click the Reply button. The e-mail address is automatically inserted in your response, and the address should be added to your Contacts list.

2. If the address isn't added to your Contacts list, click Options on the Tools menu, and, on the Send tab, select the Automatically Put People I Reply To In My Address Book check box, and click OK.

3. If you want to get the address from a message without responding to the sender, double-click the message header, and, in the window that appears, right-click the sender's name in the From line, and click Add To Address Book on the shortcut menu.

4. If you don't have a message, click the down arrow at the right of the Find button on the toolbar, click Find on the menu, and use one of the directory services in the Look In list to locate the address you want.

I can't manage my messages on the mail server

Source of the problem

Microsoft Outlook Express can work with three different mail servers: POP3, HTTP, and IMAP. (And you thought alphabet soup was kid stuff.) Each system works in its own way and impacts how your e-mail is handled. There's one big difference among the servers, however, when it comes to managing your messages. A POP3 server holds your messages until you connect, and then it downloads all the messages to your computer. After the messages have been downloaded, they're deleted from the server. With an HTTP or IMAP server, your messages are held on the server until you request some or all of them, at which time the server downloads copies of the messages and leaves the originals, undisturbed, on the server. Depending on how you work, this can cause problems in your message management. For example, if you use more than one computer for your POP3 mail, you'll have a hard time remembering which messages you downloaded on which computer, because each message appears on only one machine. If you get your messages from an HTTP or IMAP server, the same outdated messages might appear each time you connect—despite your having previously deleted them from your computer—because they still exist on the server. Fortunately, you can tell Outlook Express how you want it to work with the mail server and how the mail server should manage your messages.

How to fix it

1. Before you change any settings, make sure you know what type of mail server you're using. In Outlook Express, click Accounts on the Tools menu. On the Mail tab of the Internet Accounts dialog box, click your mail account, and click Properties. In the Properties dialog box, click the Servers tab or the Server tab (the name of the tab depends on the type of setup you have), and note the type of server you're using. Click OK to close the Properties dialog box, and repeat the process for any other mail accounts you're using. Close the Internet Accounts dialog box when you've finished. ▶

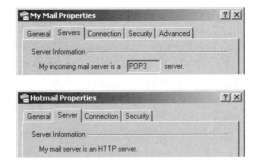

2. If you have an HTTP server, your message management is pretty simple. To delete a message or move it into a different folder, simply do so in

Outlook Express. If you're connected to the server, the changes take place immediately. If you're off line, the message is moved or deleted in Outlook Express, and it will be moved or deleted from the mail server when you reconnect. If the information isn't correctly updated on the server, click the mail server in the Folders list while you're connected, and then click Synchronize Account in the Message section. See "I spend too much time (and money) on line" on page 182 for information about synchronizing your account.

3. If your server is an IMAP server, you need to tell it how to handle your changes. On the Tools menu of Outlook Express, click Options. On the Maintenance tab, select the Purge Deleted Messages When Leaving IMAP Folders check box, and click OK. With the check box selected, any messages you've marked for deletion will be deleted immediately. If you're not connected to the server when you mark a message for deletion, the message will be deleted when you reconnect. If, instead of having your messages automatically deleted from the server, you want to manually delete the messages you've marked for deletion, clear the check box, and click Purge Deleted Messages on the Edit menu to delete the messages. ▶

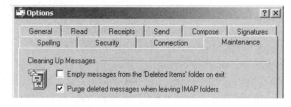

4. If your mail server is a POP3 server, your goal is probably the direct opposite of the foregoing— that is, you want to prevent your messages from being automatically deleted from the server. To do so, on the Tools menu of Outlook Express, click Accounts. On the Mail tab of the Internet Accounts dialog box, click your mail account, and click Properties. On the Advanced tab of the Properties dialog box, select the Leave A Copy Of Messages On Server check box. If you don't want to keep all your messages forever (or if you've received a message from a network adminis- trator telling you that you have too many messages stored on the server), select the Remove From Server After [ ] Day(s) check box, and specify a number of days. Note that even if you specify a large number of days, your messages might be deleted after fewer days, depending on the policies used by the mail server's administra- tor. Select the Remove From Server When Deleted From 'Deleted Items' check box if you want to coordinate what you delete in Outlook Express with what's deleted from the server. Click OK when you've finished. ▶

About that alphabet soup

If you want to impress your friends and coworkers, or if you're as curious as we are about acronyms and abbreviations, you'll be happy to know that POP3 is Post Office Protocol 3, IMAP is Internet Message Access Protocol, and HTTP is Hypertext Transfer Protocol.

I spend too much time (and money) on line

Source of the problem

Outlook Express, as you know by now, likes to work on line. You start it up, and it wants to connect; you want to read your Hotmail messages, and Outlook Express needs to be on line to retrieve each message as you select it; you create a message, and as soon as you click the Send button, Outlook Express immediately wants to connect and send the message. This urge to connect isn't a problem if your computer is always connected to the Internet or to a company intranet, but if you're paying by the minute for phone and/or ISP connections, this behavior can quickly become expensive. To reduce your costs—or simply to free up a phone line—you can set up Outlook Express to work off line most of the time, and have it connect only to retrieve all your messages at once so that you can read them off line, or to send all the mail messages you composed off line.

How to fix it

1. To break Outlook Express of its bad habit of always connecting, you'll need to deactivate some of its automatic features and tell it when to retrieve and send messages. This applies to both mail and newsgroup messages. Start Outlook Express if it isn't already running. If you're connected to the Internet, click Work Offline on the File menu. If Outlook Express asks you whether you want to hang up your modem, click Yes. You've just taken the first step toward reducing your connection charges. ▶

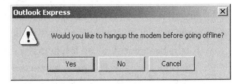

2. Manually going off line is handy, but Outlook Express still wants to be connected most of the time. You'll need to change a few settings to persuade Outlook Express to stay off line until you're ready to connect. On the Tools menu, click Options. On the General tab of the Options dialog box, clear both the Send And Receive Messages At Startup and the Check For New Messages Every [ ] Minute(s) check boxes. ▶

3. That takes care of most—but not all—of the instances when Outlook Express will connect. On the Send tab of the Options dialog box, clear the Send Messages Immediately check box. On the Connection tab, select the Hang Up After Sending And Receiving check box. Click OK when you've finished. Close Outlook Express, and then restart it to confirm that it stays off line and doesn't connect to the mail server.

4. Now you need to figure out how to get your messages sent and retrieved with as little time on line as possible. If you're using an HTTP e-mail server (such as Hotmail) or an IMAP e-mail server, you need to designate what you want to be downloaded. To do so, in the Folders list in Outlook Express, click your mail account. In the right part of the window, specify what you want to be downloaded. To retrieve messages from a particular folder, for example, select the check box for that folder in the Synchronization Settings column. To download only new messages or message headers only (the text in the list of messages that excludes the body of the messages), with the folder selected, click Settings, and click the option you want on the menu. Repeat for any other items. ▶

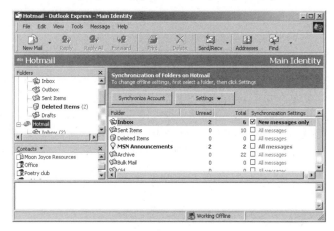

5. When you want to retrieve your messages, click either the Send/Recv button on the toolbar, or the arrow at the right of the button, and then click the mail account from which you want to retrieve your mail (if you have more than one e-mail account). Each time you need to connect, Outlook Express will prompt you to go on line, and, after you've downloaded your mail and disconnected, you'll need to click Work Offline on the File menu. If you don't do this, whenever you click a folder on an IMAP or HTTP mail server, Outlook Express will connect to the mail server. If you're using a POP3 mail server, Outlook Express will connect only when you click the Send/Recv button.

6. After you've downloaded your mail, you can read the complete text of all your messages off line, unless you set the synchronization to download message headers only. When you create or reply to a message, the message is stored in the Outbox and is sent only when you click the Send/Recv button.

7. If you did some file management while you were off line— deleted some messages, perhaps, or moved messages from one folder into another—you'll need to update the server (this applies to IMAP and HTTP servers only). To do so, click the mail account in the Folders list, and, in the right part of the window, click Synchronize. Click Work Offline on the File menu when you've finished.

Tip

For information about using different mail servers, and how to determine what type of mail server you're using, see "I can't manage my messages on the mail server" on page 180.

My e-mail messages are mixed up with other people's mail

Source of the problem

If at least one other person uses Outlook Express on your computer, in certain circumstances your messages and theirs can get mixed up in the same folders. This doesn't happen when everyone who uses the computer logs on properly, because each individual has a separate version of Outlook Express. However, if Outlook Express is used by several people who don't log on and off when they use the computer, all their e-mail messages will end up in the same folders. To make sure this doesn't happen, each person who uses the computer can create an individual identity in Outlook Express and can use that identity to keep all mail messages private and separate. If you're the only person who uses Outlook Express on the computer, but you have separate mail accounts for your business and personal mail, you might want to create separate identities to keep the two accounts completely separate.

How to fix it

1. By default, Outlook Express uses a single identity, called the Main Identity. This identity is always there, regardless of how many other identities you add. To create a new identity, in Outlook Express, point to Identities on the File menu, and click Add New Identity on the submenu. In the New Identity dialog box, type the name you want to use for the identity. If you want to keep your messages private, select the Require A Password check box. In the Enter Password dialog box, type your password twice, and click OK. When prompted, click Yes to switch to your new identity. ▶

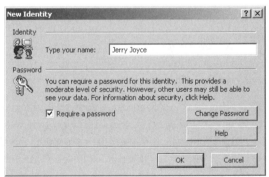

2. Creating a new identity for yourself in Outlook Express is similar to having your own private and personal copy of the program. Now you need to set up your own mail accounts. After you switch identities, the Internet Connection Wizard starts so that you can set up your connection and your accounts. The wizard lets you set up one mail account. If you want to add other mail or news accounts, click Accounts on the Tools menu. In the Internet Accounts dialog box, click the Add button, and then, on the

submenu, click the type of service you want to add. Use the Internet Connection Wizard to add the account you want. Close the Internet Accounts menu when you've finished.

3. Now that you have your new identity, you might notice that a few things are missing. For example, any mail messages that you downloaded from a POP3 server when you were using the Main Identity are no longer in your Inbox. (Note, however, that messages on an IMAP or HTTP server remain on the server, so unless you've intentionally deleted those messages, you can access them once you've added the account to your new identity.) To import messages from the Main Identity to your new identity, point to Import on the File menu, and click Messages on the submenu. On the Select Program page of the Outlook Express Import Wizard, click Microsoft Outlook Express 5, and click Next. In the Import From OE5 dialog box, click Import Mail From An OE5 Identity, click Main Identity, and click OK. Continue through the wizard, specifying which folders to import. You should now have transferred all the messages that were in the Main Identity to your new identity. Delete any messages that belong to other people who were using the Main Identity.

Warning

If you're connected to the Internet when you create a mail account that uses a POP3 mail server, Outlook Express will immediately download the messages and delete them from the mail server. To prevent this from happening, create the account off line, and read "I can't manage my messages on the mail server" on page 180 for information about preserving messages on the e-mail server.

4. Also missing from your new identity are the contacts, together with all their e-mail addresses, that you had in the Main Identity. You'll need to switch back to the Main Identity to retrieve the contacts you want. To do so, click Switch Identity on the File menu, and double-click Main Identity in the Switch Identities dialog box. In the Main Identity version of Outlook Express, click Addresses on the toolbar. In the Address Book window that appears, click Folders And Groups on the View menu if it isn't already selected. In the left pane of the window, click Main Identity's Contacts if it isn't already selected, and then drag any contact you want from the right pane onto the Shared Contacts item in the left pane. Any contacts listed in Shared Contacts will be available to all Outlook Express identities. ▶

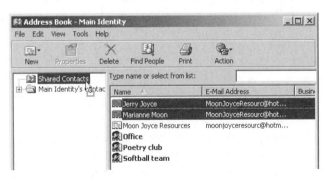

5. Close the Address Book window, and use the Switch Identity command on the File menu to return to your identity and confirm that the contacts you want from the Main Identity are now listed in your Contacts list. If you want to move the shared contacts into your private Contacts list, click the Addresses button on the toolbar, and, if the list of folders isn't displayed, click Folders And Groups on the View menu. Click Shared Contacts, and drag the contacts you want onto your Contacts folder. This way, if any contacts are deleted from the Shared Contacts list, you'll still have them in your own Contacts list.

Someone out there might be reading my mail

Source of the problem

You compose your mail, you send it off, and it zips securely from your computer to the intended recipient, right? Not even close! Your messages enjoy numerous adventures on their way to their destinations, passing through an assortment of servers and routers, and pausing here and there as they wait for the traffic to clear. These adventures, unfortunately, leave your messages vulnerable to being intercepted and read. Because Outlook Express sends your mail out as plain text messages, it can be read by anyone who can gain access to any server that handles mail. If your messages are too sensitive to be viewed by others—or if you simply detest the fact that your privacy can be invaded so easily—you can boost the security of your messages by using special cryptographic techniques.

How to fix it

1. To send a secure message, you need to encrypt it. This means the message is scrambled in such a way that, without the proper "key," no one can unscramble it. To set up this method of security, you need to have a certificate, or *digital ID,* that contains the keys to scramble and unscramble the message. Depending on network policies and/or whether you had one previously, you might already have a certificate. To see whether you do—and, if so, to set it up—on the Tools menu in Outlook Express, click Accounts. On the Mail tab of the Internet Accounts dialog box, click your mail account, and then click Properties.

   On the Security tab of the Properties dialog box, click Select in the Signing Certificate area. If there is a certificate in the Select Default Account Digital ID dialog box, you're all set. Click the certificate to select it, and click OK. In the Encrypting Preferences area of the Properties dialog box, click Select, click the same certificate, and click OK. Repeat the process for any other mail service you use. ▶

   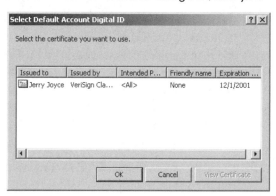

2. If you don't have a certificate, you need to get one. There are a couple of ways to do this. Many networks issue their own certificates, so check with your network administrator or help desk for information. You can also obtain a certificate over the Internet from a Certificate Authority.

Outlook Express makes it easy to do this, with direct links to suppliers. To get a certificate, on the Tools menu in Outlook Express, click Options. On the Security tab, click Get Digital ID, and follow the instructions provided to install the ID. You might have to wait until the issuing authority verifies your identity and e-mails you the details about getting the certificate. When you obtain and install it, follow the instructions in step 1 to use it.

3. Although you now have a certificate that contains your digital ID, the only way it's of any use is for other people to have the "public key"—the part of the ID that identifies you. You keep the other part of the ID—the "private key"—on your computer so that only you can decrypt the messages that were scrambled using your public key. There are a couple of ways for you to provide others with your digital ID:

- Send your business card (vCard) with your message, and have the recipient add the card to his or her address book. To send a business card, create a new contact for yourself in the Contacts list. (Don't forget to complete the information on the Digital IDs tab.) On the Tools menu, click Options, and, in the Business Cards section of the Compose tab, select the Mail check box, and click your business card. If you don't want your card included in every message you send, clear the Mail check box, and click OK. When you create a new message, your business card is automatically inserted if you selected the Mail check box, or you can insert the card in specific messages by clicking My Business Card on the Insert menu when you compose the message.

- Send a message in which you clicked the Digitally Sign Message button to add a digital signature. The recipient can then click the Digital Signature button, click View Certificates on the Security tab, and click Add To Address Book.

4. To send an encrypted e-mail message to someone whose digital ID you already have, use your Address Book to address the message, and click the Encrypt Message button. If you don't have the digital ID, use an Internet directory service or an address book or directory service on your network to find that person's e-mail address. Most services include the public key in an address.

More about encryption and digital signing

When you encrypt and send a message, you're using the public key that belongs to the message recipient, who subsequently uses a private key to automatically decrypt the message. When you send a digitally signed message, you're attaching your public key to the message, and, if the message recipient has your digital ID in an address book, he or she can use the key to verify that the message came from you and not from an impostor. Because the private key to your digital ID resides on your computer, your private key won't be available to decrypt an encrypted message that you receive on a different computer. You can export your certificate to another computer, and you can (and should) back up your certificates. To do so, log on as an Administrator, and, in the Control Panel, double-click Users And Passwords, and use the tools on the Advanced tab.

You can use your computer's power-saving features to put your monitor and your hard disk into a low power state, causing your screen to go blank; you can have a screen saver appear after a set period of time; or you can have the computer automatically go into Hibernate or Standby mode. For these useful features to work properly, however, your computer must have power-saving features that are fully compatible with Windows 2000, and all the options must be configured correctly. Otherwise, your computer might not wake up when it's supposed to, might not go to sleep on schedule, and might misbehave in other ways. We'll help you fix any problems.

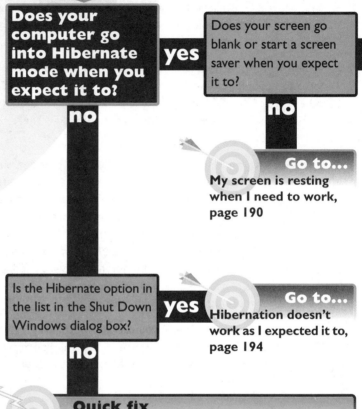

Does your computer go into Hibernate mode when you expect it to?

yes

Does your screen go blank or start a screen saver when you expect it to?

yes

no

no

Go to...
My screen is resting when I need to work, page 190

Is the Hibernate option in the list in the Shut Down Windows dialog box?

yes

Go to...
Hibernation doesn't work as I expected it to, page 194

no

Quick fix

Hibernate mode is supported for almost all computers. However, this feature can be turned on or off. You need to turn it on.

1. On the Settings submenu of the Start menu, click Control Panel.
2. Double-click the Power Options icon.
3. On the Hibernate tab, select the Enable Hibernate Support check box. Click OK.
4. If the Hibernate tab is missing, Windows has determined that your computer can't support Hibernate mode at this time, probably because of a problem with a program or device driver. You'll need to do additional troubleshooting to find the culprit.

Power options

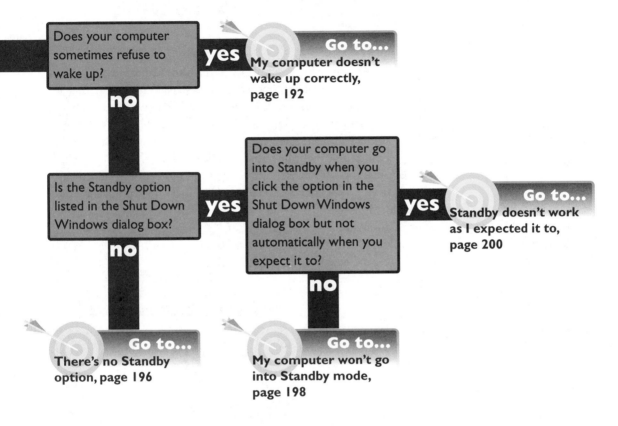

Does your computer sometimes refuse to wake up?

yes → Go to... **My computer doesn't wake up correctly, page 192**

no ↓

Is the Standby option listed in the Shut Down Windows dialog box?

yes → Does your computer go into Standby when you click the option in the Shut Down Windows dialog box but not automatically when you expect it to?

yes → Go to... **Standby doesn't work as I expected it to, page 200**

no ↓ (Is the Standby option...)

Go to... **There's no Standby option, page 196**

no ↓ (Does your computer go into Standby...)

Go to... **My computer won't go into Standby mode, page 198**

If your solution isn't here
Check these related chapters:
Faxes, receiving, page 58
Hardware installation, page 96
Mouse, page 156
Screen, page 230
Shutting down, page 242
Starting up, page 260
Or see the general troubleshooting tips on page xiii

My screen is resting when I need to work

Source of the problem

Windows has a couple of settings that control when and how your computer's screen rests. With one setting, the computer monitor goes into a low power state after a set period of time, and the screen goes blank. With the other, a screen saver appears after a set period of time, and a password might be required to deactivate it. Although these are fine tools for conserving energy and protecting your screen from prying eyes, they can be a source of incredible annoyance when suddenly, after you've paused for a moment of inspiration and a gulp of coffee, the screen goes blank and you have to wait for it to come back to life. And as maddening as this is when you're at your desk, imagine how embarrassing it can be when you're giving a presentation from your computer and, while you're answering a question, poof—everything goes blank.

How to fix it

1. On the Settings submenu of the Start menu, click Control Panel. In the Control Panel, double-click the Power Options icon. What you'll see on the Power Schemes tab depends on the type of computer you have and its capabilities. With a desktop computer, you'll see the top dialog box; with a portable computer, you'll see the bottom one. ▶

2. On the Power Schemes tab, specify the length of time the computer must be idle before it switches the monitor to a low power state and causes the screen to go blank. To do this, you can choose a predefined set of options, or power schemes; or you can change the length of time your

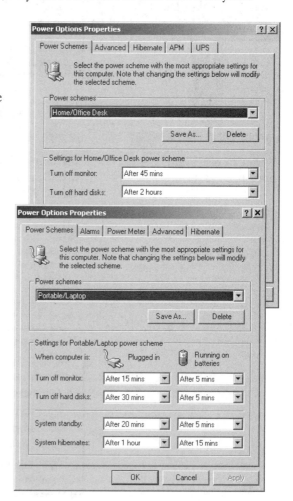

computer must be idle before the monitor is switched to a low power state. When you use a power scheme, you also change the options for the hard disk to go into a low power state and for the computer to automatically go into Standby mode (in which all systems on the computer switch to a low power state) or Hibernate mode (in which the computer is shut down without closing programs or losing information). Be sure your power scheme sets these values to the way you want your computer to work. If you manually change the values, make sure they don't conflict, or one could override the other, producing some unexpected results. Click OK when you've finished.

3. Back in the Control Panel, double-click the Display icon. On the Screen Saver tab, ▶ click None to deactivate any screen saver, or click the screen saver you want.

4. If you specified a screen saver, click the up or down scroll arrow at the right of the Wait value to set the amount of time your computer must be idle before the screen saver appears. Make sure the value represents less time than the amount of time you specified in step 2 for powering down your monitor. If the value represents more time, the computer will shut down the screen before the screen saver can appear.

5. If you want to require your user name and password to deactivate the screen saver, select the Password Protected check box. Note that if the screen saver is activated manually—for example, you use a shortcut to a screen saver file or you use a program or toolbar that starts a screen saver—the password won't be required to deactivate the screen saver.

6. If you don't like the way the screen saver looks, click the Settings button, and make your changes in the Settings dialog box. Each screen saver provides different settings, although certain screen savers have no optional settings. Close the Settings dialog box, and click the Preview button to observe your changes. Move the mouse or press any key to deactivate the preview, and if you're happy with the screen saver's appearance, click OK to close the Display Properties dialog box.

Warning

Be cautious about selecting one of the Open GL screen savers if you've set your computer to go into Standby or Hibernate mode. This type of screen saver uses some of the computer's processing power, so the computer might not go into either mode while the screen saver is running.

Tip

To make sure your screen doesn't go blank in the middle of a presentation, click the Presentation power scheme in the Power Options Properties dialog box. Click None under Screen Saver in the Display Properties dialog box.

My computer doesn't wake up correctly

Source of the problem

When your computer is in Hibernate or Standby mode, it might misbehave in several different ways. For example, it might not wake up when you want it to; it might wake up but not work in the same way it did before it went into either of these "sleeping" modes; or, worst of all, it might crash your entire system and bring forth the dreaded "blue screen of death," also known as a system Stop message. These problems can arise from a variety of situations—conflicting settings, design problems with certain computers or hardware devices, and, of course, the ubiquitous faulty device drivers. If your computer won't wake up for a fax call, see "A fax call doesn't wake the computer" on page 66.

How to fix it

1. Before you blame the computer and the system, make sure you're not inadvertently causing the problem yourself by using an incorrect way of waking the computer. Remember that Hibernate mode shuts down the computer completely, so you have to turn it back on to wake it. Then you need to wait for the system to start up and to complete all the checks the computer normally goes through when you start Windows. Finally, wait for Windows to resume and for your programs to become active again. If the computer is in Standby mode, check the computer's documentation. Some portable computers will wake from Standby when you lift the computer's lid; others require that you press the power button.

> **Tip**
>
> Once your computer starts to go into Hibernate or Standby mode, don't be in too much of a hurry either to shut down the computer or to try to wake it up. The computer needs time to record information and set the power options throughout the system. Only after the computer has finished entering Hibernate or Standby mode should you manually shut down the power (if necessary) or try to wake it.

2. If you're placing your computer in Hibernate mode, don't add or remove any hardware. If it's a portable computer, don't dock or undock it from a docking station while it's hibernating. Because you'd be returning Windows to its pre-hibernation state, the changes might not be properly detected and the system could become unstable.

3. If you're certain that you're not the cause of the problem, it's time to investigate. If the computer doesn't wake up correctly after it goes into Standby or Hibernate mode automatically, click the Shut Down command on the Start menu to manually place the computer in Standby or Hibernate mode. If, after doing so, you can wake the computer with no problem, there might be a conflict between the computer's settings and the settings you made in Windows. On the Settings submenu of the Start menu, click Control Panel. In the Control Panel, double-click the

Power Options icon, and, on the Power Schemes tab, set the length of time the computer must be idle before going into Standby or Hibernate mode to a small value (for example, two minutes for Standby or five minutes for Hibernate). If you can subsequently wake the computer after it goes to sleep automatically, try adjusting the values upward so that the computer goes to sleep when you want it to but also wakes up when you want it to.

4. If your computer still won't wake up, there could be a problem with hardware devices and their drivers. Windows attempts to determine whether your system will work correctly in Standby or Hibernate mode before it enters either mode, but sometimes a problem slips by and occurs only when the computer tries to wake up. The result can range from the computer stubbornly staying asleep to the system completely destabilizing and displaying the dreaded blue screen. In the latter case, you'll need to shut down and restart the computer. To diagnose this problem, disconnect any unnecessary devices, and then see whether the problem still exists. Also, go to *http://www.microsoft.com/hwtest/hcl* and check the Windows 2000 hardware compatibility list for your computer and all its devices. If necessary, download any updated drivers from the hardware compatibility list web site, or from the manufacturer of any troublesome device.

5. If your hardware seems blameless, the problem could be a program. If you're using a virus-protection program, check with the manufacturer about possible problems. Close your other programs before putting the computer into a sleep mode, and see whether that fixes the wakeup problem.

6. If your computer wakes up from Hibernate or Standby mode with some items not working, you might need to manually get the items working again. When the computer goes to sleep, some software support and certain connections end. When the computer wakes up, some of these items aren't reconnected or restarted. If this occurs, try turning a device on or off, or, for USB (universal serial bus)–connected items, eject the device, disconnect it, and then reconnect it. If this doesn't help, you'll need to restart Windows.

7. If your computer still won't wake up correctly, contact the manufacturer. Power control systems are still in their infancy, and appropriate corrections have been made to some software. Some computers that use the ACPI (Advanced Configuration And Power Interface) power system need to have their settings adjusted, possibly including the installation of an updated BIOS (basic input/output system). The alternative, of course, is to set your computer never to go into Hibernate or Standby mode, and, instead, to simply shut down Windows and turn off your computer.

Hibernation doesn't work as I expected it to

Source of the problem

Hibernation is a useful tool that makes it possible for you to shut down your computer without having to close all your running programs or shut down Windows. A useful tool, that is, if it works properly and if it works when you want it to. You can put your computer into hibernation in several ways: you can click Hibernate in the Shut Down Windows dialog box, you can press a button that has been designated to start Hibernate mode, or you can schedule Hibernate mode to take effect after the length of time you've specified that your computer must be idle. If certain buttons aren't assigned correctly, or if the schedule doesn't conform to your work schedule, you can modify the settings. There are several things that can prevent your computer from going into hibernation when you expect it to—a piece of hardware or its device driver, an uncooperative program, or even a bug in Windows.

How to fix it

1. On the Settings submenu of the Start menu, click Control Panel. In the Control Panel, double-click the Power Options icon. On the Power Schemes tab, either click a power scheme in the Power Schemes list to set the length of time the computer must be idle before it hibernates, or specify in the System Hibernates list the length of time the system must be idle. If you want the computer to hibernate only when you manually tell it to, click Never in the System Hibernates list.

2. Click the Advanced tab. Not all computers provide settings to control the power buttons. If yours does, click which, if any, of the power buttons you want to use to put your computer into hibernation. You'll probably want to have only one button associated with hibernation. Click OK. ▶

3. Your computer should now hibernate either on schedule or when you tell it to. This is the time to test it, so be sure to save any important documents in case things get weird.

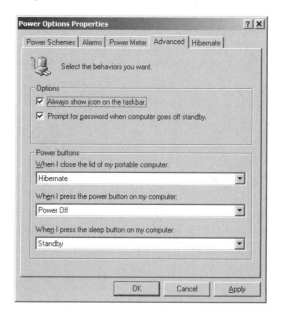

On the Start menu, click Shut Down. In the Shut Down Windows dialog box, click Hibernate, and then click OK. The computer should go into hibernation, and should either turn off its own power or tell you when it's safe to turn off the power yourself.

4. If the system doesn't hibernate, you might have a software or hardware problem. In most cases, you'll see a message telling you why your computer can't hibernate. Note that although you're trying to get the computer to go into Hibernate mode, the message specifies Standby only. ▶ You'll see the same type of message whether you're having problems with Standby or with Hibernate mode. If the problem is with a program, follow the instructions in the message. In most cases, you can solve the problem by shutting down the program before you try to get the computer to hibernate.

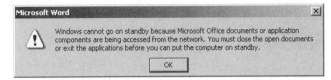

5. If the problem is being caused by a hardware device, the solution could be more difficult. Note from the message which device is causing the problem. The culprit might be a device that isn't designed to work with Windows 2000, one that's using a Windows NT 4 device driver, or one that simply has a corrupted or an incorrectly written device driver. To try to fix the problem, check with the manufacturer of the device to see whether there's an updated driver designed for Windows 2000, and, if so, install the updated driver. You should also check the Windows 2000 hardware compatibility list at *http://www.microsoft.com/hwtest/hcl* to see whether the device is compatible and whether there are any available downloads to fix the problem. For information about updating device drivers, see "The device was misidentified" on page 100. If you can't get the device to work, you'll either have to install a compatible device or learn to live without hibernation.

Tip In some circumstances, your network connection might not be reestablished when your computer comes out of hibernation. Microsoft has provided a fix for this problem in the Windows 2000 service pack. For information about service packs, see Appendix A, "Installing a service pack," on page 295.

More about hibernation

Hibernation provides you with the power-saving and security benefits of having your computer turned off, and at the same time frees you from the inconvenient and time-consuming tasks of closing all your programs and shutting down and then restarting Windows. Instead, when your computer enters Hibernate mode, all the information that's stored in the computer's memory is stored in a special location on the computer's hard disk. When you turn the computer on again, that stored information is read from the hard disk, and you're back where you were before you turned off the computer. Make sure, though, that you have the computer set to ask for a password before resuming; otherwise, anyone who turns on the computer can access the contents of your computer and anything that's accessible over the network—all in your name. For information about setting the computer to require a password before resuming, see "I'm not required to use a password to log on" on page 140.

There's no Standby option

Source of the problem

Standby is a useful power-saving mode, especially if you're using a portable computer that's running on batteries. However, Standby requires the appropriate power control system to be installed and running on your computer. If your computer isn't configured with the ACPI (Advanced Configuration And Power Interface) or APM (Advanced Power Management) power control system, or if the power management is disabled—either because of settings on your computer or in Windows, or because one or more hardware devices are interfering with the power management—the Standby option won't be available. There are also several computer configurations that can disable the Standby option.

How to fix it

1. Before you get too deeply into fixing the problem, make sure there really is a problem. Standby might be missing if your computer uses multiple processors (a "problem" many of us wish we had!). Standby *will* be missing if your computer isn't a portable computer and doesn't use the ACPI power system, if your computer is a portable computer but the APM system isn't enabled, or if you're using a VGA video driver. In these cases, it might be possible to enable APM support for a portable computer or to change the video driver.

2. To know what your computer can and can't do, you need to know what type of power management system it's using. The three possibilities are ACPI, APM, or none. To see whether your computer uses ACPI—a fairly new system—right-click My Computer on the Desktop, and click Manage on the shortcut menu. In the Computer Management window, click Device Manager. If a message tells you that you don't have sufficient security privileges, don't worry—you're just looking, not changing anything. In the right part of the window, double-click Computer. If Advanced Configuration And Power Interface (ACPI) PC is listed, your computer is using ACPI. If Standard PC is listed, your computer is using APM or nothing at all. Close the Computer Management window when you've finished. ▶

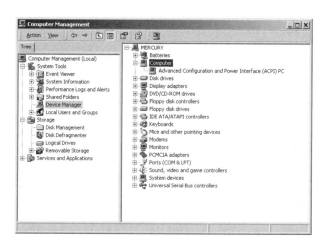

3. If the computer is using ACPI, check the items in step 1. If your computer uses multiple processors, you'll probably need to live without Standby mode, unless you want to go through a lengthy and technical procedure so that your system ends up using only one processor. That, of course, is well beyond the scope of this book. If, however, the problem is that you're using a VGA video driver, you can usually solve it by installing the correct driver for your video adapter. For information about doing this, see "The device was misidentified" on page 100.

4. If your computer isn't listed as an ACPI computer, and if it's a portable computer, you need to see whether it can use APM, and, if so, whether APM is installed. To do so, on the Settings submenu of the Start menu, double-click Control Panel. If you're not logged on as an Administrator, hold down the Shift key and right-click the Power Options icon. On the shortcut menu, click Run As, and log on as the local Administrator. If you're already logged on as a member of the Administrators group, simply double-click the Power Options icon.

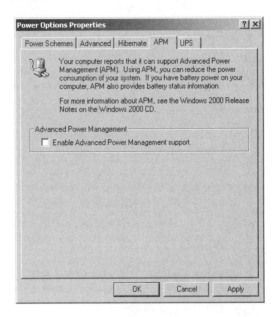

5. If there's an APM tab, click it. Select the Enable Advanced Power Management Support check box, and click Apply. Click the Power Schemes tab, and set the power scheme you want to use. Click OK. ▶

6. If there's no APM tab, either APM has been disabled in the computer's BIOS (basic input/output system) settings, or the computer can't use APM or a version of it that Windows can use (APM 1.2 or later). Consult your computer's documentation about making changes to the computer's settings, or check with the computer manufacturer about obtaining an update to the BIOS that supports APM 1.2 or later. If it's possible to enable APM in the computer's BIOS, repeat steps 3 and 4 to do so.

7. If you were successful in enabling APM, click Shut Down on the Start menu. In the Shut Down Windows dialog box, see whether Standby is listed. If it isn't, restart Windows, and check again to see whether Standby is listed now.

warning

If APM was disabled on your computer, either in the computer's BIOS or in the Power Options Properties dialog box, there might be a good reason. APM can create problems that cause your system to stop responding or that prevent you from shutting down the computer correctly. If you enable APM support and you then encounter new problems, disable the APM support and see whether this eliminates the problems.

My computer won't go into Standby mode

Source of the problem

Standby mode requires a lot from your computer. Every program and every device on the computer must comply with it, and all the settings on the computer must be at the correct levels. If Windows determines that your computer has the correct tools and configuration for entering Standby mode, it lists Standby in the Shut Down Windows dialog box. Sometimes, however, when Windows tries to go into Standby mode, it finds something that refuses to go along for the ride. In that case, Windows should tell you what's wrong so that you can try to fix it.

> **Tip**
>
> Whenever you have a problem, and especially if something in the system isn't working correctly, make sure you have a recent backup of your files. You never know what will happen when you're trying to fix a problem, and it's always wise to be prepared for the worst.

How to fix it

1. As you always should whenever you're diagnosing problems, save any open files. On the Start menu, click Shut Down. ▶

2. In the Shut Down Windows dialog box, click Standby in the list, and click OK. If Standby isn't listed in the dialog box, see "There's no Standby option" on page 196.

   Shut Down Windows

   Microsoft **Windows** 2000 **Professional**   *Microsoft*

   What do you want the computer to do?

   Stand by

   Log off Jerry Joyce
   Shut down
   Restart
   Stand by
   Hibernate

   OK   Cancel   Help

3. If Windows doesn't go into Standby mode, note the message that appears. The problem could be associated with a program, a component of Windows, or a device and its driver. Write down what the message says so that you can refer to it later.

4. If the problem is with a program, close the program before you try to start Standby. A program that's using files over the network is one that's most likely to cause problems—although almost any program can be the source of the problem. ▶

   Microsoft Word

   ⚠ Windows cannot go on standby because Microsoft Office documents or application components are being accessed from the network. You must close the open documents or exit the applications before you can put the computer on standby.

   OK

5. If the problem is a component of Windows, you're probably dealing with a bug in the system. Almost all bugs are addressed in the service packs that Microsoft releases periodically. For more information about service packs, see Appendix A, "Installing a service pack," on page 295. In some cases, there are simple workarounds. For example, if you use the Backup program to back up data to a removable disk such as a CD, and you then try to put the computer into Standby mode, you might receive an error message. In this case, all you need to do is wait a bit—about ten minutes—and then try again. ▶

6. If you receive an error message about a device or driver, you'll probably need to do more detective work. Many error messages are cryptic, to say the least. For example, a message that identifies the problem as *driver\ Driver\i740* doesn't provide much enlightenment! In this case, a specific video adapter and its driver are causing the problem. Video adapters, although frequently the cause of problems, aren't the only culprits. To try to track down the offending device, right-click My Computer, and click Manage on the shortcut menu. In the Computer Management window, click Device Manager. If you see a message about not having sufficient privileges, don't worry—you're just browsing, not making changes. Work down through the device categories, expanding the listings so that you see everything. If you find an item with a name similar to the name in the error message, it's the likely culprit. Close the Computer Management window when you've finished.

Tip
Some older devices might use Windows NT 4 drivers. Most of these drivers don't supply the proper power management to allow the computer go into Standby mode. If Windows NT 4 drivers are being used, you're likely to find them listed in the Windows Legacy section of the Device Manager.

7. If you're unable to determine which device or driver is being referenced, you can search the Microsoft Knowledge Base for its identity. Use the device identity (in this case *i740*) as the keyword in your search. For information about searching the Knowledge Base or getting other Microsoft support, see "Troubleshooting tips" on page xiii.

8. After you've figured out which device is causing the problem, the next step is to try to solve the problem, if possible. Go to either the Windows 2000 hardware compatibility list at *http://www.microsoft.com/hwtest/hcl* or the web site of the computer manufacturer to see whether an updated driver is available. If there is an updated driver, download and install it. (Note that some devices will not work in Standby mode and can't be fixed with an updated driver.) For information about installing updated device drivers, see "The device was misidentified" on page 100.

Tip
If your computer locks up or crashes when you try to make it enter Standby mode, consult with the computer manufacturer. For example, some types of portable computers might lock up if you try to go into Standby when you have a modem in use. For a quick fix, just make sure you're not using the modem (or any device that uses one of the COM ports) when you're putting the computer into Standby mode.

Standby doesn't work as I expected it to

Source of the problem

Putting your computer into Standby mode is a useful way of conserving power, and it's a real lifesaver if you're using a portable computer. When your computer enters Standby mode, everything on the computer shifts into a low power state and stays that way until you reactivate it. The computer will then power up again and be ready for you to continue doing your work. It's great when it works properly but, as you know, it can be really frustrating if, for example, the computer doesn't go into Standby mode when you expect it to—either jumping in by itself and going into Standby while you're still working, or going into Hibernate mode instead of Standby.

How to fix it

1. You first need to determine when and how Windows 2000 is set to put your computer into Standby mode. To do so, on the Settings submenu of the Start menu, click Control Panel. In the Control Panel, double-click the Power Options icon.

2. On the Power Schemes tab of the Power Options Properties dialog box, make sure that the time set for the System Standby option is less than the time set for the System Hibernates option. If the System Hibernates value is the lesser of the two, the computer will go into Hibernate mode instead of going into Standby mode. ▶

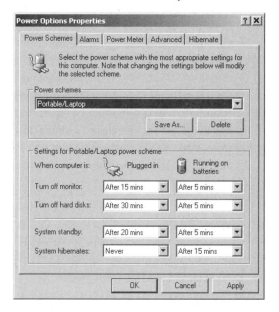

3. Click the Advanced tab. If there's a section in which you can set the action of the power buttons, click the button or the action you want to use to make the computer go into Standby mode. (Note that not all computers provide settings to control the power buttons.) Remember that even without setting any of the buttons to start Standby, you can always manually put the computer into Standby mode from the Shut Down Windows dialog box.

4. In the Options section of the Advanced tab, select the check box to prompt for a password. With this option selected, you'll have to enter your user name and password whenever the computer awakes from Standby or Hibernate mode. Without requiring a password, your system

is vulnerable to unauthorized use. Click OK when you've finished. ▶

5. Now Standby should start when you want it to. If it doesn't, there might be something else telling your system when to go into Standby mode. Check the computer's documentation to see whether there's a setting in the computer's BIOS (basic input/output system) for automatically starting Standby (sometimes called "suspend" or "sleep" mode). If the computer uses ACPI (Advanced Configuration And Power Interface), the BIOS setting shouldn't be causing a conflict, because the ACPI system should be ignoring the BIOS settings. However, if the computer uses APM (Advanced Power Management), the settings could be in conflict. If your computer uses APM, and if there's a setting in the computer's BIOS, use the computer's setup tools either to disable this feature in the BIOS or to set the length of idle time in the BIOS to be greater than the length of time you set in the Power Options dialog box. Also make sure there aren't any other programs running on your computer that are designed to control the power management. If there are any such programs, consult their documentation. Besides putting your system to sleep when you want it to stay awake, some of these programs can cause your system to become unstable.

6. Now your system should go into Standby when you want it to. Some programs and connections, however, can act quite strangely when Standby starts or when it ends. For example, some music programs that play MIDI music will act as though the computer had never gone on Standby—if the program is playing the third minute of a piece of music when Standby starts, and the computer is on Standby for ten minutes, the program will resume playing at the thirteenth minute of the music. Other programs, such as some versions of Windows Media Player, will play distorted or choppy music when Standby is ended if the program had been running before the computer went on Standby. In these cases, the fault is in the design of the program. Your best bet, if you have a program of this type, is to close it either before your computer goes on Standby or when it comes out of Standby.

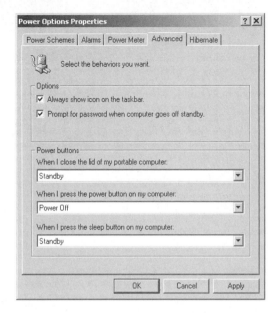

Tip

For information about determining which power management system your computer uses, see "There's no Standby option" on page 196.

Tip

When you manually start Standby mode, you might find that when you wake the computer, your modem, your VPN (virtual private network), or your ISDN connection is no longer working. If this is the case, try having the computer go on Standby automatically, and then see whether the connection you want is still working when you wake the computer.

Do you know anyone who hasn't experienced printing problems? We don't. We've probably all battled with a printer that doesn't work at all, or that seems to be working fine but nevertheless doesn't print anything, or that prints at a snail's pace and either ties up the computer for too long or takes forever to print a page or two. We've crammed a collection of these and other common but highly aggravating printing problems—and their solutions, of course—into this chapter.

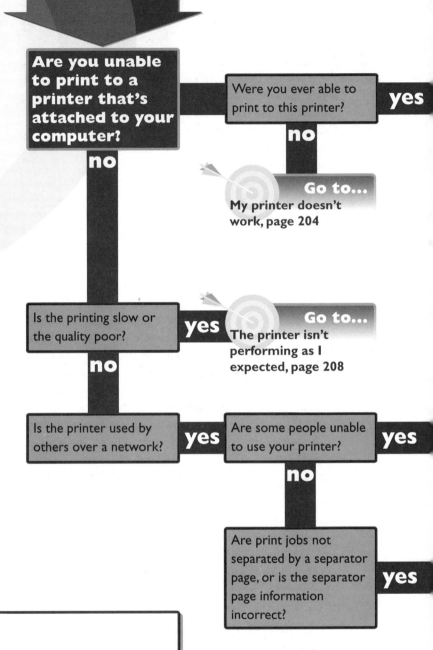

Are you unable to print to a printer that's attached to your computer?

Were you ever able to print to this printer? **yes**

no

Go to...
My printer doesn't work, page 204

Is the printing slow or the quality poor? **yes**

Go to...
The printer isn't performing as I expected, page 208

no

Is the printer used by others over a network? **yes**

Are some people unable to use your printer? **yes**

no

Are print jobs not separated by a separator page, or is the separator page information incorrect? **yes**

If your solution isn't here
Check these related chapters:
  Access to the computer, page 2
  Faxes, sending, page 68
  Hardware installation, page 96
  Printing, network, page 214
Or see the general troubleshooting tips on page xiii

Printing, local

Do documents now print to the wrong printer, or are documents sent as faxes?

yes

Quick fix
You need to select the printer when you print, or set your printer as the default printer.

1. When you print from a program, click the Print command on the program's File menu to display the Print dialog box. In the dialog box, click the printer, and then click OK.

2. If you always want the same printer designated as your printer, on the Settings submenu of the Start menu, click Printers.

3. In the Printers window, right-click the printer you want to use.

4. On the shortcut menu, click Set As Default Printer.

5. Close the Printers window.

no

Are print jobs sent to the print queue but not printed?

yes

Go to...
I try to print a document, but nothing happens, page 206

Go to...
Some people are unable to use my printer, page 212

Go to...
The separator page is wrong or is missing, page 210

My printer doesn't work

Source of the problem

If you have a printer attached to your computer, and you can't get it to work, you'll need to investigate the cause. There are several areas under suspicion here—problems with the printer itself, problems with the connection to the printer, problems with the way the printer is set up, and problems with the software that controls how the computer and the program interact with the printer. As with many of these types of problems, it's best to start with the simple and obvious possibilities first and then move along, looking at the slightly less obvious ones, and then at the more complicated ones.

How to fix it

1. You've heard it from us before, and you'll hear it again—don't overlook the obvious. Make sure that the printer is turned on, that it's on line, that it has paper and ink, and that the cable between the printer and the computer is firmly connected. If the printer is connected to a USB (universal serial bus) hub, make sure the hub is connected and is turned on. Most printers have a test button or a button combination that you can use to print a test page. Check the printer's documentation if necessary, and print a test page. If the page doesn't print correctly, you'll know there's something wrong with your printer and that it's in need of some repair.

2. If the test page comes out just fine, make sure the printer is correctly set up on your computer. On the Settings submenu of the Start menu, click Printers. In the Printers window, look for your printer. If it isn't there, you'll need to install it manually. To do so, in the Printers window, double-click the Add Printer icon to start the Add Printer Wizard. Click Next to step into the wizard, and click the Local Printer option. Select the Automatically Detect And Install My Plug And Play Printer check box if it isn't already selected, and click Next. If Windows detects the printer, it will install the proper printer drivers, and your problems will be over. If this doesn't happen, continue through the wizard, specifying the manufacturer and model of the printer and how it's connected to your computer. Use the option in the wizard to print a test page. If all goes well, you're set up and you should be able to print from your programs.

> **Tip**
>
> One of the most common and hardest to diagnose problems with a printer occurs when the cable that connects the printer and the computer goes bad. In some cases, some communication between the printer and the computer can continue, which fools Windows into thinking the printer is working correctly. If you can't figure out what's wrong, consider using a different printer cable, and see whether that solves the problem.

3. If the printer is displayed in the Printers window, click it. Either in the web content of the window or on the status bar, note the information next to the Status item. If it reads *Ready*, the

system is set up correctly and should be working. If it reads *Paused* or *Use Printer Offline*, right-click the printer, and click the checked command (Pause Printing or Use Printer Offline) to bring the printer back on line. Any documents you previously sent to the printer should now be printed. ▶

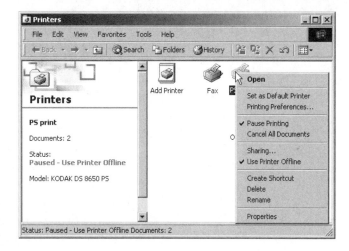

4. If the printer is set up and isn't paused or off line, the computer port you used to connect to the printer might be disabled, either in Windows or in the computer's BIOS (basic input/output system). If the port is disabled in either place, you should receive an error message. To see whether the port is disabled in Windows, right-click My Computer on the Desktop, and click Manage on the shortcut menu. In the Computer Management window, under System Tools, click Device Manager. Click OK to ignore any message you receive about permissions—you're just investigating, not making changes. Expand the Ports (COM & LPT) item if necessary, and see whether the port your printer is connected to is listed and, if it is, that it hasn't been disabled. If the port isn't listed, it either has been disabled in the computer's settings (the BIOS) or has a physical problem that Windows couldn't detect. Check the computer's documentation to see how you can enable the port in the computer's BIOS. If the port is enabled, seek professional help to find out why it isn't working. If the port is listed but is disabled, you'll need to be logged on as a member of the Administrators group to enable it. Log on, return to the Device Manager, right-click the port, click Enable on the shortcut menu, and close the Computer Management window.

5. If the port is listed and isn't disabled, there could be a problem with the device driver. To reinstall the driver and reset the entire installation, you can uninstall and then reinstall the printer. If the printer has an uninstall program, use it to uninstall the printer. If there is no uninstall program, in the Printers window, right-click the printer, and click Delete on the shortcut menu. If prompted, click Yes to confirm that you want to delete the printer. Restart the computer and see whether the printer has been detected. If it hasn't been detected, run the Add Printer Wizard. In the Use Existing Driver part of the wizard, click the option to replace the existing driver, and complete the wizard. Windows will create a new copy of the printer driver.

6. If none of this works, check with the printer's manufacturer for an updated driver or a software fix. Make sure the driver is designed for Windows 2000 and isn't a Windows NT 4 driver. If you do obtain a new driver, right-click the printer in the Printers window, and click Properties. On the Advanced tab, click New Driver, and step through the Add Printer Driver Wizard. After you've installed the new driver, print a page to verify that the printer works correctly.

I try to print a document, but nothing happens

Source of the problem

When you print a document from your computer, Windows 2000 works with the program in which you created the document. Windows creates a file that contains all the information you want printed, together with special information that controls the printer. The file is then placed in the printer queue and waits its turn for the printer to use the file and print the document—at least, that's how it's supposed to work! Sometimes, however, the print file never gets to the print queue. At other times, the file just sits in the queue and isn't printed. If there's a problem with the printer or with a Windows 2000 component that provides the printing services, you'll probably receive a message telling you about the problem. With some other problems, however, everything seems to be working correctly, except that when you stroll over to the printer expecting to retrieve and admire your document, alas, there's nothing waiting for you in the printer tray.

How to fix it

1. Make sure the problem isn't with the program you're using, and that you're not sending the print job to the wrong printer. On the Accessories submenu of the Start menu, click WordPad. Type a few words, and then, on the File menu, click Print. In the Print dialog box, click your printer in the Select Printer list, and click Print. If you see a message telling you the printer isn't ready, check to verify that the printer is turned on, is on line, has paper and ink, and is properly connected to your computer. If you've encountered and fixed any of the above problems, click the Retry button. Don't click Cancel unless you want to cancel the printing and delete the print file. ▶

Tip

If your printer isn't listed in the Print dialog box or in the Printers folder, it isn't properly set up on your computer. See "My printer doesn't work" on page 204 for information about setting up the printer, as well as information about other system problems that could interfere with printing.

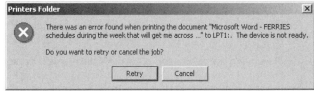

2. If you receive any other messages, possibly containing obtuse terminology such as "print subsystems not available," there might be a problem with one or more of the print services Windows provides. Try restarting Windows to see whether these services will restart and allow you to print. If this doesn't work, on the Start menu, click Run. In the Open box, type **net start spooler**, and click OK.

3. If you don't receive a message when you're trying to print, take a look to see whether the printer is receiving and holding on to the print files. On the Settings submenu of the Start menu, click Printers. In the Printers folder, double-click the printer you're using. This opens a window that displays the print queue and lists all the documents that are waiting to be printed. ▶

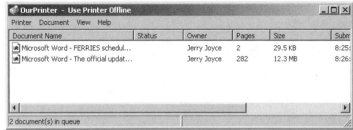

4. Note the information in the title bar of the window. If it reads *Paused* or *Use Printer Offline,* the printer has been stopped. To restart it, click Pause Printing or Use Printer Offline on the Printer menu. (If the printer has been paused or set to work off line, either of these commands will have a check mark next to it.) The printer should then begin to print.

5. If the printer wasn't paused or off line, there could be a problem with the print queue. If you've sent several documents to be printed, and none, or only some, of them—or even only part of a document—have reached the print queue, there might not be enough disk space to store the print files. To see whether this is the problem, in the Printers folder, click Server Properties on the File menu. On the Advanced tab of the Print Server Properties dialog box, note the drive that's listed in the path for the spool folder. Close the dialog box when you've finished. ▶ Double-click My Computer on the Desktop, and click the drive that was specified in the spool folder path (drive C, for example). Note either in the web content part of the window or on the status bar how much free space remains on the hard disk.

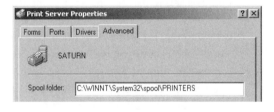

6. If there's very little free space listed (a few MB or less), try recovering some free space on the hard disk. To do so, on the System Tools submenu of the Start menu, click Disk Cleanup, and use the Disk Cleanup tool to remove extraneous files from the drive that contains the spool folder. If the Disk Cleanup tool wasn't able to free up much more space, consider backing up and deleting some files or moving them to another drive. Once you've acquired substantial free disk space, try printing again.

7. If you still can't print, try setting your system to print directly to the printer. To do so, in the Printers folder, right-click the printer, and click Properties on the shortcut menu. On the Advanced tab, click the Print Directly To The Printer option, and click OK. Try printing now. The computer should be able to print, but it will probably run a bit more slowly than usual while the printing is taking place.

The printer isn't performing as I expected

Source of the problem

When you buy a printer, you expect it to work as advertised. Keeping in mind that its abilities might have been slightly exaggerated in the sales pitch, if you find that your printer isn't doing as good a job as you had expected, the problem might not be the fault of an overzealous salesperson. Instead, lackluster printing speed and quality might be caused by the settings made for the printer in Windows, the programs you're using to create and print your documents, or even problems with your computer. Short of buying a new computer and printer, you can make a few adjustments to the way your documents are printed, although you might need to make a compromise or two between speeding up your printing and getting the best possible printed copy.

How to fix it

1. There are a couple of different types of slow printing—each as maddening as the other. One is printing that ties up your computer for a very long time while a document is being printed; the other is printing that seems to take the printer forever to spit out. To reduce the amount of time your computer is tied up with printing, you'll want to send the entire print job to the print queue (also known as the print spooler), where the print job sits and waits until the printer is available. To have the printer use the print queue in the way that is most advantageous to you, on the Settings submenu of the Start menu, click Printers. In the Printers window, right-click the printer, and click Properties on the shortcut menu. On the Advanced tab, click the Spool Print Documents So Program Finishes Printing Faster option if it isn't already selected. ▲

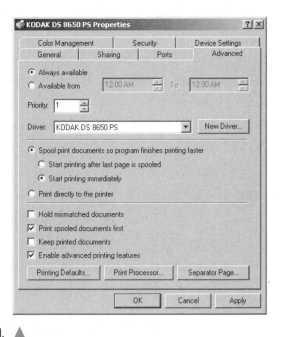

2. To speed up the actual printing of the document, click the Start Printing Immediately option. This causes the document to start printing as soon as the printer receives it, rather than waiting for the entire document to be downloaded before it starts printing.

3. Now you must decide whether you're willing to make compromises in the quality of your document to increase the speed of printing. The settings vary from one printer to another, so you'll need to consult your printer's documentation and even do a little experimentation. To change the settings for the printer, click the Printing Defaults button. In the Printing Defaults dialog box, click the Advanced button. In the Advanced Options dialog box, click an item, and make the changes you want to increase either printing speed or quality. ▶ For example, in the TrueType Font option, you can speed up printing by clicking Substitute With Device Font to use a similar font that's installed on the printer instead of downloading the TrueType font. At the cost of slower printing, click the Download As Softfont option to make sure the font used in printing is the same font, and contains the same extended characters, as the one you used on the screen.

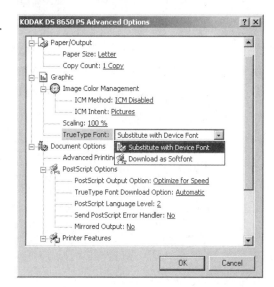

4. Before you close the printer's Properties dialog box, take a look at the different tabs. See whether there are any settings specific to your printer that you can use. When you've finished, close the dialog box and print a document. If the document doesn't print correctly, return to the printer's Properties dialog box and reverse some of your changes.

5. The settings you made in the printer's Properties dialog box are only the default settings for the printer. Many programs have their own settings for the printer. Investigate the options each program offers, and try to take advantage of settings that either decrease the printing time or increase the quality of the printing.

Different options for different printers

The options you can change for a printer are determined by its printer driver. If you see options you know your printer doesn't have, or can't find options you know it does have, make sure the correct printer driver is installed. If you have any doubts, click the New Driver button on the Advanced tab of the printer's Properties dialog box, and specify a different printer driver that's better suited for the printer you're using. Make sure, however, that the printer driver is designed for Windows 2000 and not for Windows NT 4; otherwise, the printer's performance could be seriously affected.

The separator page is wrong or is missing

Source of the problem

When you share your printer with other people on the network, figuring out which stack of paper sitting in the printer tray belongs to whom can be a horror. Even worse is the scenario in which people pick up their printing and inadvertently either leave behind a few of their own pages or walk off with a few of yours. You can't eliminate the problem, but you can alleviate it by inserting a separator page between each print job. Yes, you waste an extra piece of paper each time you print a document, but you might save paper (and time) by not having to reprint a document that someone accidentally walked away with. Windows provides a few separator pages for specific purposes. You can use these pages as is, modify them, or create custom separator pages.

How to fix it

1. Try using one of the Windows separator pages unaltered to see how it works with your printer. On the Settings submenu of the Start menu, click Printers. In the Printers window, right-click the printer, and click Properties on the shortcut menu. On the Advanced tab, click the Separator Page button. In the Separator Page dialog box, click the Browse button. Windows takes you to the system32 folder in your WINNT system folder, where all the separator pages should be stored. Click one of the existing separator page files. Use the table to decide which one you want to use. Click Open, click OK to close the Separator Page dialog box, and click OK to close the printer's Properties dialog box. Print a document, and examine the separator page. ▶

2. If the separator page is not as informational as you want, you can modify it. To do so, repeat the process in step 1 to open the Separator Page dialog box and display the list of separator pages. Right-click the page you want to modify, and, on the shortcut menu, click Open With. In the Open With dialog box, click Notepad, and clear the check box to always use this program. Click OK.

File name	What it does
pcl.sep	Switches to PCL (Printer Control Language) printing and inserts a separator page.
pscript.sep	Switches to PostScript printing (if supported) but doesn't insert a separator page.
sysprint.sep	Switches to PostScript printing (if supported) and inserts a separator page.
sysprtj.sep	Switches to PostScript printing, inserts a separator page, and supports Japanese characters.

3. In the Notepad file, before you make any changes, click Save As on the File menu. In the Save As dialog box, type a new name for your separator page, including the *.sep* file extension. In the Save As Type list, click All Files. Click Save to preserve the original file and to create a new file for your experimentation. ▶ Examine the contents of the separator file.

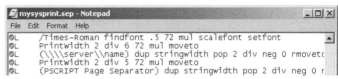

The top window shows the codes for PCL printing, and the bottom window shows the codes for PostScript printing.

4. To edit the page with PostScript code, look for the items in parentheses that correspond to the text printed on the page. These items will be printed as shown. For example, if you substitute your computer's name for *server* and your printer's name for *name,* the separator page will identify where the document was printed. You can also substitute your own text for *PSCRIPT Page Separator.* The PostScript and PCL pages both use special codes to insert information from Windows. The most common codes are shown in the table. ▶ Each code letter is always used in conjunction with another character called the "escape" character. You'll see this character in the first line of the file. For example, in the PCL file, if you wanted to change the name of the person who printed the document from block letters to normal type, you'd change the fourth line from \M\B\S\N\U to \N\U.

Code	What it does
N	Prints the name of the person printing.
D	Prints the date.
T	Prints the time.
L	Prints all the following text until it reaches the next escape character.
U	Resets printing to standard text.
n	Skips the number of lines specified by the number following the code (0–9).
I	Prints the print job number.
E	Ejects the page.
B	Prints block letters (used with S and M).
S	Prints single block letters (used with B).
M	Prints double block letters (used with B).

5. When the file is saved and closed, click the new file in the Separator Page dialog box, and click Open. Click OK, and click OK to close the dialog box. Print a document to see whether you like the results. If you later decide you don't want a separator page, return to the first Separator Page dialog box, delete the page's path and file name, click OK, and then click OK again.

Some people are unable to use my printer

Source of the problem

When you share your printer over a network, you accept the responsibility of properly administering that printer. Although a network usually works pretty well with computers that use different operating systems, sharing a printer over a network can be another story. Each operating system uses its own printer driver for each printer it uses. It's your responsibility to make sure that each of these printer drivers is available. Also, because access to a printer can be restricted, you must make sure that access to the printer is granted to those who need it, and that they can access the printer when they want to print their documents.

How to fix it

1. When people connect to a printer over a network, they can print to that printer only if the proper printer driver files are installed. When you set up a printer, its printer drivers are installed for Windows 2000 only. To make the printer available to people who are using different operating systems, you must install the drivers their operating systems require for your printer. To do so, on the Settings submenu of the Start menu, click Printers. In the Printers window, right-click the printer, and click Sharing on the shortcut menu. On the Sharing tab of the printer's Properties dialog box,

click the Additional Drivers button. In the Additional Drivers dialog box, select the check box ▲ for the type of computer and operating system you want to support for printing, and click OK.

2. Now comes the tricky part. Windows might ask you to insert the Windows 2000 Server CD. This can cause a problem; because you're using Windows 2000 Professional, not Windows 2000 Server, you might not have access to a Windows 2000 Server CD. Whether or not you have access to the CD, click OK in the Insert Disk dialog box. If you have the CD, insert it into the CD drive, and click OK in the Printer Drivers dialog box. If you don't have the CD, click the Browse button, and do any of the following to specify the location of the required files:

   ● Go to the network location where the printer drivers are stored.

- Insert the printer manufacturer's floppy disk or CD that contains the drivers and associated files, and open the appropriate folder, if necessary.

- Go to the printer manufacturer's web site and download the appropriate driver and its associated files. Be sure you download the drivers for the correct type of computer and operating system, not the drivers for Windows 2000. Store the files in a folder on your computer, and then open the folder and any subfolders, if necessary, in the Locate Files dialog box.

Tip

If you have problems configuring your printer to support other types of computers or operating systems, you can configure the support on the computer that's trying to use your printer. For information about doing this, see "The printer isn't set up for my system" on page 216.

After you've located the files using the Locate Files dialog box, click OK in the Printer Drivers dialog box to install the required files.

3. After the driver and its files have been installed, click the Additional Drivers button in the printer's Properties dialog box again if you want to install drivers for other types of computers and operating systems.

4. With the printer's Properties dialog box still open, click the Security tab. Make sure that everyone who needs access to the printer is listed or is a member of a group that's ▶ listed. Click the name of the individual or group, and, in the Permissions section of the dialog box, make sure that only the Allow check box for the type of permission you want to grant that individual or group is selected. If an individual or a group isn't listed, click the Add button, and use the Select Users, Computers, Or Groups dialog box to add the appropriate users or groups.

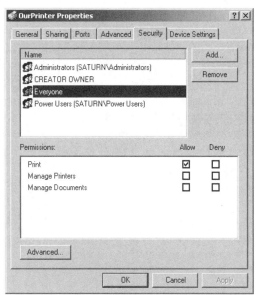

5. Click the Advanced tab. If the Available From option is selected, make sure the time range specified includes the time during which the printer will be required by all other users. If you want others to be able to use the printer at any time, click Always Available. Click OK when you've finished.

6. On the Settings submenu of the Start menu, click Control Panel. In the Control Panel, double-click Power Options. In the Power Options dialog box, make sure you haven't specified a power scheme that will place your computer in Hibernate mode. Click OK. Don't forget to leave your computer on so that other people can use your printer when you're away. For security, you can use a password-protected screen saver, or you can manually lock your computer.

When you use a printer over a network, you can run into problems that you wouldn't encounter if the printer were attached directly to your computer. For example, the network printer might not be set up to support your computer, or you might not be able to convince a program to use the printer over the network. You might have problems finding a printer that has the features you need, or you might have to wander around the building searching for your documents because they were sent to the wrong printer. Even when everything is set up correctly, your printing can be sabotaged by a misbehaving program. Once you work out the kinks, though, you'll open up your computer to all the printing resources that are available on the network.

Are you unable to print to a network printer from a program such as Notepad?

yes

no

Are documents being printed on the wrong printer?

yes

no

Are you able to print from MS-DOS programs?

no

Go to...
MS-DOS programs won't print over the network, page 218

Quick fix
You can designate a specific printer as your default printer. Unless you specify a different printer in the Print dialog box, the default printer will be used for all your printing.

1. On the Settings submenu of the Start menu, click Printers.

2. In the Printers window, right-click the printer you want to use.

3. On the shortcut menu, click Set As Default Printer.

4. Close the Printers window, and print a document to verify that it's being sent to the correct printer. If the document goes to the wrong printer, check the setup and print options settings in the program.

Printing, network

Are you unable to print to any printer on the network?

yes →

Were you unable to print immediately after you installed Microsoft Office 2000?

yes →

Quick fix
A problem with Office caused the print services to stop on your computer. You need to restart them.

1. Try restarting your computer and see whether that fixes the problem.

2. If not, on the Start menu, click Run. In the Open box, type **net start spooler**, and click OK.

no ↓

Are you unable to find a printer with the specific features you want?

yes →

Quick fix
If your network uses Active Directory, you can search for a printer by name or by feature.

1. On the Search submenu of the Start menu, click For Printers.

2. On the Features tab, specify the features you want.

3. Click Find Now.

4. Right-click the printer you want, and click Connect on the shortcut menu.

5. Close the Find Printers dialog box when you've finished.

no ↓

Go to...
The printer isn't set up for my system, page 216

If your solution isn't here
Check these related chapters:
Access to the computer, page 2
Printing, local, page 202
Or see the general troubleshooting tips on page xiii

The printer isn't set up for my system

Source of the problem

Printing on a network can be as smooth as silk—provided the printer is attached to a computer that's running Windows 2000. This is because the necessary printer drivers are already installed in Windows 2000. When you use a printer attached to a computer that's using a different operating system—Windows NT 4 or Windows 98, for example—the printer drivers aren't always downloaded automatically. In most cases, Windows will ask you if you want to install the correct drivers. In some cases, however, you'll need to install the drivers manually, and you'll also need to configure the connection to work with the print server. In extreme cases, you might need to issue arcane commands to manually force the connection to the printer and supply any required password.

How to fix it

1. Try to connect to the printer from the Print dialog box. If the Print dialog box has a Find Printer button, click it to locate the printer. If Active Directory is installed on the network, use the Directory to locate the printer. ▶

2. If you can't access the printer from the Print dialog box, you'll need to connect to the printer and install it on your computer. To do so, use My Network Places to go to the print server, and locate the printer. Open the Printers folder by clicking Printers on the Settings submenu of the Start menu. Arrange the two folders so that you can see both of them. Drag the printer from the network folder to your Printers folder.

3. If the correct drivers are available, either from the network print server or on your computer, you should be able to print. If the correct drivers aren't installed on the print server, you'll probably be asked whether you want to copy the drivers onto

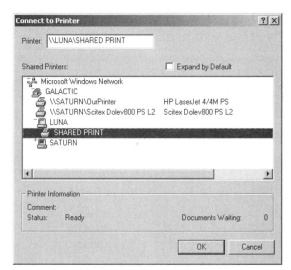

Tip

Don't overlook the obvious—if you can't find a printer, it might no longer be available. Use My Network Places to find the print server and verify that the printer is still shared.

your computer. If so, click OK, and wait for the files to be installed. ▶ (The files are usually already stored on your hard disk and simply need to be installed by Windows.) If the

correct drivers aren't available on your computer, you'll need to supply the drivers on a disk or from a network location.

4. If you aren't prompted to install the printer drivers, you'll need to force the installation of the printer. To do so, in the Printers folder, double-click the Add Printer icon to start the Add Printer Wizard. Use the wizard to install the printer as a local printer, and connect it to a parallel printer port such as LPT1.

> **Tip**
>
> If you're told that you don't have sufficient permission to add the drivers or a printer to the computer, you'll need to log on as the Administrator and try again.

After the printer is installed, right-click it in the Printers folder, and click Properties on the shortcut menu. On the Ports tab, click the printer port you used for the printer, and click Add Port. In the Printer Ports dialog box, double-click the Local Port item. In the Port Name dialog box, type the name of the print server and the printer in the form **\\\printserver\\printer**, and then click OK. Close the dialog boxes, and try printing to the printer. ▶

5. If none of the above works, there's one more way to force a printer to work with your computer. This method is especially effective if the printer is connected to a computer running Windows 95/98/Me, and if the sharing of the printer requires a password. As you did in step 4, use the Add Printer Wizard to install the printer on your computer as if it were a local printer. Then, on the Start menu, click Run. In the Open box, type **net use *lptx* \\\printserver\\printer password/persistent:yes**, where *lptx* is the printer port you specified when you set up the

printer, *printserver* is the name of the computer that is the print server, *printer* is the name of the printer, and *password* is the password required for the printer (if a password is required). Click OK. Try printing with the newly installed local printer to see whether your document prints on the network printer. ▶

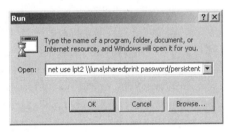

More about printer drivers

Windows uses information from the printer drivers to create a printer file that contains the information the printer needs. Without the correct drivers, the printer won't perform correctly—if it performs at all. Windows 2000 tries to keep the drivers up to date, but if you've installed printer drivers for a network printer on your computer, the drivers could be out of date. Check Windows Update to verify that you're using the most recent drivers, and especially that you're not using drivers designed for Windows NT 4. Although Windows NT 4 drivers might work, they can also cause significant printing problems.

MS-DOS programs won't print over the network

Source of the problem

Many MS-DOS programs are designed to print only to a local printer—that is, a printer that's connected to your computer using a printer port, such as the parallel printer port LPT1. If the printer you want to use is on the network, you're out of luck—unless you're devious enough to set up your system to trick the program into thinking it's printing to a local printer. What the MS-DOS program doesn't know is that the printer output is being rerouted and sent over the network to the target printer.

How to fix it

1. Make sure you can print to the network printer using a Windows program such as WordPad. This verifies that the proper printer drivers are installed and that your computer can connect to the printer.

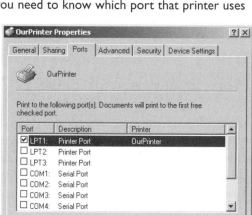

2. Open the MS-DOS program and see what your printing options are. For example, some programs will let you print to two or more parallel ports. Note the names of the ports—they should be in the form LPT1 or LPT2. ▲

3. If you have a printer attached to your computer, you need to know which port that printer uses so that you don't create a conflict between printers. If you don't know which port the printer uses, on the Settings submenu of the Start menu, click Printers. In the Printers folder, right-click the printer, and click Properties on the shortcut menu. On the Ports tab of the printer's Properties dialog box, note any port that has a printer next to it, whether or not the check box for that port is selected. Any port that has a printer is a port you can't use for redirecting your MS-DOS output. Close the dialog box when you've finished. ▶

4. Now it's time to redirect your printing from a local parallel port to the network printer. On the Start menu, click Run. In the Open box, type **net use** *lptx* **"*printserver**printer*" /persistent:yes**, where *lptx* is whichever parallel port you want to assign to the printer, and *printserver* and *printer* identify the network printer. Click OK. ▶

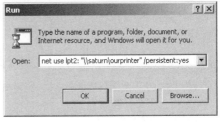

This command tells Windows to take whatever is sent to the LPT2 parallel port and send it to the network printer ourprinter *on the* Saturn *print server.*

5. Return to your MS-DOS program. Use the program's options to specify that you're going to print to the parallel port you just rerouted (for example, LPT2). Use the program's Print command to print the document. Give the network printer a little time to get around to printing your document, and then check to see whether it was printed correctly. ▶

6. If the document wasn't printed, open the Run dialog box again and check your typing. Make sure that *printserver* and *printer* are enclosed in quotation marks, and that there are two backward slashes before the *printserver* name, one backward slash before the *printer* name, and a forward slash before the *persistent* switch. Also, verify again that you can print from the Windows program to make sure the printer or network isn't off line.

Alternative printing methods

If you're unable to print from MS-DOS programs, you have a couple of alternatives, which work whether you're printing to a local or to a network printer. You can print an image of the screen contents to the printer (which is also useful if the program doesn't have a Print command). To do so, with what you want to print displayed in the program, press the key combination Shift+Print Screen. On the Accessories submenu of the Start menu, click Paint, and, in Paint, click Paste on the Edit menu. The image is now inserted into the Paint program. On Paint's File menu, click Print, and use the Print dialog box to print the image to your network printer.

The other alternative is for text only and works only in some programs. Use the mouse to select the text you want. If you can't select text with the mouse, right-click the title bar of the program, point to Edit, click Mark on the shortcut menu, and use the arrow keys to select the text. If you can't select text using either of these methods, you're out of luck. Otherwise, with the text selected, press Enter. Switch to a Windows program, such as WordPad, and paste the text. Now you can print the text to any printer.

The real work of your Windows 2000 operating system is to run your programs. When your programs won't run, your work comes to a standstill. You can get around most problems fairly painlessly, although unfortunately, in dealing with a program that suddenly locks up and refuses to respond, you'll usually lose any work you did since the last time you saved your document. Your older programs should run perfectly well in Windows 2000, but if you do encounter a program that won't run, or if you can't get an MS-DOS program to run, the problem might be that these programs violate some security aspects of Windows 2000 or are incompatible with Windows 2000. Some of the solutions to these problems are quite simple; others call for some bravery on your part.

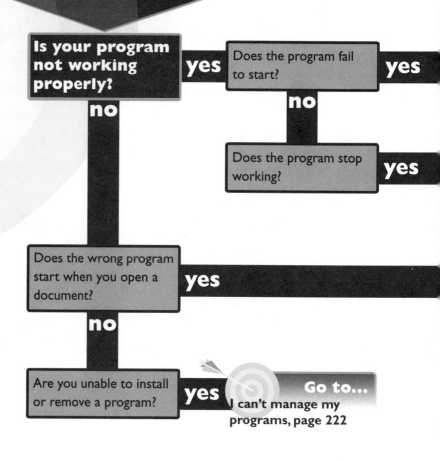

Is your program not working properly?

yes → Does the program fail to start? **yes**

no ↓

Does the program stop working? **yes**

no ↓

Does the wrong program start when you open a document? **yes**

no ↓

Are you unable to install or remove a program? **yes**

Go to...
I can't manage my programs, page 222

If your solution isn't here
Check these related chapters:
Access to the computer, page 2
Games, page 88
Mouse, page 156
Multiple monitors, page 168
Screen, page 230
Shutting down, page 242
Sound, page 250
Starting up, page 260
Start menu, page 270
Taskbar, page 278
Toolbars, page 286
Or see the general troubleshooting tips on page xiii

Programs

Did you receive a message that the program can't run in Windows 2000?

yes — **Go to...** A program that ran in an earlier version of Windows won't run now, page 226

no

Go to... My program suddenly stopped working, page 224

Is the program an MS-DOS program?

yes — **Go to...** An MS-DOS program won't run, page 228

no

Quick fix

The document type is associated with the wrong program. You can change this association.

1. Right-click the document.

2. Point to Open With on the shortcut menu.

3. If a submenu appears, click Choose Program on the submenu. If there is no submenu, click Open With on the shortcut menu.

4. In the Open With dialog box, click the program you want to use.

5. Select the Always Use This Program To Open These Files check box.

6. Click OK.

Quick fix

Program files sometimes become corrupted. You can fix corrupted files by uninstalling and then reinstalling the program.

1. Make sure that the program is compatible with Windows 2000 Professional by checking the software compatibility list at *http://www.microsoft.com/windows2000/upgrade/compat*.

2. If the program is compatible, try uninstalling and then reinstalling it to replace any corrupted files. To do so, make sure you have access to the original program installation files. Then, on the Settings submenu of the Start menu, click Control Panel.

3. In the Control Panel, use Add/Remove Programs to remove the program.

4. Restart Windows to make sure that all your settings are updated, and then use Add/Remove Programs in the Control Panel to reinstall the program.

I can't manage my programs

Source of the problem

Rarely is a computer set up so perfectly that you don't need to do some program management. For example, you might want to install the latest update of a program you already have, remove a program that's misbehaving or that you never use, or install a program that has nothing to do with work but that you just have to have on your computer. In most cases, this is a simple matter—you use the Add/Remove Programs item in the Control Panel to easily add, remove, or modify a program. However, either Windows or the program's installation process can sometimes make this operation a bit more...interesting, let's say...than it needs to be—not installing all the components you need, perhaps; not allowing you to install a program unless you have the proper permission; refusing to remove a program; or even disabling the Add/Remove Programs item in the Control Panel. Don't let it get you down. Unless you're dealing with rigid network policies, you can get around most of these setbacks.

How to fix it

1. Before you figure out how to fix the problem, make sure it really *is* a problem. For example, when you installed a program, you might have installed only part of it, so, when you try to use the program, you're prompted for the installation CD or the location of the network files. If you don't have the program CD or continuous access to the network, this will be an ongoing problem, so you'll need to change the way the program is installed. To do so, on the Settings submenu of the Start menu, click Control Panel. Double-click the Add/Remove Programs icon, and click Change Or Remove Programs in the left part of the Add/Remove Programs dialog box.

   Under Currently Installed Programs, click the program in question, and then click the Change button. ▶ Follow the instructions in the installation program to install the items you need.

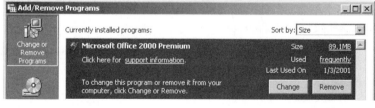

2. If you try to use the Add/Remove Programs dialog box to add, remove, or modify a program, you might not be able to do so if you don't have the proper permission. Group policies dictate what you're allowed to do, and in most cases—unless you're a member of the Power Users or the Administrators group—you can expect problems when you're trying to manage some, if not

all, programs. There are a couple of ways to approach this problem. You can ask whoever administers user accounts on your system to add you to a group that has full permission to manage programs, or you can obtain either the password for the local administrator or the user name and password of an account that is authorized to manage programs. You'll then be able to open the Add/Remove Programs item as that user. ▶ To do so, hold down the Shift key, right-click Add/Remove Programs in the Control Panel, and click Run As on the shortcut menu. In the Run As Other User dialog box, click the Run The Program As The Following User option, and log on as either the Administrator or the user account that has permission to manage programs.

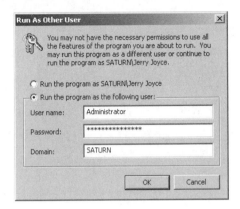

3. Windows might prevent you from removing a program—even though you have permission to do so—if there isn't enough free space on the drive. (Windows cleverly backs up a program when you try to remove it so that if anything goes wrong in the removal process, the program can be restored automatically. If there isn't enough space on the disk for that backup copy, Windows won't let you remove the program.) If this happens, on the System Tools submenu of the Start menu, click Disk Cleanup, and use the Disk Cleanup tool to remove unnecessary files from the hard disk to gain enough free space to remove the program.

4. If you're unable to use the Add/Remove Programs item at all, you might have encountered a bug. If Internet Explorer 5.5 has recently been installed on your computer, the Add/Remove Programs item can become nonfunctional. If you're not sure which version of Internet Explorer you have, you can find out by starting Internet Explorer and clicking About Internet Explorer on the Help menu. The version number is shown in the About Internet Explorer dialog box. Click OK. If you have Internet Explorer 5.5, you'll need to install a Windows 2000 service pack to fix the bug and make the Add/Remove Programs item functional again. See Appendix A, "Installing a service pack," on page 295 for details about obtaining and installing a Windows service pack.

5. If your computer is on a large network with a domain, you might see some programs listed on your Start menu that aren't really installed on your computer. This happens when the network administrator has *assigned* a program to you without installing it. Usually this isn't a problem; you click the item on the Start menu, and, presto—the installation starts. However, if your computer isn't always connected to the network, you might not have access to the installation files when you want to use the program. Even if you're always connected to the network, there'll be times when you don't want to wait for a program to be installed—when you're in the middle of a project or giving a presentation, for example. To avoid this problem, while you're connected to the network and have a little free time, try using all the programs you're going to need, and wait for any programs that aren't installed to be installed.

My program suddenly stopped working

Source of the problem

You're working away in your program and suddenly it stops. You wait, assuming the mysterious rumblings and churnings you often hear coming from the computer are keeping the computer busy. As more time goes by, you start directing muttered threats toward your computer. Finally you realize the problem isn't with your hardworking computer but that the program has seized up, locked up, frozen, stalled—whatever you call it, your program has stopped working. Depending on what happened, you might be able to work in your other programs, or everything might have come to a screeching halt. You'll probably be able to shut down the program that stopped, but you'll usually lose any work you did since the last time you saved the document. When you've shut down the program, you can take a few steps to try to prevent the problem from recurring.

How to fix it

1. The first thing you need to do is get the broken program stopped so that it doesn't interfere with Windows or with any other programs. Before you take more drastic steps, try using the program's menu to exit the program. If that doesn't work, make sure the program is active by holding down the Alt key and pressing the Tab key until the program becomes selected; then release the Alt key. If the program is displayed and active, press Alt+F4 to try shutting it down. If you can't shut it down, or if you can't get the program to respond in any way, it's time to take control.

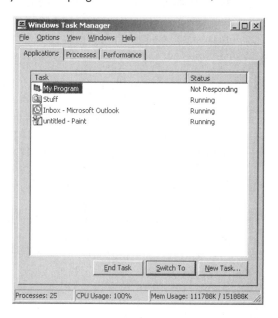

2. To force the unresponsive program to end, press Ctrl+Alt+Delete, and, in the Windows Security dialog box, click the Task Manager button. In the Task Manager dialog box, the program that's causing the problem should be shown as "Not Responding." If it isn't, click the Close button. Wait a bit, and then try to close the program again. If you can't close it, open the Task Manager dialog box again, and, if the program is now shown as "Not Responding," click it, and then click the End Task button. ▶

3. When you click the End Task button, Windows tries to shut the program down in an orderly manner. If it can't do that, you'll see the End Program dialog box. Click End Now to terminate the program. Close the Task Manager dialog box when you've finished. ▶

4. The problem with the program could be a one-time glitch or it could be a problem that will plague you as you continue to work. Restart the program and see whether you can work successfully in it. If you continue to have problems with this or any other program, shut down and then restart Windows and your computer. After you've restarted, investigate to see whether the problems have gone away.

5. If the program you're working in uses information that's stored somewhere other than on your computer, the problem could be that the connection to the information is too slow, that the quality of the connection is so poor it produces errors, or simply that the computer on which the information is stored has stopped working. If any of these conditions is causing the problem, you can have Windows temporarily store that information on your computer so that you can use it when the remote source is unavailable. To do so, use My Network Places to locate the folder in which the information is stored, right-click the folder, and click Make Available Offline. If this is the first time you've set up offline files, step through the Offline Files Wizard, specifying that you want to synchronize the files when you log on and off, and then wait for the files to be copied. If you've previously set up some offline files, the wizard won't appear and the files will be copied immediately. If you want to get an updated copy of the source information, right-click the folder, and click Synchronize on the shortcut menu. See "Windows takes a long time to shut down" on page 248 for more information about using offline files.

Warning
Using synchronized files for some programs isn't always a good idea. If you're using a database that's constantly being updated, for example, you'll find that you're working with outdated information between updates. If you're making changes to the information off line while others are using and modifying the information in its original location, you could inadvertently cause substantial problems with the different versions. For these types of situations, you should check with whoever is administering the data before you store any of the files off line.

6. If you continue to have problems, document what you've been doing, and note any new software or hardware that you've installed recently. If the program continues to lock up, contact the manufacturer of the software or hardware to determine whether you're encountering a known problem or conflict, and, if so, whether there's a software fix for the problem. You might also want to try uninstalling the problem program, restarting Windows, and then reinstalling the program, just in case any files it needed have been corrupted or deleted.

A program that ran in an earlier version of Windows won't run now

Source of the problem

Many of your older programs run perfectly well in Windows 2000, so rest assured that Windows doesn't discriminate against age. So why won't some programs run? The problem is that some of the programs that were built before Windows 2000 was created violate some of the security aspects of Windows 2000. Other programs actually discriminate against Windows 2000 by demanding to be run in a specific version of Windows. Getting around the former issue can be as simple as having yourself added to a different user group, but solving the latter problem might call for some bold and daring action on your part.

How to fix it

1. Many programs require access to the Windows Registry—the database in which Windows stores all its settings information. Windows tries to keep the Registry secure, so, when a program tries to access the Registry, Windows might block that access. The user rights you've been granted determine whether or not you have access to the Registry. If you're a member of the Power Users or Administrators group—unless group policies have been changed on your system—you have permission to access and modify the Registry, so the programs you use can also access the Registry. If you're a member of the Users or Guests group, you don't have permission to access the Registry and neither do the programs you use. If you're not allowed to run a program, you can either ask the person who administers the user accounts to add you to the Power Users group, or contact the manufacturer of the software for an update that will allow anyone to run the program.

   > **Tip**
   >
   > On the Start menu, click Windows Update, and download the Windows 2000 Compatibility Updates. These updates fix problems in many programs so that they become compatible with Windows 2000.

2. When you run an older program, you might receive an error message telling you that Windows is unable to run a 16-bit program (16-bit programs were designed for Windows version 3 and earlier). This is usually because some system files required by these programs are missing or corrupted. Installing or repairing system files can be difficult and dangerous, so consider either using a newer version of the program or contacting the manufacturer for information about any possible fixes for that program.

3. Another error message you might receive indicates that the program will run only on a specific operating system, such as Windows 95 or Windows NT 4 with a specifics service pack. In this situation, you might be able to get the program to run if you're willing to do some work, if you have access to the Windows 2000 Professional CD or the Windows 2000 support tools, and if you can log on as an Administrator. To try to fix this problem, you need a special Windows 2000 support tool called Apcompat. Before you proceed, log on to Windows as an Administrator. To see whether the support tools are already available on your computer or on the network, click Run on the Start menu, and type **apcompat** in the Open box. If you know that the support tools reside on the network, include the full path to the support tools folder on the network. Click OK. If Windows can't find the Apcompat program, insert the Windows 2000 Professional CD into the CD drive, explore the disc contents, and, in the Support folder, double-click Apcompat.

> **Warning**
>
> The *apcompat.exe* program and all the support tools are powerful enough to cause problems with your operating system if they're used incorrectly. Before you use any of the tools, save and close all your documents, back up your files, and make sure you have an up-to-date Emergency Recovery Disk. Then proceed at your own risk!

4. In the Application Compatibility dialog box, click the Browse button to locate the program (the *.exe* file) that won't run. In the Operating System section, click the operating system that the error message told you to use. Select any of the check boxes in the dialog box to correct problems, as shown in the table. Click OK when you've finished. ▶

5. If you think you'll need to use the Apcompat program frequently, copy the *apcompat.exe* file from the Windows 2000 Professional CD to your hard disk. If you want to install the Apcompat tool, along with other support tools and the Help file for all the tools, run the Setup program from the Tools subfolder of the Support folder on the Windows 2000 Professional CD.

Check box	What it does
Disable Heap Manager On Windows 2000	Eliminates memory usage problems that can stop a program, but uses memory much less efficiently.
Use The Pre-Windows 2000 Temp Path	Uses the \Temp folder instead of the standard WINNT\Temp folder to store temporary files. Some programs can't use the full path to the standard Windows 2000 Temp folder.
Correct Disk Space Detection For 2-GB+ Drives	Uses an alternative method to detect free disk space if the program couldn't be installed due to incorrect calculation of free disk space.
Make the Above Check Box Settings Permanent	Stores settings so that they'll be used whenever the program is run.

An MS-DOS program won't run

Source of the problem

Windows and MS-DOS just don't get along the way they used to, mostly because the pushy MS-DOS programs try to access the system and want to control the system hardware. In doing so, they often violate the security Windows demands of programs, and therefore Windows won't let the MS-DOS programs run. Not every problem is caused by security violations, though. Some programs just need a bit of tweaking to get them running properly. Before you do any tweaking, however, review the program's documentation to see whether there are specific settings that you should use to get the best performance from the program.

How to fix it

1. Because so many MS-DOS programs are incompatible with Windows 2000, before you try to get your MS-DOS program working, see whether it has been tested for compatibility with Windows 2000. To do so, look for your program in the software compatibility list at *http://www.microsoft.com/windows2000 /upgrade/compat*. If the program isn't listed, it might not have been tested, so check with the manufacturer to see whether the program will work with Windows 2000, or whether there are any fixes or software updates that will make it compatible with Windows 2000.

2. If you think the program should work with Windows 2000, or if you want to take the time to experiment, you can try tweaking the program's settings. To make sure the program will get all the resources it needs, close all your open programs so that they don't use up the system's resources. Use My Computer to locate the program (the .exe file). Right-click it, click Properties on the shortcut menu, and, in the program's Properties dialog box, click the Memory tab. ▶

> **Tip**
> On the Start menu, click Windows Update, and download the Windows 2000 Compatibility Updates. These updates fix problems with many programs so that they become compatible with Windows 2000.

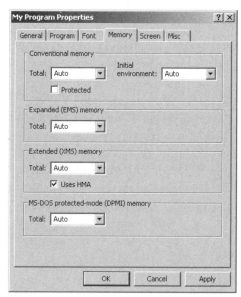

3. Check the program's documentation for the recommended amount of memory that should be allocated for the program. Set the values for each item on the Memory tab to those values. If you don't have the necessary information about the settings, set all the values to Auto. Click OK, and then try running the program. If it doesn't run, or if it causes sporadic system errors, open the Properties dialog box again, and set both the Expanded (EMS) Memory Total value and the Extended (XMS) Memory total value to 8192.

If you were experiencing system errors, select the Protected check box in the Conventional Memory section. Click OK, and try running the program again.

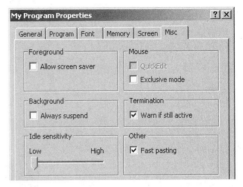

4. If the program still isn't running, open its Properties dialog box again, and click the Misc tab. Clear the Allow Screen Saver and the Always Suspend check boxes, and drag the Idle Sensitivity slider all the way to the left. Click OK, and try running the program again. ▶

5. If the program still isn't working, it's time to do some checking and some advanced MS-DOS configuration, if you're up for it. See whether the program requires special resources when it's started. These are commands that are usually placed in an *autoexec* or *config* file (the files that are used when an MS-DOS program starts). If you've discovered any commands in the documentation that you need to use, write down the exact syntax of the commands. Next you need to create the startup files that are specific to this program. To do so, find the *autoexec.nt* and *config.nt* files in the WINNT\system32 folder, and copy (remember—copy, not move) them into the folder that contains your program. Right-click the *autoexec.nt* file that you copied into the program's folder, click Open With on the shortcut menu, and use Notepad to edit the file to add the commands the program requires. Save and close the file, and then repeat the editing process for the *config.nt* file.

6. Open the Properties dialog box for the program again, and, on the General tab, click the Advanced button. In the Windows PIF Settings dialog box, enter the paths and file names of the configuration files you edited. Click OK, and then click OK again to close the Properties dialog box. Try running the program again. ▶

7. If the program still doesn't work, check with the manufacturer to see whether you need to use the Setver command to identify the version of MS-DOS in which the program is designed to run. This is a fairly complex process, so try to obtain a software utility program or a batch file from the manufacturer to make this setting. For more information about the Setver command, search Windows Help for Setver.

You turn on your computer, expecting to see certain familiar images on your screen, but, instead, you see a bunch of vertical lines or multicolored squares—or, worse, nothing at all. What's going on? In the next few pages, we'll talk about fixing these and some other fairly common screen problems: speeding up your screen's performance if it's unbearably slow; changing your screen's display settings if, inexplicably, Windows won't let you do so; reducing or eliminating any distracting flickering; and changing the size of everything on the screen to suit your comfort level. And we'll discuss a weird condition in which part of the Desktop seems to have fallen off your screen and vanished.

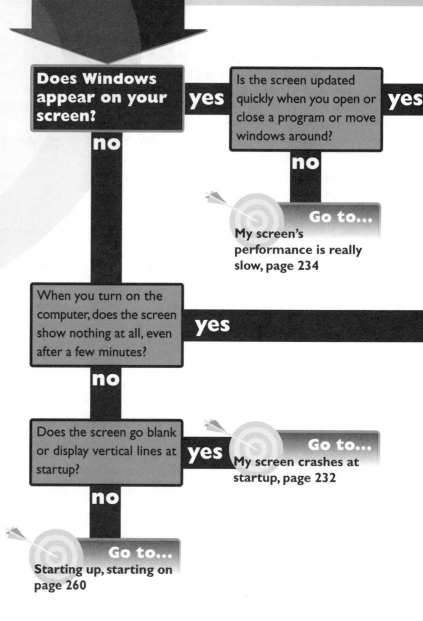

Does Windows appear on your screen?

yes → Is the screen updated quickly when you open or close a program or move windows around?

yes →

no ↓

no ↓

Go to...
My screen's performance is really slow, page 234

When you turn on the computer, does the screen show nothing at all, even after a few minutes?

yes →

no ↓

Does the screen go blank or display vertical lines at startup?

yes → **Go to...**
My screen crashes at startup, page 232

no ↓

Go to...
Starting up, starting on page 260

Can you change the display settings?

yes → Does the screen flicker, or is everything on it too big or too small?

yes →

Go to...
The screen flickers and is hard to look at, page 238

no

Go to...
I can't change my screen's display settings, page 236

no ↓

Do you see only part of the Desktop on the screen?

yes →

Go to...
Part of the Desktop is missing, page 240

no ↓

Quick fix

You should see the computer running checks and displaying messages before Windows starts.

1. Make sure the monitor is turned on and all cable connections are secure. If the computer is configured with more than one monitor, make sure all monitors are turned on and connected.

2. For a portable computer, make sure the screen isn't detached or loose, the battery is properly charged, and the computer isn't set to use a different monitor.

3. Check your computer's documentation for hardware troubleshooting methods and tools. If you can't fix the problem, get help from a reputable repair facility.

Do some items appear as multicolored squares when the computer comes out of hibernation?

yes →

Quick fix

Sometimes, with certain display adapters, some graphics elements aren't displayed after hibernation.

1. Obtain and install an updated video driver, if one is available, from the manufacturer of the display adapter.

2. To fix the problem once, shut down and restart your computer.

If your solution isn't here
Check these related chapters:
   Desktop, page 16
   Multiple monitors, page 168
   Power options, page 188
   Start menu, page 270
   Taskbar, page 278
   Toolbars, page 286
Or see the general troubleshooting tips on page xiii

My screen crashes at startup

Source of the problem

The process of displaying material on a computer screen isn't as simple as it might seem. The digital image on your computer's screen is constantly being redrawn and recalculated. To reduce the workload this involves, Windows 2000 uses a group of tools, collectively known as DirectX, to take a few shortcuts. Most of the time, these shortcuts provide an extremely fast display, but sometimes, if the display adapter isn't working as Windows expects it to, your screen display can get seriously messed up. To fix this, you can disable the shortcuts and try to figure out what's causing the problem. As in so many other situations in which you'll be making changes to the system, you need to have access to an Administrators account.

How to fix it

1. Restart Windows, and, when you see the "Starting Windows" message, press the F8 key. This displays the Windows 2000 Advanced Options menu. Use the Up or Down arrow key on your keyboard to select Safe Mode if it isn't already selected, and press Enter.

2. Once Safe Mode has started and you've logged on (if necessary), on the Settings submenu of the Start menu, click Control Panel. If you logged on as an Administrator, double-click the Display icon in the Control Panel. If you didn't log on as an Administrator, hold down the Shift key, right-click the Display icon, click Run As on the shortcut menu, and run the item as an Administrator.

3. On the Settings tab of the Display Properties dialog box, click the Advanced button. On the Troubleshooting tab, drag the Hardware Acceleration slider to the left so that it's set at None. Click OK, and then click OK to close the Display Properties dialog box. ▶

Tip

If your screen still isn't working when you start Safe Mode, your problem requires additional troubleshooting. See "Starting up," starting on page 260, for other approaches to this problem.

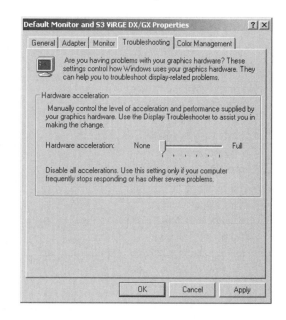

4. On the Start menu, click Shut Down, and, in the Shut Down Windows dialog box, click Restart, and then click OK. Let Windows start up in its normal mode. If the screen goes blank, or if you see vertical lines, restart the computer in Safe Mode and try some other approaches.

5. If everything is working, you can try improving your screen's performance until you break the system again. To do so, open the Display Properties dialog box as an Administrator (as you did in step 2). Click the Advanced button on the Settings tab, and, on the Troubleshooting tab, drag the slider one position to the right. Click Apply, and check to see whether everything is okay. Continue adjusting the slider and testing it until the system acts up or crashes. If you arrive at a setting that seems to improve performance, and if you think you'll be satisfied at that level, restart your computer and make sure that it starts up correctly.

6. To determine what's causing the problem, you can use a diagnostic tool designed to test DirectX. On the Start menu, click Run. In the Run dialog box, type **dxdiag** in the Open box, and click OK. In the DirectX Diagnostic Tool dialog box, use the Test buttons on the Display tab to test the different features of DirectX.

Note the status reported in the Notes section. If everything passes the test, test the other DirectX features on the Sound, Music, and Network tabs. To document your configuration, click the Save All Information button on any tab. Check with your computer's manufacturer about the results of the test and, if necessary, see whether there are any updated drivers to fix the problems. ▶

Tip

You don't need to be logged on as an Administrator to run DirectX, but unless you are you won't be able to use any of the Disable buttons to disable a certain part of DirectX. To start the diagnostic tool with Administrator rights, click Run on the Start menu, and, in the Open box, type **runas /user:domain \administratorname dxdiag**. For example, if you were using the local Administrator account on the computer named Saturn, you'd type **runas /user:Saturn \administrator dxdiag**.

More about DirectX and your system

DirectX is a general term for a group of tools that are built into Windows 2000, including DirectDraw, Direct3D, and DirectSound. Many multimedia programs use these tools to improve the quality and speed of their presentations. Sometimes, however, devices such as display adapters have problems working with these tools. The effect can be as serious as causing the display to be unreadable or as innocuous as creating a few lines or some random noises. Don't blame Windows for this inconvenience, however; it's almost certainly either a lack of proper support from some hardware device on your computer or problems in the design of a multimedia program.

My screen's performance is really slow

Source of the problem

Your computer uses a display adapter to show everything on the screen. The display adapter has its own memory and software to handle the intensive work of updating the screen whenever you make any changes. If your screen's performance has slowed down, it might be because you've set up Windows 2000 so that there's too much work for the adapter to do. Like anyone or anything with too great a workload, your adapter gets tired and slows down. To increase the speed of your display, you'll have to decrease the adapter's workload.

Although a lethargic screen is often the result of an inadequate display adapter, there can be many other causes. If you're using files over a network or the Internet, the slowness can be caused by your connection or by excessive demand on the server computer. If a program is slowing everything on your computer, the demand on the system rather than the inadequacy of your display adapter could be what's causing the poor screen performance.

How to fix it

1. Tweaking the settings will do no good if your display adapter isn't designed to work with Windows 2000. Check the most recent Windows 2000 hardware compatibility list at *http://www.microsoft.com/hwtest/hcl* to make sure that your display adapter is compatible and to see whether you have the correct drivers and settings.

2. If the adapter is compatible, try reducing some of its workload. Right-click the Desktop, and click Properties on the shortcut menu. On the Background tab, click None for your background picture, and then click Apply. Try doing some work, and see whether the screen display has speeded up.

3. If the display is still too slow, switch back to the Display Properties dialog box, and click the Web tab. If the check box to display web content is selected, clear it, and click Apply. If this increases the display speed, select the check box again, clear the check box for one of the items that's displayed on the Active Desktop, click Apply, and observe the display's performance. Continue to experiment, selecting and clearing check boxes until you find the item that slows everything down or until you've tested all the items.

4. If none of the foregoing has fixed the problem, click the Settings tab. Note your setting in the Colors list and the position of the Screen Area slider so that you'll be able to reset your values if changing them doesn't fix the problem. In the Colors list, click 256 Colors, and, in the

Screen Area, drag the slider to the left until the value shown is 640 by 480 pixels. Click Apply, confirm that you want to change the settings, click OK when prompted, and click Yes to confirm that the settings are working. Test to see whether these changes have made any improvement. If they have, experiment with these two settings to see what will work without slowing down the display. ▶

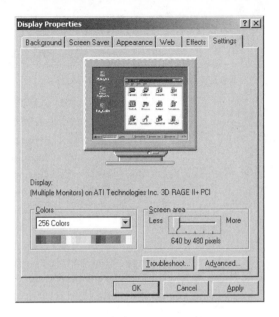

5. If the changes didn't help, on the Settings tab of the Display Properties dialog box, click the Advanced button, and, on the Adapter tab, click the List All Modes button. Note the current setting so that you can restore it later if you want to. In the list, click the item with the smallest screen area, the fewest colors, and the lowest refresh rate (the number listed in Hertz units). Click OK in the List All Modes dialog box, and then click Apply. Confirm that you want to change the settings and that the settings are working. Experiment to see whether this solves the problem. If it does, experiment with the settings in the List All Modes dialog box, but make sure you don't set the refresh rate any higher than it was before you first adjusted it.

6. If the changes didn't help, restore the screen area, colors, and refresh rate to their original settings, and close the Display Properties dialog box. Log off, and log on again as the Administrator. Open the Display Properties dialog box, and, on the Settings tab, click the Advanced button. On the Troubleshooting tab, note the position of the Hardware Acceleration slider. If it's set to Full, click Cancel, and then click OK to close the Display Properties dialog box.

7. If the Hardware Acceleration slider isn't set to Full, it might have been changed to correct a previous problem. Check the display adapter's documentation and/or with whoever administers your computer to see whether the slider should be set below Full to make your system work properly. If you're sure there's no reason for the setting to be below Full, drag the slider to Full. Click OK, and check to see whether the display is any faster. If it isn't, return the slider to its original position.

8. If any of these steps worked, you're still not quite finished. Go back through the changes you made, and experiment to see whether you can add any features while still maintaining the performance speed that's adequate for your requirements.

9. If none of these steps helped, and if you can't live with your screen's performance, consider installing a more powerful display adapter and possibly adding more memory to your system to speed everything up.

I can't change my screen's display settings

Source of the problem

It's very frustrating when Windows won't let you do something you've done over and over again with no previous problem. For example, you've never had any difficulty making changes to your screen in the Display Settings dialog box but suddenly, for no apparent reason, either the changes you make immediately revert to the previous settings or you're simply unable to access some of the settings. You might feel as though Windows is trying to drive you crazy or engage you in a power struggle, but it's really just having a problem with a setting, a piece of hardware, or a driver. However, you can show Windows who's boss by fixing the problem and then setting up your screen the way you want it.

How to fix it

1. Right-click the Desktop, and click Properties on the shortcut menu. If, on the Settings tab, you find very limited choices for colors and screen area—or if there are no choices at all— there might be a problem with the driver for the display adapter. Before you go any further, do the following:

   Tip

   If you have problems with your display adapter, check the hardware compatibility list at *http://www.microsoft.com/hwtest /hcl* to see whether the adapter is designed to work with Windows 2000, whether there are new drivers for it, or whether there are special installation notes.

   ● Make sure you're not trying to use settings that your adapter and/or your monitor aren't designed to display on your screen. Check the documentation for the adapter and the monitor to see what each can display.

   ● Verify that the display adapter is correctly identified in the Display section of the Settings tab. If it's not correctly identified, turn to "The device was misidentified" on page 100.

   ● Check to make sure the adapter isn't disabled in the computer's setup (the BIOS, or basic input/output system). If necessary, consult your computer's documentation for information about changing settings in the BIOS.

   ● Make sure that any cable between the computer and the monitor is firmly connected. A loose cable might cause the monitor to be incorrectly identified.

2. If you're still having problems, check with the manufacturer to see whether there's an updated Windows 2000 driver for the adapter. If one is available, download it. If the Advanced button on

the Settings tab is grayed (unavailable), the computer is probably using a driver that was designed for Windows NT 4.

3. To change drivers, you must be logged on as a member of the Administrators group. If you're not currently logged on as an Administrator but you have an Administrators account, open the Control Panel, hold down the Shift key, and right-click the Display icon. Click Run As on the shortcut menu, and log on as an Administrator. On the Settings tab of the Display Properties dialog box, click the Advanced button. On the Adapter tab, click the Properties button. On the Driver tab of the adapter's Properties dialog box, do either of the following: ▶

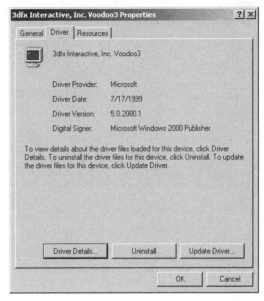

- If you have an updated driver, click the Update Driver button, and complete the Upgrade Device Driver Wizard to install the driver you downloaded.

- If you don't have a new driver, click the Uninstall button. This removes the driver, and, when you restart, Windows reinstalls the original driver, replacing any defective driver.

4. Restart the computer when prompted and see whether you can adjust the settings now. If you continue to have problems, make sure the display adapter is functioning correctly and that it doesn't have a loose connection. The manufacturer might have software available that you can use to test whether the adapter is working correctly.

Tip

Don't worry if you can't adjust the screen settings when your computer is in Safe Mode. Because Safe Mode is designed for fixing problems, the computer uses a generic VGA video driver that has very limited capabilities, so you can't adjust settings in this mode. If you're in Safe Mode, your Desktop will be black, and you'll see Safe Mode labels on all four corners of the screen.

More about settings

The adapter and the monitor on your system talk to the computer and tell it what each is capable of doing. Windows uses the driver for the adapter to implement this information. If you're using the wrong driver, or one that's out of date, you can expect problems. The capabilities of an adapter are limited by the amount of memory it has. The greater the number of colors you're using, and the larger the screen area, the more memory the adapter needs. When you combine a high number of colors with a large screen area, you're asking the display adapter to use a lot of memory, and some adapters simply don't have enough memory. If you need to use more colors and a larger screen area than your adapter can handle, you'll probably need to upgrade the adapter.

The screen flickers and is hard to look at

Source of the problem

One complaint almost all computer users have is how difficult it is to stare at that flickering screen all day long. Whether you have to move closer to the screen or farther away from it to read its contents, that flickering makes your work more difficult than necessary and decreases your efficiency. What can you do? Your screen flickers because all screens flicker. However, you can usually change the rate at which the screen is redrawn so that you no longer see the flickering. After you've made the screen easier to look at, you can also make it easier to read by increasing or decreasing the size of everything on it.

How to fix it

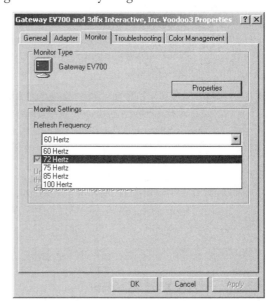

1. To eliminate the screen's flickering, you need to change the Refresh Frequency of the monitor—that is, the rate at which the screen is redrawn. To do so, right-click the Desktop, and click Properties on the shortcut menu. On the Settings tab of the Display Properties dialog box, click the Advanced button.

2. On the Monitor tab, make sure the Hide Modes That This Monitor Cannot Display check box is selected, and click a higher rate in the Refresh Frequency list. Click Apply. ▶ Click OK when you're notified that the new settings will be used, and then click Yes when you're asked whether you want to apply the settings. If you don't click Yes within 15 seconds, the new settings will be discarded and the old settings will remain. This is a safeguard so that if you make a setting that disrupts the screen and are then unable to click Yes, the setting will be discarded.

3. If the flicker is still there, repeat step 2 until you've eliminated the flicker or reduced it to an acceptable level. Click OK to close the Advanced Properties dialog box, and then click OK to close the Display Properties dialog box.

4. After you've fixed the flicker, you might still be straining to read what's on the screen because everything is so small, or you might be moving your chair back because a dialog box is so huge

that it covers the entire screen. You can adjust the size of everything by changing the screen area. Of course, this doesn't change the actual dimensions of the screen area; it changes the screen resolution, gaining more "virtual" area by shrinking the size of everything. Right-click the Desktop, and click Properties on the shortcut menu. On the Settings tab, drag the Screen Area slider to the left to make screen items larger or to the right to make them smaller. Click OK in the Display Properties dialog box. Click OK when you're notified that the new settings will be used, and click Yes when you're asked whether you want to apply the settings. ▶

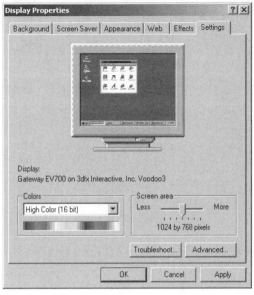

5. If you've increased the screen area, you might find that the text in the windows, on the taskbar and menus, and so on is too small to read. To enlarge it, right-click the Desktop, and click Properties on the shortcut menu. On the Appearance tab, in the Scheme list, click one of the Large or Extra Large schemes—Windows Standard (Large), for example. Click OK to make everything much easier to read.

Some refreshing information, and more about the screen area

The refresh rate is the frequency with which the screen is redrawn. A monitor with a 60 Hertz refresh rate redraws the screen 60 times a second. Normally you don't notice the continuous flicker because the rate of change is so fast that it all merges into a constant image, just as the individual frames of a movie merge into a continuous picture. Sometimes, though, your eyes can discern the pattern of change and you notice every few times the screen is redrawn. That's when you see the flicker. A minor adjustment of the refresh rate can either eliminate the flicker or make it worse.

When you adjust the screen area, you're telling Windows how much to expand or compress items. The dimensions you see—800 by 600 pixels, for example—mean that the screen is 800 pixels wide by 600 pixels tall. When Windows displays an item—unless the item is minimized—its dimensions are defined in pixels and fitted to the dimensions of the screen. An item that's 400 pixels wide occupies half the width of a screen whose width is 800 pixels. If you increase the screen area to 1280 by 1024 pixels, that same item occupies less than a third of the screen (it's still 400 pixels wide, but every pixel on the screen is smaller). Obviously, your monitor can't grow when you increase the screen area, so everything on the screen is smaller.

Warning

A refresh rate that's too high can damage a monitor. If Windows correctly identified your monitor, only refresh rates that won't damage it are listed. If the monitor isn't correctly identified, check its documentation for a range of valid refresh rates. If you use a refresh rate that isn't normally listed for that monitor, you do so at your own risk.

Part of the Desktop is missing

Source of the problem

Windows 2000 organizes itself on your computer screen by placing everything on the Desktop. This is the normal arrangement you expect to see, but sometimes, because of certain settings and configurations, part of the Desktop seems to have fallen off the edge of the screen and disappeared. This is an alarming situation when the very items you need to access have vanished. No matter how hard you try to peer around the corner of your monitor, you can't find the missing material. What you need to do is figure out what caused this strange condition, and then determine whether it's a feature you can utilize or a problem you need to solve.

How to fix it

1. The first possible culprits to consider are your monitor's physical settings. Most monitors are equipped with controls that let you adjust the size, shape, and location of the image on the screen. You'll usually find these controls somewhere on your monitor in the form of little buttons or wheels. Consult the documentation that came with the monitor to see how to make the adjustments you want. Try adjusting the image so that your Desktop fits on the screen and you can see everything. It should take very little adjusting to determine whether these controls are the source of the problem.

   > **Tip**
   > If, after you've adjusted the settings on your monitor, the same problem occurs the next time you start up, you probably didn't save the new settings. Check the monitor's documentation for information about saving any changes you make.

2. If your monitor is adjusted correctly but the problem persists, check to see whether your computer uses a "virtual" Desktop. This is not really part of Windows 2000, but it's a commonly used tool—especially in portable computers—to create more Desktop space without making everything on the Desktop too small. With a virtual Desktop, part of the Desktop is stored in the computer's memory and isn't displayed on the screen. To see whether your computer does have a virtual Desktop, try moving the mouse to one side of the screen and observing whether the Desktop scrolls to show the hidden area while hiding part of the Desktop on the opposite side of the screen. If your computer does have this feature but you don't like it, you can reduce the screen area by right-clicking the Desktop, and then clicking

   > **Tip**
   > The virtual Desktop requires substantial coordination between the display adapter and the monitor. You'll see this feature only on systems that are specifically designed to support it, so don't spend time trying to get it to work on your computer if it isn't built in.

Properties on the shortcut menu. On the Settings tab, drag the slider in the Screen Area section to the left to reduce the screen area, and then click OK. You might need to experiment with the Screen Area setting to eliminate the virtual Desktop while preserving enough working area on the Desktop. You might also need to check your computer's documentation for any other information about changing settings for the virtual Desktop.

3. If you're still looking for the source of the problem, however, check to see whether your computer is set up to work with multiple monitors. Right-click the Desktop, and click Properties on the shortcut menu. On the Settings tab of the Display Properties dialog box, see whether there's more than one monitor displayed. If there is, click the monitor that isn't selected. (The selected monitor is the one you're using, and it has a dark border around it.) This should make the Extend My Windows Desktop Onto This Monitor check box active. Clear the check box, and click OK. ▶

4. If the problem isn't being caused by multiple monitors, there could be some miscommunication going on among the computer, the adapter, and the monitor. Right-click the Desktop, click Properties on the shortcut menu, and, on the Settings tab, drag the slider in the Screen Area section to the left to reduce the screen area. Click OK. If you can now see your entire Desktop, you'll probably need to use this screen area setting as your default setting.

5. If you've investigated all the foregoing possibilities but none of them has fixed the display problem yet, you probably need to look at some other, more remote, possibilities. If, for example, your computer is set up to use a switchbox to switch between monitors, you might need to replace the switchbox. You might be able to test this by connecting the monitor directly to the computer instead of through the switchbox. Failing that, check with the manufacturer of the switchbox. Also, you should check with the manufacturers of both the display adapter and the monitor for possible updated drivers and other fixes specific to that hardware.

Tip

Don't dismiss the possibility that your computer has been set up for multiple monitors simply because you have only one monitor sitting on your desk. If your computer has been configured to use more than one monitor, Windows assumes those other monitors are there and spreads the Desktop out onto the other monitors—even if they're not there. For more information about setting up and using multiple monitors, see "Multiple monitors," starting on page 168.

We've probably all encountered a frustrating situation in which Windows either refuses to shut down when you want it to or shuts down when you don't want it to. Who's the boss here anyway? In the former case, you might have to assert your authority by forcing Windows to shut down; in the latter, you'll need to do some detective work to determine whether Windows really has shut down or is in Hibernate or Standby mode, or whether—because of a power failure or a discharged battery—the computer has shut itself down without shutting down Windows. And if Windows does shut down when you want it to but takes an agonizingly long time about it, there are a few simple steps you can take to speed things up.

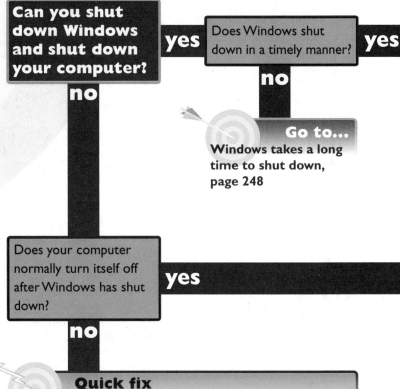

Can you shut down Windows and shut down your computer?

yes

Does Windows shut down in a timely manner?

yes

no

Go to...
Windows takes a long time to shut down, page 248

no

Does your computer normally turn itself off after Windows has shut down?

yes

no

Quick fix

Power management must be working properly on your computer for automatic shutdown to take place.

1. See "Power options," starting on page 188, for information about troubleshooting the power management on your computer.

2. On the Start menu, click Shut Down, click Shut Down in the list in the Shut Down Windows dialog box, and click OK.

3. If you can't get the power management working correctly on your computer, or if the power management is enabled but the computer still doesn't turn itself off, turn it off manually only after you see a message that it's safe to turn off the computer.

If your solution isn't here
Check these related chapters:
    Programs, page 220
    Starting up, page 260
Or see the general troubleshooting tips on page xiii

Shutting down

Does Windows sometimes shut down by itself?

yes → **Go to...** I'm working, and Windows suddenly shuts down, page 246

no

Do you lose data or settings when you shut down Windows?

yes →

Quick fix

When Windows is shut down correctly, it makes sure that all your data and settings are saved.

1. If a program consistently loses data when you shut down, save all the data and close the program.

2. If you're normally connected to a network, make sure you're properly connected.

3. On the Start menu, click Shut Down, click Shut Down in the list in the Shut Down Windows dialog box, and click OK.

4. Wait for Windows to shut down and for the computer to turn itself off. Turn off the computer manually only after you see a message that it's safe to turn off the computer.

Is a single program or the entire system not responding?

yes → **Go to...** I can't shut down Windows, page 244

no

Quick fix

System policies might not allow you to shut down the computer.

1. Check with whoever administers system policies to see whether you're allowed to shut down the computer. If you don't have this permission, ask to be added to a group that does.

2. If you're denied permission, log off, and ask someone who does have permission to log on and to shut down Windows and shut down the computer for you.

I can't shut down Windows

Source of the problem

Windows 2000 is an extremely resilient system. If something goes wrong, Windows usually finds and fixes the problem—shuts down a misbehaving program, for example, or disables a hardware component—and then continues without interruption. Occasionally, though, either Windows can't take care of a problem, or Windows itself is the problem. In these circumstances, the best solution is to shut down Windows and restart the computer so that everything gets reset—the best solution, that is, provided you *can* shut down Windows. Sometimes Windows just refuses to shut down, and, on rare occasions, the system is locked up so badly that you can't even tell Windows to shut down. Fortunately, there are ways to force Windows to shut down. We'll start with the least drastic step and gradually proceed to the ultimate and most undesirable one: turning off the computer without shutting down Windows.

How to fix it

1. On the Start menu, click Shut Down. In the Shut Down Windows dialog box, click Shut Down in the list, and click OK. If the only option available in the list is for you to log off, it means that you're not allowed to shut down Windows. Group policies can be set to prevent members of certain groups from shutting down Windows. You'll see this most frequently on a large corporate network, but the policy can be set on an individual computer too. If you must shut down the computer, log off, find a member of a group that has permission to shut down Windows, and have him or her log on and shut down Windows for you.

2. If the Shut Down option is in the list in the Shut Down Windows dialog box but Windows doesn't shut down when you click the option, you need to find the reason. When Windows shuts down, it shuts down all open programs and windows. If a program doesn't respond to the order from Windows to shut down, Windows won't shut down. Look for any messages about running programs. If you have a program open in which there are unsaved changes, you'll be prompted to save them. If you don't respond to the prompt, Windows gives you the option of forcing the program to shut down and losing the unsaved changes. Click Cancel, locate the message about saving your data, save the changes, close the program, and then try again to shut down Windows.

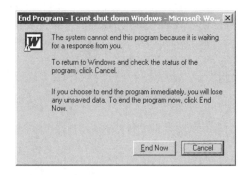

3. Other programs can also refuse to shut down, either because an element of the program, such as a dialog box, is open, or because the program itself is busy and must complete a task before it can be shut down. Again, if Windows displays the End Program dialog box, click Cancel, close any open dialog boxes or other elements, wait for any tasks to be completed, save any unsaved data, and then close the program. To make sure that you won't have any further problems with running programs, close all open programs and windows, and try to shut down Windows again.

4. If you can't close a program but you're sure that the program isn't busy doing what it's supposed to do, try shutting down Windows from the Start menu, and see whether Windows will automatically end the program. Any unsaved information in the program, however, will probably be lost. ▶

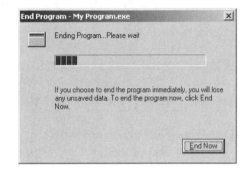

5. If Windows doesn't try to shut down the misbehaving program, you'll need to manually end the program, along with any other misbehaving programs and Windows components, before you can shut down Windows. To do so, press Ctrl+Shift+Esc to open the Task Manager, and, in the Task Manager dialog box, click the program that won't shut down, and then click End Task. Repeat for any other item that isn't responding. Again, any unsaved information in the program will probably be lost. Close the Task Manager when you've finished, and try again to shut down Windows. For more information about shutting down a misbehaving program, see "My program suddenly stopped working" on page 224.

6. If the computer is unresponsive and you can't manually shut down your programs, or if you can't even open the Start menu to shut down Windows, you can try forcing Windows to shut down. Press Ctrl+Alt+Delete to display the Windows Security dialog box. Click the Shut Down button, and try shutting down Windows. If you can display the Windows Security dialog box but Windows still won't shut down, click the Task Manager button, and try shutting down any misbehaving programs as in step 5. When you've finished, close the Task Manager dialog box, press Ctrl+Alt+Delete to display the Windows Security dialog box again, click Shut Down, and try again to shut down Windows.

7. If Windows still refuses to shut down, or if you were unable to display the Windows Security dialog box, you have a couple of choices. You can call for help, and hope that someone with the right tools will be able to shut down the item that's causing the problem so that you can recover unsaved data from your other programs. The other choice is to turn off the computer. If you do this, you'll lose not only any unsaved information in your programs but any settings that you recently made in Windows.

I'm working, and Windows suddenly shuts down

Source of the problem

You're working at your computer, you turn away for a minute to look at something or speak to someone, and poof—for no apparent reason, Windows is shutting down. You know *you* didn't do anything to make it shut down. What's going on here? This type of shutdown can have several causes—none of them particularly benign, of course. Some of the little things that can cause a shutdown are easy to remedy, and others can be quite confusing, so we'll try to help you find the problem.

How to fix it

1. Are you sure that Windows really did shut down? Windows 2000 uses special power-saving modes that can act automatically and can make it appear that Windows has shut down. Press a key on the keyboard, and see whether the computer comes back to life. If nothing happens, press the power button on the computer. If the screen appears almost immediately, or if a Computer Locked dialog box appears, the computer has gone into Standby mode. If the computer goes through its standard startup process, but, instead of seeing a message that Windows is starting up, you see a message that Windows is resuming, you'll know that the computer had gone into Hibernate mode. To adjust the scheduling of these modes, see "Power options," starting on page 188.

2. Another possibility is that your computer shut down without Windows having been shut down. Make sure there wasn't a power failure or that your computer wasn't accidentally turned off or disconnected from its power outlet. Also, if you're using a portable computer, make sure the computer's battery hasn't completely discharged. If, when you turn on your computer, Windows starts and then pauses to run a check of the computer's disk, you can be fairly certain that the computer was turned off without Windows having been shut down. If the computer doesn't restart at all, recheck the power outlet and the connections, and make sure the battery has had enough time to recharge. If the power appears to be in order, you might be experiencing a major hardware failure that will require a service call.

3. If you're certain that Windows really did shut down, think about what you were doing just before the shutdown happened. Did you do anything to make Windows think you wanted to shut down? For example, if there were no programs running and no windows open and you pressed Alt+F4, you used the keyboard shortcut that shuts down whatever is running—in this

case, Windows. If you then pressed Enter, you did the equivalent of clicking OK in the Shut Down Windows dialog box. Other key combinations will shut down Windows too—for example, pressing Ctrl+Alt+Delete, pressing S, and then pressing Enter. If Windows will start up for you, try repeating what you did before it shut down.

4. If you were using the On-Screen Keyboard, the problem might have been caused by a strange design quirk. If the screen area for your display is set to 640 by 480 pixels, and if you click the Windows key on the left side of the On-Screen Keyboard, the Start menu opens, and the Shut Down command on the menu—which just happens to sit beneath the left Windows key—will be clicked. If you press or click Enter, Windows will shut down. Even if your screen area is set at a different resolution, you might experience the same problem if you've moved the On-Screen Keyboard from its startup position. To avoid this anomaly, move the On-Screen Keyboard away from where the Start menu will appear when it's opened.

Tip

Were you suddenly logged off? You can be logged off without Windows being shut down for many of the same reasons described here. You can also be logged off if you're authorized to be connected during specific hours and are still logged on after that time period.

5. What if Windows really *did* shut down through no action of your own? On a network with a domain, a network administrator can usually shut down your computer from another computer. In other instances, Windows might shut down if a security policy has been violated or if the security of your computer can't be monitored. Windows can also shut down if one of its services has stopped unexpectedly. If an administrator shut down your computer, see whether the shutdown was a planned one for maintenance or for some other reason. If the cause was a security violation, expect a visit from those who control and enforce network security. If the problem was with a service, restart the computer and see whether that solves the problem. If it doesn't, you might have a hardware failure or problems with your Windows files that you'll need to troubleshoot.

6. A sudden shutdown can also occur if your computer is connected to a UPS (an uninterruptible power supply) whose power has gone out and the battery the UPS is using is running down. This applies to the type of UPS that's configured to work with your operating system and that's connected to your computer through a serial port as well as with a power cord. In this case, all you can do is wait for the power to be restored. To confirm that the UPS is set to shut down your computer, or to modify the UPS response to a power failure, on the Settings submenu of the Start menu, click Control Panel. In the Control Panel, hold down the Shift key, right-click Power Options, click Run As on the shortcut menu, and log on as the Administrator. On the UPS tab of the Power Options dialog box, click Configure, and inspect and, if necessary, modify the settings. If the Configure button is grayed (unavailable), the UPS either isn't connected or doesn't interact with the computer and can't shut down the computer on its own.

7. If none of the foregoing seems to be a likely reason for your computer to have shut down, you should be concerned that it might have been infected with a virus. Consult your anti-virus software's documentation for information about scanning and repairing your system.

Windows takes a long time to shut down

Source of the problem

The day is done, and it's time to get away from that computer. You don't want to leave until it's properly turned off, in case something goes wrong. You wait, occasionally hearing the whirling of a disk and other indecipherable clicks and clanks emanating from the computer's innards. Finally, after what seems like an eternity, Windows shuts down, the computer turns itself off, and you can escape. Diligence always has its price, but waiting and waiting for Windows to shut down seems like an excessive price to pay. And it is. You might be able to shorten the shutdown process yourself, or, failing that, you might need to send a few gentle words of complaint in your network administrator's direction.

How to fix it

1. One of the greatest contributors to a lengthy shutdown is the time it takes for Windows to go through every program that's open, checking to see whether there's any unsaved data; asking you whether you want to save the data, and, if you do, saving the data; and, finally, closing the program. Multiply the time this process takes by the number of open programs, and you quickly get the picture! If you want to get out of the office fast, save your documents regularly, close a program when you've finished with it, and close any programs that are still open when you're ready to shut down. Windows still has plenty to do—it has to shut down all the programs that run behind the scenes.

2. Another major shutdown slowdown occurs if you use files off line and your system is set up to synchronize the files when you log off. Windows updates all the files in all the folders that are set up to be used off line. Depending on your setup, you might also be updating web pages, which isn't really very useful when you're shutting down. To change when your files are to be synchronized, or to specify which ones are to be updated, on the Accessories submenu of the Start menu, click Synchronize. In the Items To Synchronize dialog box, click Setup. On the Logon/Logoff tab of the Synchronization Settings dialog box, either clear the check box to synchronize when you log off, or select the check box to ask before synchronizing, or do both if you want to synchronize selected folders when you log on. Click OK, and then click Close to close the Items To Synchronize dialog box. ▶

3. If you turned off the check box to synchronize when you log off, you might want to synchronize your files manually. To do so, on the Accessories submenu of the Start menu, click Synchronize. In the Items To Synchronize dialog box, clear the check boxes for the items you don't want to synchronize, and then click the Synchronize button. ▶

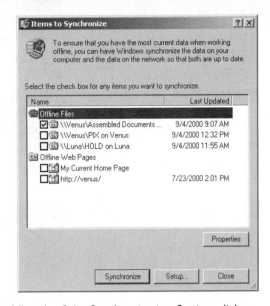

4. If you kept the check box to synchronize when you log off selected, and you selected the check box to ask before synchronizing, the Items To Synchronize dialog box will appear when you log off or shut down so that you can specify which items to synchronize. If you want your files synchronized automatically, but not when you're logging off, in the Items To Synchronize dialog box, click the Setup button, and, on the On Idle tab of the Synchronization Settings dialog box, specify whether you want your files to be synchronized when your computer is idle; or, on the Scheduled tab, create a schedule for the updating of the files. Close the dialog boxes when you've finished.

5. Another factor—one that you probably can't do anything about—can affect shutdown. A network administrator can create a program called a *script*, which dictates that certain actions take place when you shut down the computer. Almost anything can be included in the script, so you're completely at the mercy of its author. If your computer goes through a seemingly endless series of steps before it shuts down, ask the powers that be whether a shutdown script is being used, and, if so, whether it can be modified so that it doesn't take so long to shut down the computer.

6. Sometimes it doesn't just *seem* that your computer takes forever to shut down—it really does! That is, the system gets hung up and the shutdown process simply stops, although it appears to be continuing. If you try to shut the computer down but, after you've had a couple of cups of coffee and taken a stroll around the office, the computer hasn't shut down and there seems to be no disk activity, the computer is probably stuck. See "I can't shut down Windows" on page 244 for information about dealing with this situation.

Tip

Consider placing your computer in Hibernate mode instead of shutting it down if you're going to be the next person who uses it. Windows usually goes into Hibernate mode faster and starts up more quickly than it does when you shut down Windows. Just remember to require a password when the computer comes out of hibernation so that your information is protected.

In this chapter, we'll explore the various reasons why your computer's sound system might not be working properly and why you can't play, hear, or record what you want. You'll find troubleshooting techniques here that take you through a step-by-step process of elimination: making sure the sound system and speakers are hooked up properly, checking for missing software components, verifying that the system is compatible with Windows 2000, and so on. We'll also look into what you can do to improve poor sound quality when you participate in conference calls using a communications program such as Microsoft NetMeeting. And if your system won't let you listen to Beethoven or Brubeck while you work, we'll help you figure out why the CD drive won't play music.

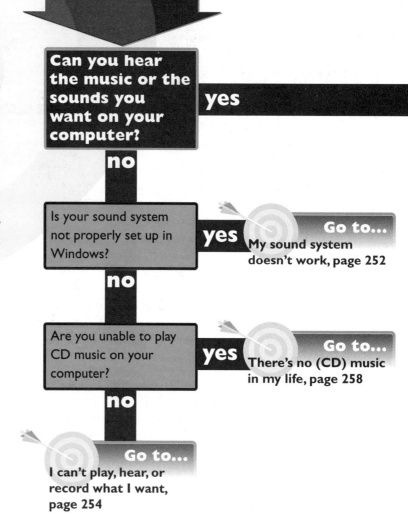

Can you hear the music or the sounds you want on your computer?

yes

no

Is your sound system not properly set up in Windows?

yes

Go to...
My sound system doesn't work, page 252

no

Are you unable to play CD music on your computer?

yes

Go to...
There's no (CD) music in my life, page 258

no

Go to...
I can't play, hear, or record what I want, page 254

If your solution isn't here
Check these related chapters:
Games, page 88
Hardware installation, page 96
Taskbar, page 278
Or see the general troubleshooting tips on page xiii

Are your speakers not working as well as they should?

yes → **Quick fix**

Windows sets up your speakers as stereo desktop speakers. If you're using a different type of speaker, let Windows know so that you can get the best possible sound.

1. On the Settings submenu of the Start menu, click Control Panel.

2. Hold down the Shift key, right-click Sounds And Multimedia, click Run As on the shortcut menu, and log on as the Administrator.

3. On the Audio tab of the Sounds And Multimedia Properties dialog box, click Advanced in the Sound Playback section.

4. On the Speakers tab of the Advanced Audio Properties dialog box, click the type of speakers you're using in the Speaker Setup list. Click OK, and then click OK again to close the Sounds And Multimedia Properties dialog box.

no

Do you hear an echo in voice communications on your computer?

yes → **Go to...**

Voices echo or sound choppy in Internet or conference calls, page 256

no

Is that logon music too loud or too annoying?

yes → **Quick fix**

When Windows is installed, it's set to play a logon sound. You can turn down the volume, change what's played, or set it so that nothing is played.

1. On the Settings submenu of the Start menu, click Control Panel. In the Control Panel, double-click Sounds And Multimedia.

2. On the Sounds tab of the Sounds And Multimedia Properties dialog box, drag the Sound Volume slider to adjust the volume.

3. In the Sound Events list, click Start Windows. In the Name list, click the name of a sound you want to play, or click None to start Windows with no sound. Click OK.

My sound system doesn't work

Source of the problem

In the not-too-distant past, computers didn't play music, help you carry on voice communications, or even add sound effects to a game. Instead, you heard an occasional beep when you did something the operating system didn't like, and a lot of buzzing and crackling as your modem tried to make a connection. Today, of course, you expect great sound from your computer. So why isn't your sound system working? We'll explore some possibilities.

How to fix it

1. Make sure your system is hooked up correctly, with the speakers properly connected to your computer, turned on, and—if they use external power—plugged in. If the speakers have their own volume control, make sure the volume is set high enough to be heard. If the components are all in order, make sure the computer is set up for sound and that the volume used by Windows isn't turned down too low or completely muted. Double-click the Volume icon on the taskbar. If there is no Volume icon, on the Entertainment submenu of the Start menu, click Volume Control. If you receive an error message, your sound system isn't properly set up, software components are missing, or the sound system isn't compatible with Windows or is disabled or malfunctioning. ▶

2. If the Volume Control does appear, depending on the setup of your computer and sound system, you should see Volume Control, Wave, and—with integrated speakers such as those in a portable computer—PC Speaker sections. If, in any of these sections, a Mute or Mute All check box is selected, clear it. Drag the Volume slider toward the top of each section to make sure the volume is high enough to be heard. Close the Volume Control after you've made your settings. ▶

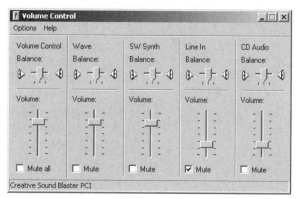

3. Now you need to test the system to see whether it works at all. On the Entertainment submenu of the Start menu, click Sound Recorder. In Sound Recorder, click Open on the File menu, and open a sound (.*wav*) file to play. Usually you'll find sound files in the Media subfolder of the WINNT folder. Click the Play button. If the slider moves from left to right, you should hear the sound. If you don't, something is still wrong with your sound system. ▲

4. To make sure the problem isn't with the speakers—excluding USB (universal serial bus) speakers—try plugging your headphones either into the port where you normally connect the speakers or into the headphone port on a portable computer that has internal speakers. Because the volume might be set high, hold the headphones away from your ears so that you aren't deafened, and use Sound Recorder to play a sound. If you don't hear anything, try again with the headphones closer to your ears. If you still don't hear anything, reconnect your speakers, and be confident they're not the source of the problem.

5. Before you go any further, you need to find out whether there's any known problem that prevents your sound system from working with Windows 2000. Be aware that many sound systems might work with only limited capabilities or might not work at all. Check your computer's documentation to note the manufacturer, model, and type of your sound system, and then check the Windows 2000 hardware compatibility list at *http:/www.microsoft.com/hwtest/hcl*. Also check with the manufacturer of your computer and/or sound system. Many sound systems require updated software to make them work properly.

6. If your sound system is compatible with Windows 2000, your next step is to see whether it was properly installed. Right-click My Computer on the Desktop, and click Manage on the shortcut menu. In the Computer Management window, click Device Manager. If you receive a notice that you don't have the necessary permission to make changes, click OK, and ignore the message—you're just checking, not making changes. Double-click the Sound, Video, And Game Controllers item if it isn't already expanded. You'll probably see several items listed. Find the item that matches your main sound system, and double-click it. If there's a problem listed in the Properties dialog box, see "The device doesn't work" on page 102. If your sound system isn't listed, Windows didn't install it properly, and you'll need to install it. See "The device wasn't detected" on page 98 for information about manually installing the hardware. If you need to update the software for the sound system to make it compatible, see "The device was misidentified" on page 100 for information about installing updated drivers. Close the Computer Management window when you've finished.

I can't play, hear, or record what I want

Source of the problem

There are all sorts of audio files and formats around, and many different tools available for playing and/or recording them. Unless you use the proper program and device, you won't get the results you want. For example, if you want to make a recording that includes sounds from an audio tape, you might need to configure your sound system so that you can record what's being played when you hook up a tape player to the Line In port of your sound system. Or, if you want to play MP3 music from the Internet, you'll need to use a program that can retrieve the music and play that type of audio file. To play, hear, or record what you want, you'll need to configure your system correctly, using the best program for the job.

How to fix it

1. If you don't hear anything when you're supposed to—you're sure your speakers are turned on and that your sound system works, and you play some music or use your sound system to chit-chat on the phone instead of using a telephone handset—you need to check the settings for the device you're using. If you see a Volume icon on the taskbar, double-click it. If there is no Volume icon, on the Entertainment submenu of the Start menu, click Volume Control. If you see a section for the device you're using in the Volume Control, make sure the Mute check box is cleared. Also make sure the Mute All check box is cleared in the Volume Control section, and that the Volume slider is set to a high volume.

2. If you don't see your device, click Properties on the Options menu. Click the Playback option if it isn't already selected, and select the check box for the type of device you're using. Click OK, and adjust the volume control for the device. ▶

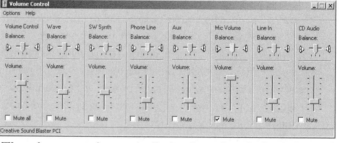

The volume controls you can display depend on the hardware and software installed on your computer. Above are a few of the many different items that can be displayed in the Volume Control.

3. If you don't see your device in the Volume Control, or in the list of devices in the Properties dialog box, the device might not be installed or might use a generic control. For

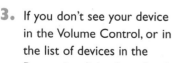

example, the volume for playing a sound file using Sound Recorder is controlled by the Wave Volume section. See "The device wasn't detected" on page 98 for information about determining whether a device is installed and working properly.

Tip

Many programs use their own volume controls. Make sure the sound isn't muted or set too low in the program.

4. What if you're trying to record your melodious voice, or any other sound or music, but nothing happens? If you're sure that any exterior component is attached correctly, verify that the device is enabled as an input device. To do so, open the Volume Control as you did in step 1. Click Properties on the Options menu, and click the Recording option. Make sure the check box for the device is selected, and click OK. In the Recording Control, make sure the Mute (or, in some Recording Controls, the Select) check box is cleared for the device, and that the volume is adjusted to the level you want. Close the Recording Control when you've finished. ▶

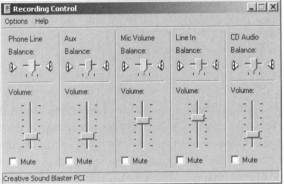

5. If you can't play a certain type of audio file, you might not have the correct tool. Windows Media Player supports many different music and other multimedia formats. To see which formats are supported, on the Entertainment submenu of the Start menu, click Media Player. If you have Media Player version 6.4, click Options on the View menu to display the Options dialog box. If you have Media Player version 7, click Options on the Tools menu to display the same dialog box. On the Formats tab, inspect the available formats. For details about each format, click the listed item, and, in the Description area, note the different file types that are supported. If the format you want isn't listed, you might need to obtain different software. Some proprietary formats, such as those used by RealNetworks, work only on specific players. In most cases, any web site that requires a specific player will provide a link to a location from which you can download the player.

Tip

Windows Media Player version 7 supports several formats that aren't supported by Media Player version 6.4. To see which version you have, on Media Player's Help menu, click About Windows Media Player. On the Start menu, click Windows Update to download an updated version of Media Player.

6. If you have the proper devices and programs to play or record the sounds or music you want, but your sound system still refuses to cooperate, there could be a problem with the way your sound system interacts with Windows. Some sound cards are simply unable to accomplish a specific task when running in Windows 2000, despite being designed to do so and despite the fact that they can accomplish that task when installed on a computer running Windows 95/98/Me. Check the Windows 2000 hardware compatibility list or contact the manufacturer for any known problems with your particular sound system.

Voices echo or sound choppy in Internet or conference calls

Source of the problem

Windows 2000 provides communications programs such as Microsoft NetMeeting and Phone Dialer that make it possible for you to conduct verbal discussions using your computer. You can stay at home and work in your slippers instead of having to wear a business suit; you can avoid the torture and expense of airline travel; or you can just save money on long-distance calls. There are many communications, telecommuting, and teleconferencing programs that all work in similar ways, and they're revolutionizing the way we work—that is, when they work properly. However, if important conversations are cut off in midsentence or if all you hear is the echoing of your own voice, you'll need to remedy the situation. Some problems of this nature are associated with the resources a program requires, others are hardware related, and yet others simply need the correct settings.

How to fix it

1. If you're using your program over a network, you should normally have adequate resources to conduct a full conference call, including the use of video. However, if your network is overloaded, its performance will suffer. The end result can vary depending on the program you're using, but what often happens is that the transmission of voices or other information stops temporarily until enough has been transmitted so that the information can be played (known as *caching* information), or parts of the transmission are lost, resulting in choppy sound or video. If you encounter these problems, try either reducing the amount of data transmitted—for example, terminating video and using voice only—or rescheduling the call to a time when the network should provide better performance.

2. If you're connecting to people outside your network, find out what connections they're using. The conference, unfortunately, will be controlled by the slowest and least powerful connection on the call. For example, if you're on a network but you're calling someone who's using a modem, the communications will be governed by the speed and capabilities—or lack thereof—of the modem. Again, the best strategy is to reduce the amount of data being sent, and to make sure the person using the modem optimizes its settings.

3. If you're connecting to a call using a modem, make sure you have the correct settings for that modem. Most programs provide an option for specifying the speed of your connection, often called the Bandwidth. If you specify a connection that's faster than the speed at which you

normally connect, you could lose information, the sound or video might be choppy, and you could even cause the program to stop responding. If you specify a connection that's slower than the speed at which you normally connect, you'll probably be able to send only very little information, and features such as video might be disabled by the program or produce an image of very poor quality. ▶

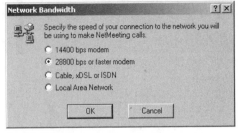

In NetMeeting, you can specify your connection speed so that the program doesn't try to send too much information too fast.

4. If one voice or both voices are silenced when you're connecting by modem and having a two-way conversation, your modem might not be adequate to handle the call, or you might have incorrect settings for the call. Check your computer documentation for information about the modem. If it's a *half-duplex* modem, the sound can travel in one direction only, so you can't talk and hear someone else talking at the same time. If the modem is a *full-duplex* modem, the sound should be able to travel in both directions simultaneously. Some modems provide a setting to enable full-duplex communications, so, if your modem is a full-duplex one, make sure it's set up correctly. If you have a half-duplex modem, you'll either have to learn to live with its limitations or obtain and install a Windows 2000–compatible full-duplex modem.

5. If you're using a microphone and speakers in your calls, you'll hear that annoying echo when the microphone transmits the sounds it picks up from the speakers. To eliminate the echo, you have to prevent the sounds from your microphone from being played over the speakers. If you see a Volume icon on the taskbar, double-click it. If there's no Volume icon, on the Entertainment submenu of the Start menu, click Volume Control.

6. In the Volume Control, you need to adjust the settings for the microphone playback. These settings aren't always displayed in the Volume Control. To display them, click Properties on the Options menu. In the Properties dialog box, click the Playback option if it isn't already selected, and then select the Mic Volume check box (and the Digital Recording Control check box, if it's present) in the Show The Following Volume Controls list. Click OK.

7. In the Mic Volume (or the Digital Recording Control) section of the Volume Control, select the Mute check box. Close the Volume Control when you've finished. Your echo problems should now be eliminated. ▶

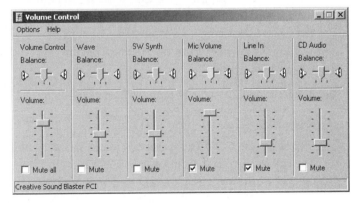

There's no (CD) music in my life

Source of the problem

Your computer is a great CD player. Of course, it's too bulky and expensive to be used for that purpose only, but if you want a little musical accompaniment while you work, drop in your favorite CD, and you're all set—provided, of course, that your computer is set up for multimedia and your CD drive is set to play music. If your computer can play other types of multimedia, such as sound (.*wav*) or MIDI (.*mid*) files, you'd assume that it could play CD music. If you can't get any music out of your CD drive, you might be able to fix it by changing a setting or two, or you might find that the CD drive hasn't been configured to play music.

How to fix it

1. Verify that your computer can play sounds and music. On the Entertainment submenu of the Start menu, click Sound Recorder. (Sound Recorder is a basic sound-recording and playback program that comes with Windows 2000.) On Sound Recorder's File menu, click Open, and open a sound (.*wav*) file to play. You'll usually find sound files in the Media subfolder of the WINNT folder. Click the Play button. If the slider moves from left to right, you should hear the sound. If you don't, see "My sound system doesn't work" on page 252 to figure out what's wrong with your sound system. Close Sound Recorder when you've finished.

2. If your sound system is working, the next step is to find out what's wrong with the CD drive. If you see a Volume icon on the taskbar, double-click it. If there's no Volume icon on the taskbar, on the Entertainment submenu of the Start menu, click Volume Control. If, in the CD Audio section of the Volume Control, the Mute check box is selected, clear it, and then drag the Volume slider upward to increase the volume. Close the Volume Control when you've finished.

3. If there is no CD Audio section, click Properties on the Options menu. In the Properties dialog box, click the Playback option if it isn't already selected, and then select the CD Audio check box in the Show The Following Volume Controls list. Click OK, and then adjust the settings in the CD Audio section. ▶

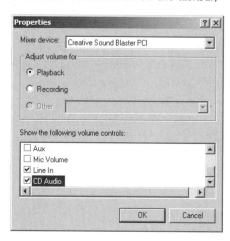

4. Insert the music CD into the CD drive, close the drive, and wait for the CD to start playing. Depending on the software that's installed on your computer, you might see the CD Player, Windows Media Player, or a third-party CD player that was installed. If an icon for the player appears on the taskbar, click it. There might be a dialog box waiting for your response before the player will start the CD. If so, respond, and close the dialog box, and the CD player should start playing.

Tip

Only Windows Media Player version 7 (or later) is capable of playing CDs. If you have an earlier version of Media Player, you can use CD Player to play your music.

5. If a CD player doesn't start after you insert the CD, on the Entertainment submenu of the Start menu, click CD Player. If the CD doesn't start playing, click the Play button.

6. If the CD appears to be playing but you don't hear anything, there might be a problem with a setting, and you'll need to do a bit of experimenting. On the Settings submenu of the Start menu, click Control Panel. In the Control Panel, hold down the Shift key, right-click the System icon, click Run As on the shortcut menu, and log on as the Administrator. On the Hardware tab of the System Properties dialog box, click Device Manager. In the Device Manager window, double-click the DVD/CD-Rom Drives item to expand it, and then double-click your CD drive.

7. On the Properties tab, make sure the CD Player Volume slider is set to High. Here's where you have to experiment. If the Enable Digital CD Audio For This CD-ROM Device check box is selected, clear it. If it's not selected, select it. Click OK, and try playing your CD. If the problem still exists, return to the Device Manager window, double-click your CD drive, and, on the Properties tab, select the cleared check box or clear the selected check box to reverse your previous change. Click OK, close the Device Manager window, and click OK to close the System Properties dialog box. ▶

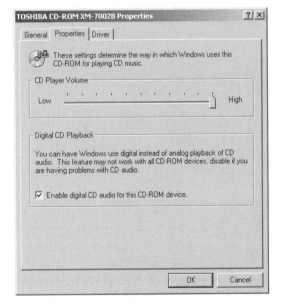

8. If you still can't get the CD to play, you need to see whether there are any hardware problems. Try to read a non-music (data) CD using My Computer. If you can't read it, you'll need to have the CD drive checked to see whether it has failed. If the CD has a headphone port, connect your headphones, turn up the manual volume control, and play a music CD. If you can hear it, have the system checked to make sure the audio cable from the CD drive to the sound system is connected and working, and that both the CD and your sound system are fully compatible with Windows 2000. If you can't hear any music, have the CD drive checked.

If you can't start Windows, you're in trouble! Is it a hardware problem or a software problem, or are those computer gremlins at work again? And if you can't start the computer, how can you fix what ails it? We'll explore the possibilities and help you find some answers. We'll also look into why Windows might be starting up at a snail's pace, and why a hardware profile can be a marvelous time saver at startup if you use your computer in different configurations with different hardware.

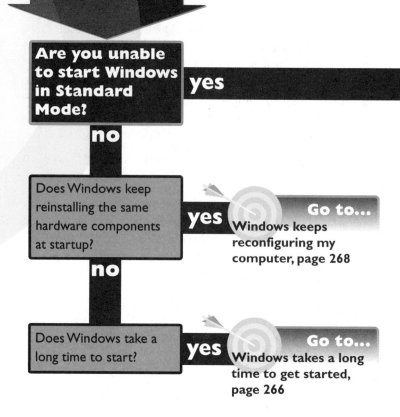

Are you unable to start Windows in Standard Mode?

yes

no

Does Windows keep reinstalling the same hardware components at startup?

yes

Go to...
Windows keeps reconfiguring my computer, page 268

no

Does Windows take a long time to start?

yes

Go to...
Windows takes a long time to get started, page 266

If your solution isn't here
Check these related chapters:
    Dual boot, page 46
    Logging on, page 136
    Multiple monitors, page 168
    Screen, page 230
    Shutting down, page 242
Or see the general troubleshooting tips on page xiii

Starting up

Can an Administrator start Windows in Standard Mode? — **yes** → **Quick fix**

Someone has changed the permission that allows data to be read from the disk. This can result in an error message when you try to log on, or you might see only the wallpaper or a blank screen.

1. Start Windows, and log on as the Administrator.

2. In My Computer, right-click the drive that contains the operating system (often drive C), and click Properties on the shortcut menu.

3. On the Security tab, click Everyone if it isn't already selected. Select the Read check box if it isn't already selected, and then click OK.

4. Double-click the drive to open it. Right-click the folder that contains the operating system (usually the WINNT folder), and click Properties on the shortcut menu. Repeat step 3 for this folder.

5. Restart the computer, and log on as you normally would.

no

Can you start Windows in Safe Mode? — **yes** → **Go to...**

Windows won't start correctly, page 262

no

Is your computer on a network with a domain? — **yes** → **Quick fix**

You have a serious problem that's probably beyond the scope of anything you should be trying to fix.

1. Make sure the computer and the monitor are both turned on, and that all cables are firmly attached.

2. If there's power to the computer and the monitor, write down anything you might have done to the computer just before it failed.

3. Don't try to do anything to the computer. Contact the network administrator to get help.

no

Go to...

I can't repair the computer because I can't start it, page 264

Windows won't start correctly

Source of the problem

Despite all the safeguards built into the system, there are many ways to break Windows. Not only can you mess it up by deleting essential files or making the wrong settings, but hardware or software that isn't fully compatible with Windows 2000 can do some evil things to the system. For example, you might try using an old device driver for your modem because there are no Windows 2000 drivers available for the modem. Some drivers might work just fine, but others will cause a system failure. If you used software to create your own CDs on a computer running Windows 98, you might find that your system locks up when you install the software on a computer that's running Windows 2000. Although there's no substitute for checking the software and hardware compatibility lists before you install or modify anything on your computer, Windows does provide a couple of other safeguards. If the system isn't working correctly, you can try starting Windows using the settings that worked previously. If that doesn't work, you can usually start the system in Safe Mode, with only minimal features available, and then try to fix the problem.

How to fix it

1. Start Windows. When you see the "Starting Windows" message on the black screen, press the F8 key. (Depending on your computer, you might need to do this very quickly.) If your computer is set up to run more than one operating system, you can press the F8 key when you're prompted to select an operating system. When you press the F8 key, the Windows 2000 Advanced Options menu appears, offering you several choices. Use the Down arrow key to select the Last Known Good Configuration item, and press Enter. In the Hardware Profile/Configuration Recovery menu that appears, you can select a different hardware profile if your computer has one, or you can start with the default profile. If you created a backup profile before making any major hardware changes, and if you've since reversed the hardware changes, select the backup profile, and press Enter. Otherwise, wait for the default profile to be used and for the computer to start.

> **Tip**
> For information about creating and using hardware profiles, see "Windows keeps reconfiguring my computer" on page 268.

2. If Windows starts normally, reverse whatever you did that caused the problem. If you installed a program, remove it. If you installed a hardware driver, remove it. If you discover that whatever you did has already been reversed, be happy—it means that Windows ignored the cause of the problem when you started up using the previous configuration.

3. If Windows didn't start normally, restart the computer, and press the F8 key to return to the Windows 2000 Advanced Options menu. Now you must select the startup option you want. Determine what you need to do, use the arrow keys to select the appropriate option, and then press Enter to start Windows in the mode you selected.

- **Safe Mode:** Starts Windows with no network connections and without most of its drivers. Use this option to correct settings, remove programs or drivers, or fix network problems.

- **Safe Mode With Networking:** Starts Windows with network connections but without most of its drivers. Use this option if any resources you need are on the network, or if someone is going to try to fix your computer from another computer on the network.

- **Safe Mode With Command Prompt:** Starts Windows without network connections, without most of its drivers, and with the command prompt only. Use this option only if you have special utilities that run from the command prompt and/or you have detailed instructions about repairing your computer from the command prompt. Repairing the system from the command prompt is not for the timid.

- **Enable Boot Logging:** Starts Windows normally, and records startup information to the *ntbtlog.txt* file (in the WINNT folder). It's useful in diagnosing the startup problem. If the system fails to start correctly, restart in Safe Mode, and examine the log.

4. Log on to the computer as the Administrator, and change the settings or remove the program or driver that's causing the problem. Then restart the computer and see whether it will start in Standard Mode.

5. If you were unable to correct the problem in Safe Mode, you need to go to the next level of repair. If your computer is on a large network with a domain, get help from your network administrator. If you're on a small network or you have a stand-alone computer, insert the Windows 2000 Professional CD, restart Windows, and try to get the computer to boot from the CD (some computers require you to press a key to boot from the CD). If the computer doesn't boot from the CD, shut down Windows and the computer, insert the first of the four Windows 2000 Professional Setup disks into the floppy disk drive, and restart the computer. Step through the setup process, and, in the Welcome To Setup section, press R to begin the repair process. In the Windows Repair Options section, press R to use the emergency repair process. Specify whether you want to use the automatic or the manual repair process, and whether you want to use your emergency repair disk, if you have one. Complete the process, restart Windows, and see whether you've repaired the problem.

> **Tip**
> If you don't have the Windows 2000 Professional Setup disks, see "I can't repair the computer because I can't start it" on page 264 for information about creating the disks.

6. If none of the foregoing has solved the problem, you might need to repeat the repair process, this time choosing to install a new copy of Windows. However, consult a repair professional first, because this is the last resort.

I can't repair the computer because I can't start it

Source of the problem

There are two ways to start your computer when you need to use the Microsoft Windows 2000 Professional CD to repair the operating system. If your computer supports it, you can insert the CD and boot directly from it. If your computer doesn't support booting from the CD, you'll need to use a set of four floppy disks to start the system. If you can't find the boot disks, don't worry—you can create a whole new set of the disks from the Windows 2000 Professional CD. Regardless of the way you start your computer, you'll enter Windows 2000 Setup, where you can either reinstall Windows 2000 or use repair tools to fix a serious problem.

How to fix it

1. The first step is to assemble the pieces you need to work with. You will, of course, need the Windows 2000 Professional CD. If you need to create the Setup disks, you'll need four blank formatted floppy disks and access to a working computer. (You can also use disks that contain material you don't need any more—the process of creating the Setup disks will delete anything on the disks.) Label each disk as "Microsoft Windows 2000 Professional Setup Disk," and number the disks consecutively.

2. If your computer can boot from a CD, and if the computer is turned off, turn it on; if it's running, restart it. As soon as the computer has power, quickly place the CD in the CD drive. Watch the screen for any instructions about booting from the CD (usually a message telling you to press any key). Wait for the computer to start and for Windows Setup to start. Follow the instructions to run the parts of Setup that you want to use.

3. If you need to create the Setup disks, insert the Windows 2000 Professional CD into the CD drive of any computer running Windows or MS-DOS. If you're prompted to log on as another user, click the option to log on as yourself. (You don't need Administrator permission to create these disks.) If you're asked whether you want to upgrade your operating system, click No to cancel any automatic installation. (This might occur if you're using a computer that's running an operating system other than Windows 2000.)

> **Warning**
>
> In a corporate network environment, Windows is usually set up using special deployment tools over a network or from a specially designed CD. If you need to fix the system, but you didn't install Windows 2000 on your computer and don't have the Windows 2000 Professional CD, check with the network administrator about the methods and tools he or she uses to repair problems. Trying to run the Setup program on a system that was set up over a network can cause serious problems.

4. If the Microsoft Windows 2000 Professional CD window appears, click Browse This CD. If this window doesn't appear, in My Computer, double-click the CD. ▶

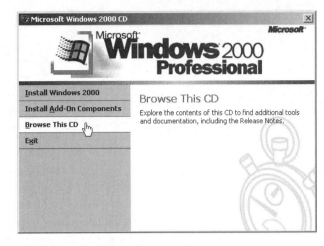

5. In the folder window for the CD, double-click the BOOTDISK folder. Double-click MAKEBOOT in the BOOTDISK folder. When the Command Prompt window opens, type the letter of the floppy disk drive (usually **a**), insert the first floppy disk into the drive, and press any key. Wait for the information to be copied, and then insert the second floppy disk when prompted. Repeat for the remaining two disks, making sure to insert them in the correct order.

When all four disks have been created, close the BOOTDISK folder window and close the Microsoft Windows 2000 Professional CD window. ▶

6. Return to your broken computer. Insert the Microsoft Windows 2000 Professional Setup Disk 1 into the floppy disk drive, and start the computer. Follow the instructions, placing each disk in the drive as needed. When prompted, place the Microsoft Windows 2000 Professional CD in the computer's CD drive, and follow the instructions for repairing the existing installation or installing a new copy of the operating system. If you install a new operating system, you might lose many of your settings and might need to reinstall your programs. Installing a new copy of the operating system should be your last resort.

More about booting

Booting from the CD is by far the quickest way to start Setup and the repair process. Although most computers that support Windows 2000 will boot from a CD, some have had this option disabled in the computer's setup (the BIOS, or basic input/output system). If your computer won't start from the CD, check its documentation to see whether it does support booting from the CD and, if so, how you can enable booting from the CD in the computer's settings.

Windows takes a long time to get started

Source of the problem

You arrive at your desk, turn on your computer, and wait for Windows to start up so that you can log on and get to work—and you wait…and you wait…and you wait. Why is it taking so long? Well, it does take Windows a little time to load the items that it needs to function properly, but that time can be greatly affected one way or the other by the speed of your computer and your network connections, and especially by the way you've set up the computer. You can usually speed up Windows' startup time by tweaking those settings so that Windows doesn't have to work so hard to get started.

How to fix it

1. Start Windows, and watch as it starts up. Note what it does and where it seems to slow down. If, for example, you're logging on to a network, see whether it's that process that causes a major slowdown. If you're dialing in to the network, you should expect a delay, depending on the speed (or lack thereof) of the connection and the time the server takes to verify your account. If you have a direct connection to a network that has a domain, the logon should be fairly quick. If it's slow, ask the network administrator whether it's possible to speed up the network logon.

2. Most startup delays occur immediately after you've logged on. At that point, Windows is working on all the extra, time-consuming tasks it's been assigned—displaying the contents of open windows, for example, and restoring network connections. To prevent an open folder window from appearing when you start Windows, close all your folder windows before you log off or shut down Windows. To eliminate or reduce the number of network connections that Windows has to restore, disconnect any network drives you don't need. To do so, in My Computer, right-click the mapped network drive, and click Disconnect on the shortcut menu.

   > **Tip**
   >
   > Don't leave a CD or a removable disk in its drive unless you need it. When Windows starts, it tests each drive, and, if it finds a CD or a disk, it reads the contents, which adds to the startup time.

3. The next step is to determine which programs are starting automatically when Windows starts, and to prevent them from doing so if you don't always need them at startup. On the Programs submenu of the Start menu, point to Startup, and examine any programs listed on the submenu. These are the programs that start automatically when you start Windows or when you log on. Drag any program you don't need at startup from the Startup submenu into another location on the Start menu. You'll be able to start the program when you need it by clicking its name on the

Start menu. If you do leave programs in the Startup folder, make sure they're not configured to run tasks that could take a long time (otherwise, be prepared to wait uncomplainingly for the task to be completed). For example, if you have a mail program in the Startup folder and you've configured it to download an address book each time it starts, the startup time will increase substantially.

4. Not all programs that start automatically are shown on the Startup submenu. To see which other programs are set to start when Windows starts, on the System Tools submenu of the Start menu, click System Information. In the left pane of the System Information window, double-click the Software Environment item to expand it, and then click Startup Programs. In the right pane of the window, note the programs that are listed, and then close the System Information window. Most of these programs probably do need to start when Windows starts, but, if you identify a program that shouldn't be included, check the program's documentation for information about preventing it from starting automatically. Sometimes you'll need to uninstall and then reinstall the program, using different installation choices so that it isn't set to start automatically. ▶

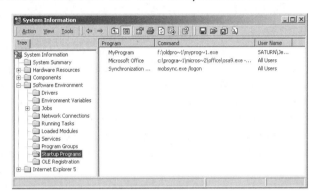

5. Programs can be scheduled to run in other ways too. To see whether a program is scheduled to run when you log on, on the System Tools submenu of the Start menu, click Scheduled Tasks. In the Scheduled Tasks window, see whether a task is scheduled to be run at logon. If so, right-click the task, and click Properties on the shortcut menu. In the dialog box that appears, either clear the Enable check box on the Task tab to prevent the task from being run, or, on the Schedule tab, reschedule the task, and then click OK. Close the Scheduled Tasks window when you've finished. ▶

6. Yet another way a program can be set to run when you start Windows is with a logon *script*—a set of special instructions that are run at logon. If you created the logon script, we'll assume that you know how to edit it to remove unnecessary programs. If you didn't create the script, don't try to modify it—you could create a situation in which you can't log on at all. Instead, try to obtain an updated script from the network administrator or from the person who created the logon script.

7. Another long delay in logging on can occur if your computer is set to use offline files, either from your network or the Internet. For information about modifying the way offline files are synchronized, see "Windows takes a long time to shut down" on page 248.

Windows keeps reconfiguring my computer

Source of the problem

When you add hardware to or remove it from your computer, the change is usually detected when you start Windows, and Windows makes the proper adjustments to your system. This is usually a good thing. However, if you routinely use your computer in two or more different configurations, this repetitive detection and reconfiguration can be annoying and time consuming. For example, if you use a scanner connected to a serial port in one configuration, and you use the same serial port for a modem in another configuration, you'll have to spend time working with Windows to configure one of the devices each time you change the configuration and restart Windows. Fortunately, Windows provides a simple and convenient way to avoid this problem: you can create a separate hardware profile on your computer for each different configuration you use. When you start Windows, all you need to do is select the profile you want to use, and Windows is all set without installing, uninstalling, or disabling support for different pieces of hardware.

How to fix it

1. Windows usually starts with a single profile on your computer that records your current configuration. This profile will be your starting point, so make sure the computer is configured properly for one of your configurations. If you made any changes to the configuration, restart the computer. Log on to the computer as the Administrator.

2. What you're going to do is copy your main profile and then modify it to create a second profile. To copy the profile, right-click My Computer, and click Properties on the shortcut menu. On the Hardware tab, click Hardware Profiles. In the Hardware Profiles dialog box, click your current profile if it isn't already selected, and click Copy.

3. In the Copy Profile dialog box, accept the proposed name or type a descriptive name for the new profile, and click OK. In the Hardware Profiles Selection section, click the option to wait

until you select the profile. Click OK to close the Hardware Profiles dialog box, and click OK again to close the System Properties dialog box.

4. Although you've created a new profile, any hardware changes you make now will be stored in the original profile. To set up your new profile, shut down Windows. Make any hardware changes you want, and then start the computer and Windows. During the startup process, you'll see the Hardware Profile/Configuration Recovery menu. Use the Down arrow key to select the profile you just created, and press Enter.

5. Log on as the Administrator, and do whatever you need to do to configure the hardware on the computer exactly as you want it. Test your setup to verify that everything is working properly.

6. If you'll be using one profile most of the time, right-click My Computer, and click Properties on the shortcut menu. On the Hardware tab, click the Hardware Profiles button. Click the profile that you want to be your default profile, and use the Up arrow, if necessary, to move the profile to the top of the list. In the Hardware Profiles Selection section, click the option to automatically use the first profile, and set the number of seconds to a value long enough to allow you to select a profile at startup. ▶

7. If at some point you find that you use one profile exclusively, and you'd prefer not to see the Hardware Profile/Configuration Recovery menu at startup, you can delete the profile you no longer use. To do so, right-click My Computer, click Properties on the shortcut menu, and, on the Hardware tab, click the Hardware Profiles button. In the Hardware Profiles dialog box, click the profile you don't use, and click the Delete button. Click OK, and then click OK again.

Hardware profiles are for special situations

Profiles are used primarily with portable computers, but they can be used in any system on which you have two or more configurations. A portable computer that has a docking station usually has two profiles—one for when the computer is docked and the other for when it's undocked. In most cases, Windows creates these profiles automatically. When you start the computer or change the docking state, Windows usually detects whether the computer is docked and selects the appropriate profile. Create additional profiles only if you're having problems. You can also create a profile before you make extensive changes to your system. That way, if the system doesn't work correctly after the changes, you can restore the hardware setup to the way it was, and then start Windows using the profile for the original configuration.

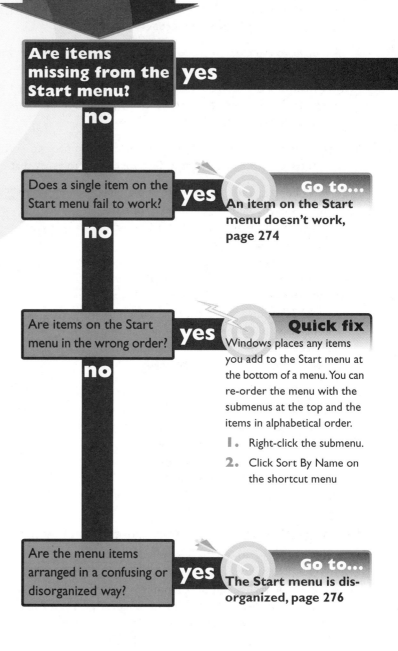

If your Start menu isn't organized the way you want—if it's lacking the items you use all the time and cluttered with those you seldom use—a few mouse clicks will tailor it to your needs. If any items aren't working properly—often the result of a broken connection between the Start menu short-cut and its file—here's where you'll find out how to diagnose and fix the problem.

Are items missing from the Start menu?

yes

no

Does a single item on the Start menu fail to work?

yes

Go to...
An item on the Start menu doesn't work, page 274

no

Are items on the Start menu in the wrong order?

yes

Quick fix

Windows places any items you add to the Start menu at the bottom of a menu. You can re-order the menu with the submenus at the top and the items in alphabetical order.

1. Right-click the submenu.
2. Click Sort By Name on the shortcut menu

no

Are the menu items arranged in a confusing or disorganized way?

yes

Go to...
The Start menu is disorganized, page 276

Are there ≳ symbols at the bottom of a submenu?

yes

Quick fix

You're seeing the personalized menus that Windows adapts based on your usage.

1. To see the entire contents of the menu, click the ≳ symbol, or just wait a few seconds until Windows displays the entire menu.

2. To always display the full menu, right-click a blank spot on the taskbar, click Properties, and, on the General tab, clear the check box option to use personalized menus.

3. Click OK.

no

Are you logged on as you usually are?

yes

Go to...

Some items I want aren't on the Start menu, page 272

no

Quick fix

The Start menu is personalized for each user, and the settings can be stored on the network or on the individual computer.

1. On the Start menu, click Shut Down, click Log Off, and click OK.

2. Log on as usual.

If your solution isn't here

Check these related chapters:

Desktop, page 16

Programs, page 220

Screen, page 230

Starting up, page 260

Taskbar, page 278

Or see the general troubleshooting tips on page xiii

Some items I want aren't on the Start menu

Source of the problem

There are several reasons you might not be able to find one or more of the items you want on the Start menu. For example, a program you need might not be installed on the computer you're using. In that case, you need to install it, and Windows 2000 will probably add it automatically to the Start menu. If, however, the item you need is already on your computer, you can add it to the Start menu for easy access. The item doesn't have to be a program—it can be a document that you use frequently or a folder that you work in every day.

Tip

When you add an item (a program or a document) to the Start menu, Windows creates a shortcut to the item, and it's the shortcut that's added to the Start menu. If you move, rename, or delete the shortcut, the original item isn't affected.

How to fix it

1. To add an item to the Start menu, use My Computer to locate the item, and then drag it onto the Start button. If you want the item to appear in the top section of the main Start menu, release the mouse button. If you want to place the item on a submenu of the Start menu, hold down the mouse button until the Start menu opens. Then drag the item onto the submenu until it opens, move the item onto the submenu, and release the mouse button.

2. If the name of the item isn't appropriately descriptive, right-click the item, and click Rename on the shortcut menu. Type a descriptive name for the item, and click OK.

3. To change the way you open or start an item, right-click it on the Start menu, and click Properties on the shortcut menu. In the item's Properties dialog box, set any options you want. For example, if you always want a particular document to open in a maximized window, click Maximized in the Run list. If you add a descriptive comment, it will appear when you point to the menu item for a moment or two. Click OK when you've made your changes. ▶

4. If you want items other than programs or documents on the Start menu, you'll need to adjust some Windows settings. On the Settings submenu of the Start menu, click Taskbar & Start Menu. On the Advanced tab, select or clear items in the list to display or hide those items on the Start menu, and click OK when you've finished. ▶

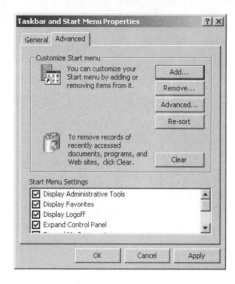

- ● Display Administrative Tools: Creates a menu item on the Programs submenu whose submenu contains all the administrative tools you can normally access from the Administrative Tools item in the Control Panel.

- ● Display Favorites: Creates a menu item on the Start menu whose submenu contains the items listed on the Favorites menu of a folder window.

- ● Display Logoff: Creates a menu item on the Start menu to log off the current user. Functions in the same way as clicking Shut Down on the Start menu and then clicking Log Off in the Shut Down Windows dialog box.

- ● Expand Control Panel: Creates a submenu for the Control Panel on the Settings submenu. The submenu displays all the items normally displayed in the Control Panel.

- ● Expand My Documents: Creates a submenu for the My Documents item on the Documents submenu. The submenu displays all the items in your My Documents folder.

- ● Expand Network And Dial-Up Connections: Creates a submenu on the Settings submenu for the Network And Dial-Up Connections item. The submenu shows the network, the remote connections, and the Make New Connection Wizard items that are usually shown in the Network And Dial-Up Connections window.

- ● Expand Printer: Creates a submenu on the Settings submenu for the Printers item. When opened, the submenu shows the printers and the Add Printer Wizard items that are usually shown in the Printers window.

- ● Scroll The Program Menu: Adds a vertical scroll bar if there are more items on the Programs submenu than can be displayed on the screen at one time.

More about expanding items on the Start menu

When you expand a Start menu item, you gain quick access to the items in the folder but you lose quick access to the folder's window. However, you can always open a folder in its own window from some other location in Windows—for example, by double-clicking the My Documents icon on the Desktop or by right-clicking the menu item and then clicking Open on the shortcut menu.

An item on the Start menu doesn't work

Source of the problem

The items that appear on the Start menu and its sub-menus are actually only shortcuts to the original programs or documents. If anything has happened to the files to which these shortcuts are connected—for example, if the connection to a file has been lost, or if the record of the connection is lost or damaged—the menu item won't work correctly. What you need to do is reestablish the connection between the shortcut and the file.

How to fix it

1. Make sure that any disks or network connections you usually use are in place and connected.

2. On the Start menu, click the item that isn't working. When the Missing Shortcut dialog box appears, wait while Windows searches for the shortcut. ▶

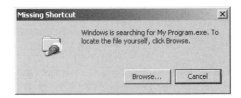

3. If Windows finds the file, the shortcut is reestablished. If Windows can't find the file, the Problem With Shortcut dialog box appears. If it indicates that Windows found a similar file, examine the file's name and location. If this is the correct file, click the Fix It button. The shortcut link should be reestablished, and you'll just need to make sure it works. If this isn't the correct file, however, click Delete It if you want to get rid of the menu item, or click Cancel if you want try to reestablish the link to the item. If the dialog box notifies you that Windows didn't find a similar file, click Yes to delete the item, or click No to try to reestablish the link. If you deleted the menu item, you've eliminated your problem. ▶

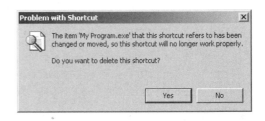

4. On the Start menu, right-click the item that isn't working, and click Properties on the shortcut menu. On the Shortcut tab, note the name of the file in the Target item. If the Target button is grayed (unavailable), click the General tab, and note the location of the file. If the entire location isn't displayed, point to the location, and wait for it to be displayed. Use My Computer to navigate to the location.

5. Search the folder for the file or for the shortcut to the file. Also check to see whether the folder (or any other possible folder) has been renamed. Double-click the Recycle Bin on the Desktop, check to see whether the file was deleted, and restore it if you find it there. If you can't locate the file, click the Search button in the folder window, and search your computer or your network locations for the file.

6. If you find the file or the shortcut, double-click it to open or run it. If it won't run, you'll need to troubleshoot that file. If it does run, open the Start menu, click the item, and, when the Missing Shortcut dialog box appears, click Browse. Locate and click the file, and then click Open.

7. After the shortcut connection has been reestablished, click the item on the Start menu. If the link again fails to work, the file might be corrupted, incorrectly installed, or associated with the wrong type of program, or some of its components might be missing. Again, you'll need to do more troubleshooting on that file.

8. If you still can't locate the file, either ignore its presence on the Start menu and hope that at some point you'll connect to the correct location and that the menu item will work, or simply right-click the item and choose Delete to remove it from the Start menu. Remember that if you do delete the item, you're deleting only the shortcut, not the program or the document itself.

9. If you want to restore a deleted item to the Start menu, you'll need to make a new shortcut to the item. If the item is a program, use its setup program to reinstall it. Windows should automatically add the item to the Start menu. If the item is a document, use your backup files to restore the file, and then add it to the Start menu.

To prevent this

Programs that are added to the Start menu are installed using a setup program. If you delete a program from a folder instead of uninstalling it, the program will remain listed on the Start menu, and you might find that some other programs aren't working properly. This is because you might have deleted some shared files. To remove a program, always use the Add/Remove Programs item in the Control Panel.

More about Start menu shortcuts

The items on the Start menu are shortcuts to files; they're not the files themselves. The file you want to use can be a program, a document (such as a Word document or a data file), or even another shortcut. The purpose of the Start menu shortcut is simply to tell Windows where the file you want is located. If you move a file, Windows tries to locate it for you based on several properties, including date, type, and file size. If you delete a file or move it to a location that becomes inaccessible, such as a removable disk or a dial-up network connection, Windows won't be able to locate the file for you.

And you'll be glad to know that not every problem occurs because of your own actions. Sometimes, when a shortcut goes awry, it's simply one of those rare glitches in Windows. More often, however, it's an indication that there might be a problem with a hardware device such as a disk drive, or that your system has been infected with a virus. If the problem seems inexplicable or if it keeps recurring, scan your computer for viruses, and back up all your data again.

The Start menu is disorganized

Source of the problem

As the Windows 2000 operating system hums along perfectly for months on end, and as you add or delete programs, your computer can accumulate many items on the Start menu and its submenus, often in a very disorganized way. How did the menus become such a disorganized mess? For some reason, most—we won't say all—programmers are convinced that their program is the most important one on your computer, so they want that oh-so-vital program to be placed on the first submenu, if not on the main Start menu itself. If you spend a lot of time trying to figure out where the items you need are hiding, it's time to take control of the Start menu. You can reorganize it for your own convenience, grouping items by the way you use them, and moving the programs least important to you into distant subfolders or even removing them from the Start menu.

> **Tip**
> To make changes to your personalized Start menu and to the items shared by everyone who uses the computer, make the changes to your own settings, and then, in the Start Menu folder that's located under the All Users folder, make the changes that you want to apply to all items.

How to fix it

1. Right-click the Start button, and click either Explore or Explore All Users on the shortcut menu. The Explore command lets you make changes to your personal settings on the Start menu, and the Explore All Users command lets you make changes to the items shared by all users of the computer. The Explore All Users command is available only if you're logged on as a member of the Administrators group.

2. In the Folders area (the left part) of the window that appears, expand the list of subfolders under the Start Menu folder. Each folder represents a submenu of the Start menu. Click to select the folder in which you want to create a submenu. ▶

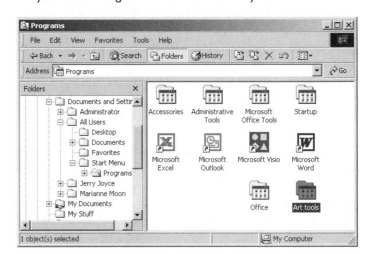

Right-click in the right part of the window, point to New on the shortcut menu, and click Folder on the submenu. Name the new folder, using the name you want to appear on the Start menu. Continue adding folders to create any other Start menu submenus you want.

3. Open the Start menu, but don't close the window (you might need it later). Find the items you want to include in each new folder, and drag them into the new folders. To move an item from an expanded submenu to an unexpanded one, drag the item back to the main menu, and, still holding down the mouse button, drag the item onto the destination submenu. Still holding down the mouse button, wait for the submenu to open, drag the item onto the submenu, and release the mouse button. Continue moving items until the Start menu is organized as you want it. ▶

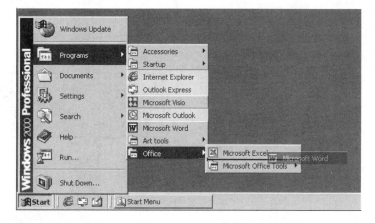

4. If any of the items aren't arranged in the way you want, return to the folder window with the items displayed. Add any new folders, move folders into other folders to create another set of submenus, or move a subfolder out of a folder to move a submenu into a higher-level subfolder. Return to the Start menu to continue your arrangement of the existing items. Drag any other items you want to add from folders or from the Desktop onto the Start menu and then onto the submenus where you want them. If, after you've completed your arrangement, some empty folders remain, return to the folder window and delete them. Close the window when you've finished.

5. On the Start menu, open a submenu and right-click it. On the shortcut menu, click Sort By Name to organize the menu items. Repeat for the other submenus.

More about the Start menu

The Start menu is actually a combination of two menus: the one that's your personalized menu and the one that's listed for All Users. Sometimes the changes you make to the Start menu will affect only your personalized Start menu; at other times they'll affect anyone who uses the computer. Windows will notify you if the changes you make will affect all users. Like almost everything in Windows, changes to the Start menu can be influenced by network policies. Also, your own personalized Start menu items will follow you from one computer to another only if you have a roaming profile and if the computer you're using is set up to accept roaming profiles. If you don't have a roaming profile, your personal settings will be stored only on the computer you're using.

Your Windows 2000 taskbar is a marvel of flexibility and efficiency. If you don't like its size or location, you can make it bigger or smaller, and you can move it to any one of the four sides of your screen. You can add toolbars to it in whatever configurations you prefer. If you want to, you can maximize your screen area by hiding the taskbar when you're not using it and having it reappear only when you need it. If the icons that are displayed in the status area of the taskbar aren't helpful to you, you can remove the ones you don't need and add the ones that are most relevant to your work.

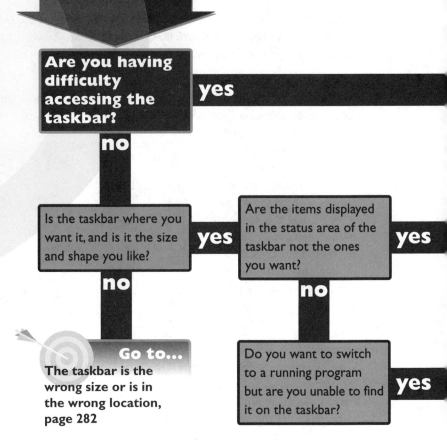

Are you having difficulty accessing the taskbar?

yes

no

Is the taskbar where you want it, and is it the size and shape you like?

yes

no

Go to...
The taskbar is the wrong size or is in the wrong location, page 282

Are the items displayed in the status area of the taskbar not the ones you want?

yes

no

Do you want to switch to a running program but are you unable to find it on the taskbar?

yes

If your solution isn't here
Check these related chapters:
    Date and time, page 10
    Desktop, page 16
    Programs, page 220
    Start menu, page 270
    Toolbars, page 286
Or see the general troubleshooting tips on page xiii

Taskbar

Can you see the taskbar on your screen?

yes

no

Quick fix

If you can see the taskbar but nothing happens when you click it, Windows might be busy doing something else, your mouse might not be working, or Windows might be locked up.

1. Press Ctrl+Esc to open the Start menu. When it opens, click outside the Start menu, and then click a blank spot on the taskbar. If the Start menu opens but nothing happens when you click the mouse, see "Mouse," starting on page 156, for information about diagnosing mouse problems.

2. If the Start menu doesn't open, Windows is probably locked up. See "I can't shut down Windows" on page 244 for information about dealing with a locked-up computer.

Go to...

The taskbar is missing, page 280

Go to...

The items I want aren't on the taskbar, page 284

Quick fix

Some programs are designed not to show up on the taskbar; others can be difficult to detect if the taskbar buttons are very small.

1. Hold down the Alt key and keep pressing the Tab key to cycle through the running programs.

2. If you can't find the program, right-click a blank spot on the taskbar, and click Task Manager on the shortcut menu.

3. On the Applications tab, click the program you want, and click Switch To.

4. Close the Task Manager.

The taskbar is missing

Source of the problem

The taskbar is a control center for your computer. You can use it to switch between programs, access the Start menu, and check the status of your devices. Sometimes, however, the taskbar disappears. If its disappearance is associated with other problems—for example, nothing happens when you double-click a Desktop icon—you probably have a system-wide problem and need to do some troubleshooting. If, however, everything else is working fine and the only problem is that the taskbar is hiding somewhere, you'll need to find it and, if necessary, move it and change some settings so that you won't have problems with the taskbar again.

How to fix it

1. If you have no idea where the taskbar might be, press the Ctrl+Esc key combination. This will make the taskbar appear and will also open the Start menu. If your keyboard has a Windows key, you can press the Windows key to open the Start menu. ▶

2. If your computer is configured with more than one monitor (multiple monitors), and if you don't see the taskbar,

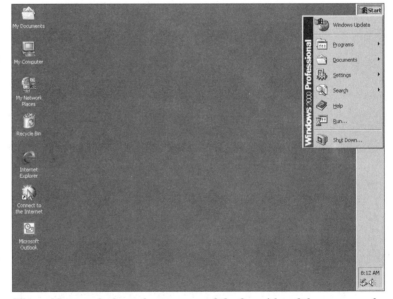

The taskbar can be located at any one of the four sides of the screen, and, if you're using multiple monitors, on any monitor.

turn on all the monitors. If any of the monitors don't display your Desktop, right-click a blank spot on the Desktop of the main monitor, click Properties on the shortcut menu, and, on the Settings tab of the Display Properties dialog box, activate the inactive monitors. Close the dialog box, and press the Ctrl+Esc key combination again. (Multiple monitors is a feature of Windows that lets you spread your Desktop across several monitors. It's a very handy feature for special tasks, such as working on multiple programs simultaneously, but it can be difficult to set up. We discuss multiple monitors in "Multiple monitors," starting on page 168.)

3. On the Setting submenu of the Start menu, click Taskbar & Start Menu to display the Taskbar And Start Menu Properties dialog box. ▶

4. Select the Always On Top check box so that the taskbar won't be obscured by any other windows.

5. Clear the Auto Hide check box to make the taskbar visible at all times, and click OK.

6. If the taskbar is located on a monitor that isn't your primary monitor (for multiple monitors), or is at a side of the screen where you don't want it, point to a blank spot on the taskbar, and drag the taskbar to the edge of the Desktop where you want it.

7. If you want to maximize your screen area by hiding the taskbar when you don't need it, right-click a blank spot on the taskbar, and click Properties on the shortcut menu. In the Taskbar And Start Menu Properties dialog box, select the Auto Hide check box. Make sure the Always On Top check box is selected, and click OK. Click anywhere on the Desktop or in a window, and confirm that the taskbar disappears.

8. Move your mouse pointer to the edge of the screen where the taskbar is hiding, and wait for the taskbar to reappear. Move the mouse pointer off the taskbar, and observe that the taskbar once again disappears.

More about playing hide-and-seek with the taskbar

The taskbar is important for navigating around Windows and accessing programs and documents, but it can take up valuable space on your screen. You can't make the taskbar go away for good, but you can regain the screen area it takes by using either or both of two options. If the Always On Top option isn't selected, you can place portions of a window on top of the taskbar, and the taskbar won't pop up on top of the window. To access the taskbar, you simply move the window out of the way. If you prefer to hide the taskbar when you're not using it, it's best to have the Always On Top option selected so that you can always "unhide" the taskbar.

If you attach a toolbar to the taskbar, the toolbar will be hidden whenever you hide the taskbar. If, instead of attaching a toolbar to the taskbar, you "dock" the toolbar on one side of the screen, the toolbar won't be hidden when you hide the taskbar. A docked toolbar is one that's placed near the edge of the screen. The edge grabs the toolbar and stretches it out to the entire length or width of the screen. An undocked, or "floating," toolbar acts like a little window, so you can move it around, change its size vertically or horizontally, and place it behind other windows. You can also right-click a docked toolbar and then select the Auto Hide option for the toolbar, whether or not you have the taskbar set to disappear. The taskbar, unlike the toolbars, cannot float; it can only be docked.

The taskbar is the wrong size or is in the wrong location

Source of the problem

You can move or resize the taskbar, and you can add toolbars to it. The developers of Windows 2000 built this flexibility into the system so that you could tailor the taskbar to your individual working style. This flexibility, though, can result in a taskbar that's difficult to access, takes up too much room on the screen, or is so condensed that you can have difficulty finding the items you're looking for. However, it's quite simple to drag the taskbar—and its toolbars, if they're attached—around your screen until you find the place where you're most comfortable working with them and can determine the size at which you can most easily see everything they contain.

How to fix it

1. If you want to move the taskbar into a different location, point to a blank spot on the taskbar and drag it to another side of the computer screen. The taskbar can be located at any of the four sides of your screen or, if you're using multiple monitors, at the edge of any one of the screens in use. Any toolbars that are attached to the taskbar remain attached and are moved with the taskbar to the new location.

2. If you've placed the taskbar at the left or right side of the screen, drag the inside edge of the taskbar to widen it so that you can see the text on the buttons. The taskbar will always be stretched to the entire length of the screen. ▶

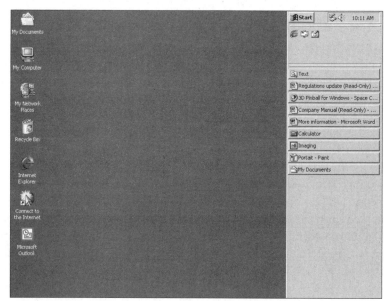

The taskbar and its associated toolbars at the right side of the screen

3. If you've placed the taskbar at the top or bottom of the screen, drag the inside edge of the taskbar to widen it. The result will be that any toolbars attached to the taskbar will be moved into one or more separate rows, providing more space for the taskbar icons. If you have too many taskbar icons to fit into a single row, drag the taskbar further to make it even wider and then display the taskbar icons in two rows. ▶

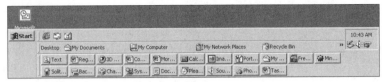

4. If the taskbar (and its attached toolbars) is too wide, drag the inside edge of the taskbar to decrease its width. To maximize the area of the taskbar when the toolbars are on the same line, double-click the small vertical "raised" bar on the taskbar. To manually set the length of the taskbar, drag the raised bar. ▶

The taskbar and its associated toolbars at the bottom of the screen

5. If you don't like the arrangement of the taskbar and the toolbars, you can rearrange them. To re-order the taskbar and the toolbars, keep dragging the raised bar on the taskbar or on a toolbar to the right until you've moved it to the right of the taskbar or to the right of another toolbar. Continue dragging items to the right until you've rearranged everything to your liking. (You can rearrange items by dragging them to the left, but this tends to be more difficult and somewhat prone to failure, so it's best to always drag to the right.) ▶

More about making the taskbar and the toolbars do your bidding

The taskbar and its associated toolbars can provide you with access to almost everything on your computer, on the network, and even on the Internet. The trick is to set the taskbar up in the way that works best for you.

Some people think that one of the taskbar's most appealing and useful features is its ability to disappear when you don't need it and reappear when you do. (There are also those of us who feel that this is an absolutely maddening feature and want no part of it!) If you like playing hide-and-seek with the taskbar, you'll like the Auto Hide feature. To read about using Auto Hide, see "The taskbar is missing" on page 280.

If you want your arrangement of the taskbar and its associated toolbars to be as compact as possible, you can modify the way the toolbars are displayed. For example, you can display only the icons instead of including a text description of each item. And you don't have to attach the toolbars to the taskbar. The toolbars work independently of the taskbar, and you can place them in different parts of the screen. You can even create your own customized toolbars to simplify your work. We discuss toolbars in "Toolbars," starting on page 286.

The items I want aren't on the taskbar

Source of the problem

On the taskbar is a section—variously called the system tray or the status area—that usually displays the time and an array of icons. These icons can be very useful, as they often display the status of a program or other operation, and they can provide a quick link when you want to make changes to your settings or control the operations of a program. Depending on your settings and the programs that are installed on your computer, however, the time might or might not be displayed, and the icons you see might not necessarily be the ones you want displayed.

How to fix it

1. To display the time on the taskbar, right-click a blank spot on the taskbar, click Properties on the shortcut menu, select the Show Clock check box, and click OK. The clock provides three functions: it displays the time when you look at it; it displays the date when you point to it for a second or two; and, when you double-click it, it displays the Date/Time Properties dialog box, where you can change the date and the time or specify the time zone you're in.

2. Removing an icon from the taskbar might require some detective work. To determine the purpose of an icon, point to it and wait for a description of the icon to appear. If the icon was placed on the taskbar by its program, consult the documentation or the Help file that came with the program for information about disabling the icon. If you want to experiment, right-click the icon. If you see a Properties, a Settings, or an Options item on the shortcut menu, click it, and see whether there's an option that lets you remove the icon from the taskbar.

> **Tip**
>
> The icons displayed in the status area of the taskbar fall into two categories: those that Windows places there to change the settings or to display the status of a device or program, and those that other programs place there. You can control most of the Windows icons, but the icons from other programs can be difficult or impossible to remove without uninstalling the program that placed them there.

3. Windows displays some icons automatically. You can display other icons that might make your work a little easier. At the right are the most common ones that you can display or hide, and ▶ following, in the same order, are details about how to display the icons on the taskbar:

- Volume: Double-click the Sounds And Multimedia icon in the Control Panel. On the Sounds tab, select the Show Volume Control On The Taskbar check box, and click OK.

- Locale: Double-click the Regional Options icon in the Control Panel. On the Input Locales tab, select the Enable Indicator On Taskbar check box, and click OK. You must have at least two items in the Input Language list to be able to select this check box.

- Power Meter: Double-click the Power Options icon in the Control Panel. On the Advanced tab, select the Always Show Icon On The Taskbar check box, and click OK. You'll see different icons depending on whether the computer is plugged in or is using a battery.

- Unplug Or Eject Hardware: Double-click the Add/Remove Hardware icon in the Control Panel. Step through the wizard to unplug or eject hardware, and, on the final page of the wizard, select the Show Unplug/Eject Icon On The Taskbar check box.

- Network Connection (including Internet connections): Right-click My Network Places on the Desktop, and click Properties on the shortcut menu. In the Network And Dial-Up Connections window, right-click the network connection, and click Properties on the shortcut menu. On the General tab, select the Show Icon In Taskbar When Connected check box, and click OK.

- CPU Usage: Right-click a blank spot on the taskbar, and click Task Manager on the shortcut menu. Minimize the Task Manager if you want. Whenever the Task Manager is open, the CPU Usage icon is displayed.

- Fax: Double-click the Fax icon in the Control Panel. On the Status Monitor tab, select the Display Icon On Taskbar check box, and click OK.

More about those helpful taskbar icons

You'll probably see other Windows icons on the taskbar, such as the Printer icon when you're printing a document, and the Synchronize icon when you're working with network files off line. These are helpful items that you can use to help manage your work. If you need help figuring out which program has created an icon, and if right-clicking the icon doesn't help, right-click a blank spot on the taskbar, and click Task Manager on the shortcut menu. On the Applications tab of the Task Manager, you'll see which programs are running. Try closing one program at a time to see whether the icon goes away. Be sure, however, to close only the programs that you know are running locally on your computer. Don't close any system programs or programs that are required for safe and stable usage. In other words, close programs at your own risk, first making sure that you've saved any open documents and files.

Some of the programs that create icons are placed in the Startup folder on the Programs submenu of the Start menu, so they start when Windows does. If you want to eliminate any of those icons, and if you don't need the corresponding program to start automatically, move the program out of the Startup folder and into another location on the Start menu. The program won't start automatically, but you can start it by clicking it on the Start menu.

Windows 2000 provides you with toolbars that appear in your folder windows and toolbars that are associated with the taskbar. As you might expect, you can display or hide any of the toolbars, depending on the way you like to work. You can customize most of the existing toolbars by adding the tools you need and deleting those you don't use, and by modifying the way the toolbar buttons appear—specifying, for example, whether you want to see large or small icons on the toolbars and whether you want to include text descriptions for the buttons. If your work involves specialized requirements that the existing toolbars can't meet, you can create the most useful toolbars of all—your own—and can tailor them to your exact needs.

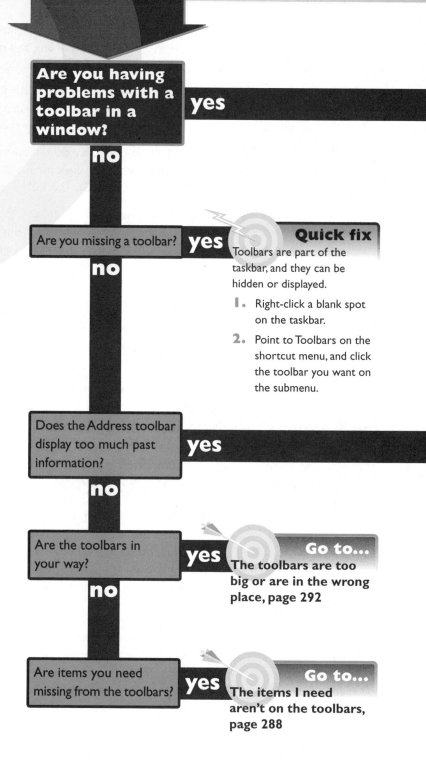

Are you having problems with a toolbar in a window?

yes

no

Are you missing a toolbar? **yes**

no

Quick fix

Toolbars are part of the taskbar, and they can be hidden or displayed.

1. Right-click a blank spot on the taskbar.

2. Point to Toolbars on the shortcut menu, and click the toolbar you want on the submenu.

Does the Address toolbar display too much past information?

yes

no

Are the toolbars in your way? **yes**

no

Go to...
The toolbars are too big or are in the wrong place, page 292

Are items you need missing from the toolbars? **yes**

Go to...
The items I need aren't on the toolbars, page 288

Is a toolbar you want missing from a folder window?

yes

no

Can you not find the items you want on the toolbars?

yes

Go to...
I can't find the items I want on the toolbars, page 290

Quick fix

There are four toolbars that can be displayed in a folder window. There are also five Explorer Bars that work in a manner similar to that of a toolbar.

1. Right-click a blank spot on a toolbar or on the menu bar.

2. On the shortcut menu, click an unchecked toolbar to display it or click a checked toolbar to hide it.

3. To display the Search, Favorites, History, Folders, or Tip Of The Day Explorer Bar, on the View menu, point to Explorer Bar, and click the one you want. Other than the Tip Of The Day Explorer Bar, you can have only one Explorer Bar open in a single window.

Quick fix

If the history of what you've accessed from the Address toolbar is too revealing to others or is no longer relevant, you can clear the list. By doing so, however, you'll delete other histories, including the list of recently used documents shown in the My Documents subfolder of the Start menu.

1. Right-click the taskbar, and click Properties on the shortcut menu.

2. On the Advanced tab, click the Clear button.

3. Click OK to close the dialog box.

If your solution isn't here
Check these related chapters:
Or see the general troubleshooting tips on page xiii

The items I need aren't on the toolbars

Source of the problem

The toolbars that are associated with the taskbar—the ones adjacent to the taskbar, floating on the Desktop, or docked at one side of the Desktop—are useful tools and great time savers. However, their basic settings don't always provide all the tools you need. You can remedy this situation either by adding the items you want to the existing toolbars or by creating your own custom toolbars. When you design your own toolbars, you specify every item on a toolbar, from programs to documents to printers. Custom toolbars can make your work go so smoothly that you might never use the standard Windows toolbars again.

How to fix it

1. You can add only specific types of items to each of the existing toolbars. The Desktop toolbar displays the items that are sitting on your Desktop (even if the icons are hidden by the Active Desktop settings). To add an item to the Desktop toolbar, you place the item on the Desktop. You can, however, reverse the process—that is, you can place an item on the Desktop toolbar, and the item will be added to the Desktop. For example, if you drag a web site address from the Address toolbar onto the Desktop toolbar, the shortcut to that web site will be added to the Desktop and will appear on the Desktop toolbar.

2. The Links toolbar is designed to provide links to web pages, and it comes with a few predefined links. Surprisingly, the Customize Links button doesn't let you customize the Links toolbar but instead takes you to a web page about customizing. This doesn't mean that you can't add or delete links, nor does it mean that you can add links only to web pages. To delete links that you don't want, right-click the link on the toolbar, click Delete on the shortcut menu, and, if you're asked to confirm the deletion, click Yes. To add a link, drag an item (or a shortcut to it) onto the Links toolbar. Windows will create a shortcut to the item or to the shortcut. You can also drag the buttons on the Links toolbar to reposition them. Note that the Links toolbar on the Desktop is connected to the Links toolbar in a folder window and in Internet Explorer. Any changes you make to a Links toolbar will appear on all the Links toolbars. ▶

On this floating Links toolbar, some items have been added, some renamed, and some deleted. The links don't have to be links to web pages.

3. The Address toolbar can, by definition, contain only addresses. Those addresses, however, can lead to a variety of locations. Although the Address toolbar is handy for quickly going to web pages, you can also use it to go to a folder on your computer or on the network. To do so, though, you need to include the folder's full path, so it's usually easier to get to a location by using My Computer. However, if someone sends you a document or an e-mail message that contains the address of a web page or a shared folder, but that address isn't formatted as a link that you can click, you can copy the address in the document (select the address, and press Ctrl+C), click in the Address toolbar, and press Ctrl+V to paste the address. Then press Enter or click the Go button to go to that location.

4. The Quick Launch toolbar can be invaluable because it can contain almost any type of item. To add an item to the Quick Launch toolbar, simply locate the item and drag it onto the toolbar. Unless you have the toolbar set to display text—which helps identify the items but takes up substantial space—you'll need to carefully select which items you add so that you can tell which is which. Because programs use immediately recognizable icons, it's usually a good idea to limit your additions to programs or items such as My Documents or Control Panel, whose icons are easily identifiable without text labels. ▶

The Quick Launch toolbar, docked with the taskbar, shows the distinctive icons of programs, along with some special folders.

5. The most versatile toolbar of all is the one you create yourself. To create a toolbar, you use a folder in which you place all the items you want on the toolbar, and then you tell Windows to create a toolbar based on that folder. To do so, either create a folder in a secure location on your computer, or use My Computer to locate an existing folder that you want to use. Open the folder and place in it only the items you want on the toolbar. If you created shortcuts, or if there are files without good descriptive names, rename them. When the folder contains all the items you want on the toolbar, click the Up button on the folder's Standard Buttons toolbar to move to the parent folder. Now drag the folder onto the taskbar. Right-click the name of the new toolbar, and click a command on the shortcut menu to customize the toolbar by displaying or hiding names or modifying the size of the buttons.

Warning

Unlike other toolbars that contain only shortcuts to items, a custom toolbar contains direct connections to the items in the folder. Therefore, if you delete an item from a custom toolbar, you could be deleting a document or a program. To prevent the accidental deletion of programs or important documents, the folder you use to create a custom toolbar should contain shortcuts only.

6. If you want the toolbar to be a floating toolbar, drag it onto the Desktop. Use the toolbar just as you use any other toolbar. If you move a file or folder onto the toolbar, you'll be adding that item to the folder that's the source of the toolbar. If you close your custom toolbar, it will be deleted, so don't close it until you're sure you won't need it again. However, when you do close it, the contents of the folder still exist and are unchanged. When you want to use the toolbar again, you simply drag the folder back onto the taskbar.

I can't find the items I want on the toolbars

Source of the problem

The four toolbars that appear in your folder windows are the Standard Buttons, Address Bar, Links, and Radio toolbars. You can hide or display these toolbars, move and arrange them, and even customize some of them. You might sometimes have problems accessing certain items on a toolbar if your arrangement of the toolbars hides the items you want, or if the items you want simply aren't on any of the toolbars. To remedy this problem, you can hide the toolbars you don't want and rearrange the remaining toolbars so that there's enough room to display the items you want. You can customize the Standard Buttons toolbar if you want either to display additional items or to hide items you don't use, and you can also modify the way the buttons appear on the toolbar.

How to fix it

1. Double-click My Computer on the Desktop. Right-click a blank spot on one of the toolbars or on the menu bar. On the short-cut menu, click a checked tool-bar name to hide that toolbar or click an unchecked tool-bar name to display that toolbar. ▶

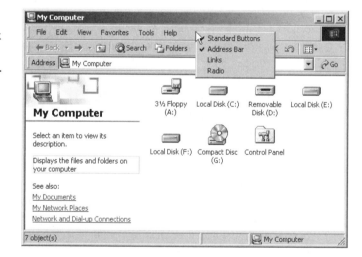

2. If the toolbars are crowded onto one or two lines, you can either expand the toolbars you want to use and compress the other toolbars, or you can move the toolbars onto separate lines. To expand a toolbar, double-click the "raised" vertical bar at the left of the toolbar. This maximizes the length of that toolbar and minimizes the length of the other toolbars. To adjust a toolbar to a specific length, drag the raised bar. You can also click the double chevrons (>>) to see the hidden buttons. ▶

3. If you'd rather see the entire toolbar on a separate line, point to the raised bar at the left of the toolbar, and, when the mouse pointer turns into a two-headed arrow, drag the toolbar down below the other toolbars. ▲

4. If items are missing from the Standard Buttons toolbar, if there are items on it that you never use and want to remove, or if you simply don't like the way the toolbar looks, you can modify it. To do so, right-click a blank spot on the Standard Buttons toolbar, and click Customize on the shortcut menu.

5. In the Customize Toolbar dialog box, click an item in the Available Toolbar Buttons list that you want to add to the toolbar, and then click Add. Continue adding any other items you want. To remove an item from the toolbar, click it in the Current Toolbar Buttons list, and click Remove.

6. When all the items you want on the Standard Buttons toolbar are in the Current Toolbar Buttons list, you'll probably want to organize the list. The order of items from top to bottom in the list determines the order from left to right in which the buttons are displayed on the toolbar. To change the order in the list, click an item you want to move, and then click the Move Up or the Move Down button. Continue moving items in the list until everything is arranged as you want. ▶

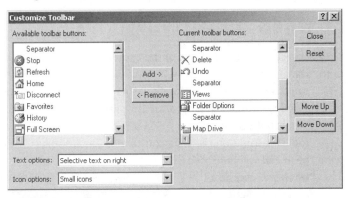

7. If you want to make changes to the appearance of the buttons on the toolbar, use the Text Options list at the bottom of the dialog box to specify whether you want text descriptions for any, some, or all of the buttons. In the Icon Options list, specify whether you want to see small or large icons on the toolbar. Click Close when you've finished.

8. If you don't like the results of the toolbar customization, return to the Customize Toolbar dialog box, and either modify the items in the various lists or click the Reset button to restore the Standard Buttons toolbar to its default layout.

Tip

For information about customizing the Links toolbar, adding items to other toolbars, and creating your own toolbars, see "The items I need aren't on the toolbars" on page 288.

The toolbars are too big or are in the wrong place

Source of the problem

Windows 2000 provides four toolbars associated with the taskbar: these are the Address, Links, Desktop, and Quick Launch toolbars. Although these toolbars are very useful and can, in fact, be invaluable, they can also get in your way and take up a lot of room on your screen. To make the toolbars efficient tools rather than obstacles to your work, you can change their size, shape, and location, and you can even redesign them by reaching a compromise between the size of a toolbar and the amount of information you want it to display. You can also set your toolbars to be hidden from view when you don't need them and to reappear when you do.

How to fix it

1. Look at the arrangement of the toolbars and decide what you want to be displayed and what you want to modify. If there's a toolbar you never use, close it. (When you close one of the Windows toolbars, the toolbar isn't lost but is simply hidden.) To close a toolbar, right-click a blank spot on the taskbar or on a toolbar, point to Toolbars on the shortcut menu, and click the toolbar's name on the submenu to close it. A toolbar with a check mark next to its name is open and will be closed when you click it; a toolbar without a check mark is closed and will be opened when you click it. ▶

> **Tip**
>
> If you have a custom toolbar, it will be lost when you close it. The contents of the folder on which the toolbar was based, however, remain intact.

2. When only the tool-bars you want are open, you can move or resize the remaining toolbars to fit your working style. To maximize the length of a toolbar, double-click the "raised" vertical bar at the beginning of the toolbar. Double-click the raised bar again to minimize the toolbar's length. To move a toolbar, point to the raised bar and drag the toolbar to the location you want. If you drag the tool-bar along the same line occupied by the other toolbars, it will change in relationship to those toolbars or to the taskbar. If you

> **Tip**
>
> Toolbars have their own terminology. A toolbar that's connected to the edge of the Desktop is "docked"; a toolbar on the Desktop that has its own title bar is "floating."

drag the toolbar away from the adjacent toolbars and onto the Desktop, it will become a separate floating toolbar, which looks like a little window. You can move a floating toolbar any-

where on the Desktop, and you can resize it by dragging one of its sides. To move a floating toolbar, drag it by its title bar. To turn a floating toolbar back into a docked toolbar, drag it to one side of the Desktop until it becomes docked. ▶

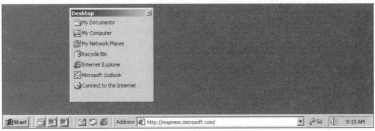

In this situation, the Desktop toolbar was moved onto the Desktop to become a floating toolbar, and it was then resized. The docked toolbars and the attached taskbar were rearranged and resized.

3. You can customize a toolbar's appearance to get it out of your way or to help you figure out how to use it. ▶ To customize a toolbar, right-click the raised bar or a blank spot on the toolbar that you want to modify, and do any of the following:

The floating Quick Launch toolbar is set to show text. The Desktop toolbar is set to show no title, no text, and to use large icons.

- Click Show Title on the shortcut menu to hide or display the name of the toolbar. (This option works only for a docked toolbar.)

- Point to View on the shortcut menu, and click an icon size on the submenu. (This option isn't available for the Address toolbar.)

Tip

For more information about controlling toolbars that are attached to the taskbar, see "The taskbar is the wrong size or is in the wrong location" on page 282.

- Click Show Text on the shortcut menu to hide or display the text descriptions of the icons. (This option isn't available for the Address toolbar.)

- Click Always On Top on the shortcut menu if it's unchecked to make sure the toolbar is always visible, or click the option if it's checked to be able to place windows on top of the toolbar. (This option isn't available when the toolbar is docked with the taskbar.)

- Click Auto-Hide on the shortcut menu if it's unchecked to make the toolbar disappear when you don't need it and to make it reappear when you move the mouse to the edge of the Desktop where the toolbar is docked; or click the option if it's checked to make sure that the toolbar is always visible. (This option is available only for toolbars docked at a side of the Desktop that doesn't contain the taskbar.)

Installing a service pack

Although Windows 2000 Professional is a great operating system, it's not perfect. To remedy problems that have been discovered since the program was created, Microsoft provides service packs that contain fixes for bugs in the operating system, that resolve unexpected interactions with different software and hardware, and that even contain some updated software to work with new technology. Windows service packs are inclusive—that is, the most recent one contains all the fixes that were included in all previous service packs, so you need to install only the current service pack. You've probably already seen several references to service packs throughout this book. If you've determined that you need a service pack, here's how to obtain and install it.

Setting up

Take a look to see whether you have a service pack already installed, and, if so, which one. Double-click My Computer on the Desktop, and, in the My Computer window, click About Windows on the Help menu. In the About Windows dialog box, you'll see the version number and build number of Windows. If there's a service pack installed on your computer, it will be noted next to

the build number. Otherwise, no service pack has been installed. Click OK to close the dialog box.

You can quickly see whether you already have a service pack installed, and, if so, which one.

To install a service pack, you'll need to do a little preparation. There's always some risk when you modify your system, so it's wise to prepare for the worst. Your first step is to create a new ERD (emergency repair disk), and then to back up your entire system. For information about creating an updated ERD, see Appendix B, "Editing the Registry," on page 297. To back up your system, use the Backup program on the System Tools submenu of the Start menu, or use whatever backup method has been provided to you on your network. You'll also need to know how much free disk space you have, because installing the service pack can take a large amount of disk space. In My Computer, click the drive on which you're going to install the service pack, and write down the amount of free disk space you have—you'll need this information later.

Installing

You can obtain a service pack from several sources, so choose the most convenient one.

- Download the service pack from Windows Update (on the Start menu, click Windows Update) or from the Microsoft Windows web page at *http://www.microsoft.com/windows*. On the web site, download and install only the elements you need, or download the entire service pack so that you can install it on your computer and/or other computers on your network. Installing only the elements you need requires the least free disk space of any download method.

- Install the service pack from a network location to which it has already been downloaded. Ask your network administrator for the location and for any installation instructions.

- Ask the network administrator to install the service pack on your computer during non-office hours.

- Obtain the service pack on a CD from Microsoft, and install it from the CD. The CD might contain other elements that aren't part of the downloaded service pack, so explore the CD for all the features it contains. Check the Windows web site for details about ordering the service pack CD.

Before you continue, read the documentation that came along with whichever method you used to download the service pack. Pay particular attention to the amount of free disk space that's required. Make sure you've disabled any virus-protection software that's running on your computer, and then proceed with installing the service pack, following the instructions provided in the documentation.

Note that you have the option of backing up your current files so that you can uninstall the entire service pack if you have problems. Accept this option unless you don't have enough disk space to back up the system. However, without backing up the system, you'll be unable to uninstall the service pack if you encounter problems.

If you installed the service pack successfully but are experiencing problems that you think might be caused by the service pack, check the service pack documentation on the Windows web site to see whether there's a known problem with the service pack or with the item that's misbehaving. If you can't resolve the problem, you can uninstall the service pack, provided you backed up the files to enable uninstalling when you installed the service pack. To uninstall the service pack, in the Control Panel, double-click the Add/Remove Programs icon, and, in the Add/Remove Programs dialog box, click the service pack, and then click the Change/Remove button. Confirm that you want to remove the service pack, and follow the instructions on the screen.

Editing the Registry

We really hope this book is helping you solve any problems you've run into with Windows 2000, but if you've struggled with a question we haven't covered, and if you've sought advice elsewhere, you might have been told to edit the Registry. You'll notice that nowhere in this book have *we* suggested that you edit the Registry. Why? Because the Registry is *very* scary, and because, in most cases, you can solve a problem by making changes to settings or by using tools that make changes to settings. In doing so, you keep the Registry protected from experimentation, mistyping, or general misunderstanding of the task at hand. However, there are some problems—usually specific to a particular program or piece of hardware—that might require you to make edits directly in the Registry.

So what *is* the Registry? It's a hidden database that Windows uses and maintains to keep track of all your settings. When you start up, Windows reads the Registry. When you make changes to your system, Windows updates the data in the Registry. When you shut down your computer and wait for Windows to save your settings, it's updating the Registry. Sometimes, when you try to repair your system, you're using the Registry without realizing it—for example, if you start Windows using the Last Known Good

Configuration option, you're using a special feature of the Registry that restores the previous Registry settings. And if you use the Repair feature of Windows, you're using a copy of the Registry—either on the ERD (emergency repair disk) or one that's stored in a Repair folder on your hard disk. As you can see, messing up the Registry is definitely not a good idea. However, if you really need to work directly with the Registry, your first safety measure should be to back it up.

Back it up

Before you back up the Registry, make sure everything is working correctly. If you've messed up your system, fix it, and then back up the Registry. If you've already edited the Registry and made a mess of it, it's too late to back it up. You'll have to restore the old Registry first, using the Windows Repair process and losing any changes you've made since the last time the Registry was backed up. When everything is working correctly, back up the Registry using the Microsoft Windows Backup program.

To create your backup, on the System Tools submenu of the Start menu, click Backup. On the Welcome tab of the Backup program window, click the Emergency

Repair Disk button, and follow the instructions on the screen. Be sure to use a blank disk, and label it with the date. It's important to keep your existing ERD in addition to the one you're creating now until you're certain there are no problems with your current Registry settings.

While you're creating the ERD, you also have the option of backing up the Registry to the Repair folder on the hard disk. This is a good safeguard—you can use this copy of the disk if you can't find your ERD when you're repairing your Windows installation. And while you're busy backing up, it's a good idea to back up your entire system if you haven't done so recently.

Edit with caution

After you've created your backup copies of the Registry, you can proceed with the editing, using the special tool that Windows provides. You will, of course need to be logged on as the Administrator, although special permission can be assigned for editing the Registry. If necessary, check with whoever normally administers your computer. Note that most instructions about editing the Registry include some type of disclaimer that tells you how dangerous it is to edit the Registry, and that you need to do so very carefully and at your own risk. Take these messages seriously! Making the wrong entries can mess up your system so badly that you could lose access to Windows and to your hard disk. If you're willing to take

the risk, make sure you have precise directions from a reliable source about what to edit and how to do it, and that the process has been thoroughly tested.

To start the Registry Editor, click Run on the Start menu. In the Open box, type **regedt32**, and press Enter. With the Registry Editor open, follow the directions you've been given to make your changes. You'll probably have been given a "key"—a database item that contains data for a specific purpose—in the editing instructions. A key in the Registry Editor is represented by a folder, which might have subkeys in it. An easy but sometimes time-consuming way to find a specific key is to use the Find Key command on the View menu. Type the key name exactly as it was given to you, and click Find Next. If the key that's found isn't the one you're looking for, keep clicking Find Next until you locate the correct key. Then click Cancel, double-click the item to be changed, make the change, and then close the Registry Editor. Your change is saved automatically.

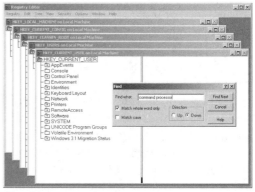

Searching for the key that you want to edit is the easiest way to locate the correct item in the very large and complex Registry.

Gathering information

In the world of troubleshooting, your greatest ally is information. The correct information does more than just help you figure out what's wrong. You can use it to document your system when it's working correctly so that you'll be able to reconfigure the system without creating conflicts with the current configuration. You can also use the information to restore your settings if you've made some unwise changes. In many cases you'll need to be logged on as an Administrator to access the information.

Use the tools

The following tools can be helpful, although some of them gather too much information to be of any practical use—most of it written in codes and terminologies that surely only an engineer could love.

System Information

The System Information tool collects all sorts of information in one place. It's often used when someone is trying to fix your computer over a network or on the Internet. It's useful for getting basic information

about your computer and all the elements connected to it. The nice thing is that you can save the results to a text file, from which you can then extract the information that's relevant to your needs. For example, if you want to install some hardware for which you must manually set the IRQs (hardware interrupt requests), you can print a list of the IRQs the computer is currently using and then set the hardware to a free IRQ. There are many other uses for the information, so it's handy to keep the full text file available on a floppy disk. That way, you can access it from another computer if your computer is shut down or won't start.

To obtain the information about your system, on the System Tools submenu of the Start menu, click System Information. In the

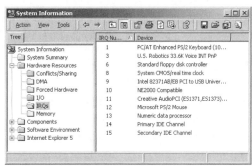

The System Information tool provides technical information about your computer system.

left pane of the System Information window, click the item you're interested in, and then read the information in the right pane. For example, to see a list of the IRQs your computer is using, click IRQs under Hardware Resources.

To save the information you're currently viewing to a text file, select the item in the left pane, and click the Save Text Report button on the toolbar. To create a master file of all the information the System Information tool can record, click the System Information item at the top of the left pane, and click the Save Text Report button. You'll probably have to wait a few minutes as the information is gathered up and written to a text file.

Task Manager

You're probably familiar with using Task Manager to shut down a program that's misbehaving, but it's also a good place to gather information on how your system and your programs are functioning. On the Performance tab, you'll see a graphic representation of your CPU and Memory usage. CPU usage is a measure of how much computing your computer is doing at the moment. If the CPU usage is very high, expect your system to slow down. To learn more about the various statistics, use the Help menu to search for each item.

The Processes tab of Task Manager identifies any program that's overtaxing your system. You won't recognize all the items—some are programs that Windows runs behind the scenes. You should, however, be able to identify many of the programs and establish whether one is hogging most of the CPU or memory usage.

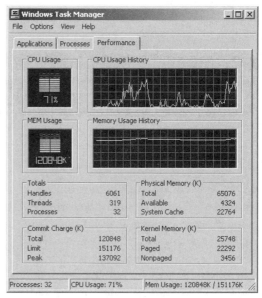

The Performance tab shows graphs and data that tell you how hard your computer is working.

Computer Management

We've discussed Computer Management several times in this book. Besides using it to monitor shared folders, fix the hardware on your computer, and manage the users on a computer, it also provides useful technical

The Computer Management window displays details about your hard disks and drives, and provides access to many other reporting tools.

information about your computer's hard disks and removable storage, plus access to logs that we'll discuss later. To open the Computer Management window, double-click Administrative Tools in the Control Panel, and then double-click Computer Management. For information about your hard disks and how they're set up, click Disk Management under the Storage item. Click Logical Drives to see how all your drives are set up, including any network drives that you've created. To see a list of the removable media on your computer, click Physical Locations under Removable Media.

View the logs

Windows maintains logs that record information about the way the system operates and that note any problems. There's also a log that records data when a program or the system becomes unstable. Much of this information won't be of use to you, but you might find tidbits here and there that will help you figure out what's wrong. These logs, however, are valuable to technicians when they're diagnosing a problem.

Event Viewer

Event Viewer is a tool for viewing the Applications log, the Security log, and the System log.

Event Viewer displays logs that contain information about events such as warnings and errors.

● The Applications log records events related to the programs running on your computer—the programs Windows uses, as well as those you use.

● The Security log records Windows security events. Security audits must be activated in the network group policies or the local security policy. Use the Local Security Policy item in the Administrative Tools folder to activate security auditing on your computer.

● The System log records all the events that occur on your computer.

To use Event Viewer, double-click Administrative Tools in the Control Panel, and double-click Event Viewer in the Administrative Tools window. To see a list of recorded items, click the log in the left pane. To see details of a log entry, double-click the entry in the right pane. You can save the log to a file so that you can send it to a technician or view it at leisure if you enjoy reading log files. To save a log, click it in the left pane of Event Viewer, and click Save Log File As on the Action menu. In the Save As dialog box, you can save the log in one of three formats: as an Event Log, as a text file, or as a comma-separated (delimited) text file. Save the log as an Event Log if you'll be sending it to a technician for help—the Event Log format can be opened in Event Viewer and contains more information than does a file saved in text format.

Note that these logs fill up fairly quickly and stop recording events when they're full. If you receive a message that a log is full, open Event Viewer, click the log in question, save its contents, and then click Clear All Events on the Action menu.

Services

Services isn't exactly a log, but it works like one. It lists all the services that are set up on the computer, and tells you if they're running and whether they're configured to start manually or automatically. Services differs from a log in that you can double-click a service and manually start or stop it, change how it's started, and even change what happens if the service either doesn't start or suddenly stops. You probably won't want to use any of these features—you can cause unexpected results when you change the settings for a service. To view the list of services, double-click Administrative Tools in the Control Panel, and, in the Administrative Tools window, double-click Services. Check the status of any service in question, and then close the Services window.

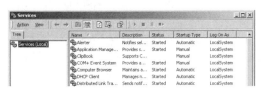

The Services window shows the status for all the services Windows has installed.

Dr. Watson

This tool starts automatically when there's a major problem with the system, and it writes a log that documents the problem. The log, as you might expect, is written for repair technicians, and is therefore mostly indecipherable. If you want to take a look at it and see whether there's anything you can get from it, search your hard disk for the file *drwtsn32.log*, and open it in Notepad. In most cases you'll want to include this file when a technician is working on your problems from a remote location.

Crash records

This information is strictly for repair technicians and can't be read without special tools. What is saved, however, is customizable. To set up the way information about your system is to be recorded, while you're logged on as the Administrator, right-click My Computer, and click Properties on the shortcut menu. On the Advanced tab of the System Properties dialog box, click Startup And Recovery. In the Write Debugging Information section of the Startup And Recovery dialog box, click the type of log you want.

The Small Memory Dump provides a snapshot of what went wrong, keeps a record of every crash you've had, and is often all that's needed by a technician. If you're asked to provide more information the next time the system crashes, specify a different type of memory dump—being aware that you'll be creating very large files. A full memory dump uses the same amount of disk space as the number of MB of memory you have, plus one additional MB. For example, if you have 128 MB of memory, the memory dump file will be approximately 129 MB. If you need to send the file to a technician, you'll find the dump file in the folder specified in the Dump File box.

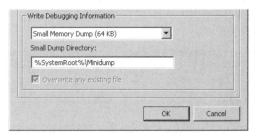

Use the Startup And Recovery dialog box to set up the type of information dump that's recorded when your computer crashes.

Index

cluttered, 16, 20–21
color schemes, 18
customizing, 18–19
displaying only portions
    on screen, 231
folders on, 21
folder status of, 21
icon size and fonts, 18
missing items, 17, 22–23
moving files off, 21
on multiple monitors, 169
patterns on, 19
performance and, 19
problems fitting on screen,
    240–41
screen area size, 231, 238–39
shortcuts on, 16
tiling windows on, 83
troubleshooting flowchart,
    16–17
turning off Active Desktop, 27
undoing severe house-
    cleaning, 21
virtual Desktop, 240
web content on, 18
Desktop toolbar, 23, 288, 292
Details view, 80, 85
detecting
free disk space, 227
misidentified hardware, 100–101
modems, 147, 148–49
mouse devices, 158–59
multiple monitor adapters, 170
new hardware, 96–99
printers, 204
wheels on mouse devices, 161
Device Manager symbols, 102
devices. See hardware; modems;
    mouse devices; USB devices
Device Troubleshooting
    Wizard, 103
DHCP (Dynamic Host
    Configuration Protocol)
    servers, 114
diagnosing problems, xiv
diagnostic tools
DirectX Diagnostic tool, 91, 233
querying modems, 150
diagrams. See troubleshooting
    flowcharts
dialing, operator-assisted, 151
dialing failures, 147, 150–51
dialing, on-demand, 119, 121

dialing rules, 35, 151, 152
dialog boxes displayed on wrong
    monitors, 174–75
dial tone, waiting for, 151
dial-up connections
dialing rules, 35
game performance, 94
ICS host computers, 113, 119
modem connection speeds, 106
modem troubleshooting, 146–47
on-demand dialing, 119, 121
to other computers, 152–53
remote connection problems, 31
repetitive dialing, 34
slow modem performance, 154
troubleshooting flowchart,
    28–29
using instead of ICS
    connections, 112, 116–17
wrong connection to Internet,
    116–17
digital business cards (vCards), 187
digital IDs, 186
digital signatures, 187
Direct3D, 233
DirectDraw, 88, 233
directories, file-sharing permissions
    and, 7
DirectSound, 233
DirectX Diagnostic tool, 91
DirectX software
Administrator logon and, 233
checking installation of, 91
conflicts with games, 90
cursor problems and, 93
diagnostic tools, 233
role in screen display, 232
sound adapters and, 91
strange mouse pointers and,
    166–67
upgrading software for, 89
disabled dual booting, 46
disabled hardware icon, 102
disabled Heap Manager, 227
disabled modems, 148
disabled ports, 205
disassembling mouse devices, 162
disconnecting
from MSN, 35
unwanted disconnections, 28,
    34, 119
USB hubs, 126
discount hours for faxing, 73

Disk Cleanup tool, 107
Disk Defragmenter program, 37
disk drives. See hard drives
display, screen. See screen display
display adapters
AGP and PCI adapters, 173
compatibility, 171, 234, 236
cursor problems and, 93
DirectX and, 90
disabled, 168
Hibernate mode and, 231
nonfunctioning secondary
    monitors, 170–71
onboard or integrated, 173
primary and secondary, 173
slow performance, 234–35
displaying
Active Desktop items, 23, 25
administrative tools on Start
    menu, 273
clock on taskbar, 10
CPU usage on taskbar, 285
e-mail messages, 179
Explorer Bars, 287
faxes, 58, 64–65
fax icon on taskbar, 285
fax printer icon, 69
file extensions, 49
file information in folders,
    80–81
files to be deleted, 38
folder windows, 78–81
font problems, 133
fonts on web sites, 108–9
international characters on web
    sites, 105, 110–11
keyboard shortcuts, 134
last user's name in logon,
    144–45
locale information on
    taskbar, 285
Log Off command on Start
    menu, 273
missing Desktop icons, 22
modem command logs, 150
mouse pointers correctly, 93
network connection icon on
    taskbar, 285
pictures on Desktop, 19
power meter on taskbar, 285
Start menu Favorites, 273
Start menu submenus, 271
system files, 49

keyboards, *continued*
  troubleshooting flowchart, 124–25
  wireless, 126
keyboard shortcuts and key commands. *See* shortcuts and key commands
keypads, 129, 135
keys
  e-mail certificates, 186
  public, 187
  in Registry, 298
keystrokes, repeated, 131
Knowledge Base, xvii, 199

labeling removable disks, 36–37, 44–45
languages
  adding language files, 110
  problems entering special characters, 124, 128–29
  switching keyboard to other languages, 129
  on web sites, 105, 109, 110–11
  wrong characters are displayed, 132–33
LAN settings, 116–17
laptop computers. *See* portable computers
large text and icons on screen, 19, 80, 231, 238–39
Large Windows scheme, 239
Last Known Good Configuration
  Registry and, 297
  starting up with, 127, 262
last user's name, 145
layout of faxes, 68, 72–73
leaving copies of messages on servers, 181
left-handed mouse use, 160
Like Current Folder option, 79
limiting access
  dial-up access, 29
  encrypted files, 56–57
  to files or folders, 9
  logging on, 2–3
  network files, 6–7
  to printers, 213
  remote connections, 30–31
  removable media, 44–45

line delays in data transfers, 153
line ends in data transfers, 153
line feeds in data transfers, 153
Line In port, 254
lines on screen instead of startup, 230
links. *See also* shortcut icons and menu commands
  to items on Start menu, 274
  on Links toolbar, 288
Links toolbar, 288, 290, 292
listing
  all screen modes, 235
  compatible software, 34
  currently installed programs, 222
  file names in folders, 80
  removable media drives, 301
  services on computers, 302
List view, 80
local accounts
  accounts on other computers, 143
  changing computer settings, 4
  logging on, 136–37, 138
  new accounts, 139
local area connections (ICS), 114–15, 121
locales, regional, 129, 285
local groups, 5
local printer ports, 217
local printers
  nonfunctional, 204–7
  troubleshooting flowchart, 202–3
local security policies
  changing logon policy, 144
  defined, 45
  listing, 145
  local permissions, 44
  log files, 301
locating. *See entries beginning with* finding
location of temporary files, 227
locked-up or frozen computers. *See* crashes
log files, 263, 301–2
logging off
  forced logoffs, 247
  logoff command on Start menu, 273
  no Shut Down option available, 244
  synchronizing files, 248

logging on
  accessing computers without permission, 137
  automatic remote connections, 32–33
  dial-up connection trouble-shooting flowchart, 28–29
  logon scripts, 267
  networks and, 142–43
  not requiring passwords, 137, 140–41
  permission denied, 2–3
  problems accessing networked computers, 29
  problems logging on, 138–39
  remote connections, 29, 30–31
  running as other user, 5
  slow startups and, 266
  someone else's name is listed, 144
  Start menu and, 271
  time or date problems, 11
  troubleshooting flowchart, 136–37
logical drive information, 301
logon scripts, 267
losing
  file information, 81
  file or folder security settings, 9
loud logon music, 251
lowercase characters in passwords, 138
low power management levels, 67, 190
LPT ports. *See* parallel ports
L (repair option), 51

M (repair option), 51
main identity for e-mail, 184
MAKEBOOT program, 265
managing power options. *See* power management
manual functions
  answering fax calls, 60, 63
  checking e-mail, 182
  dialing modem calls, 151
  Standby or Hibernate mode, 192
  updating Active Desktop, 24, 25
  updating folder display, 77

manual repair process, 51, 263
manufacturers' names for hardware, 99, 101, 149
MAPI (Messaging Application Programming Interface), 61
marking messages as unread, 179
maximized windows, starting up with, 272
MCI drivers, 89
MCI-DVD drivers, 89
members of groups, 4–5
memory. *See also* free space on hard drives
  conventional, expanded, and extended memory, 229
  disabling Heap Manager, 227
  disk-drive needs, 38
  display adapters and, 237
  MS-DOS programs and, 228
  printing and, 209
  Small Memory Dump log, 302
  Task Manager information, 300
menus
  enlarging on screen, 239
  expanding submenu contents, 273
  navigating through with keyboards, 134
  shortcuts defined, 275
  Start menu shortcuts, 272, 274–75
Messaging Application Programming Interface (MAPI), 61
microphones, 257
Microsoft Direct3D, 233
Microsoft DirectDraw, 88, 233
Microsoft DirectSound, 233
Microsoft Exchange, 61
Microsoft Intellipoint, 158, 160
Microsoft Internet Explorer. *See* Internet Explorer
Microsoft Knowledge Base, xvii, 199
Microsoft Management Console, 44–45
Microsoft NetMeeting, 152, 256, 257
Microsoft Network (MSN), 35
Microsoft Office, 215
Microsoft Outlook, 61, 117
Microsoft Outlook Express. *See* Outlook Express

Microsoft Press Troubleshooting web site, xvii
Microsoft web sites, xvii
Microsoft Windows 95/98/Me
  compatible programs, 227
  drivers, 101
  dual booting, 46, 50–51
  problems accessing hard drives, 47
  reinstalling, 46
  shared folders and, 143
Microsoft Windows 2000 Compatibility Updates (Windows Update), xvii, 217, 226, 228, 296
Microsoft Windows 2000 Professional
  forcing Windows to shut down, 245
  problems starting, 260–65
  program compatibility, 221
  Registry, 226, 297–98
  slow startup, 266–67
  troubleshooting assistance, xiv
  updating, 217, 226, 228, 296
  Windows 2000 Support tools, 227
Microsoft Windows 2000 Professional CD, 51, 264, 265
Microsoft Windows 2000 Server, 30
Microsoft Windows 2000 Server CD, 212
Microsoft Windows 2000 service packs, xvi
  drivers on, 101
  game bug fixes, 88, 93
  identifying installed service packs, 295
  installing, 295–96
  obtaining, 296
  problems after installation, 296
  uninstalling, 296
Microsoft Windows Backup tool, 40, 53, 57
Microsoft Windows Desktop. *See* Desktop
Microsoft Windows Indexing Service, 42–43
Microsoft Windows Media Player, 201, 255, 259

Microsoft Windows NT 4
  drivers, 101, 199, 217, 237
  compatible programs, 227
  screen display drivers and, 237
Microsoft Windows Update, xvii, 217, 226, 228, 296
mic volume settings, 257
MID files, 258
MIDI music, 201, 258
minute clock format, 14
misbehaving machines. *See* crashes
misidentified hardware, 100–101
missing
  icons, 22–23
  items on Start menu, 272–73
  shortcuts, 274
  taskbar, 279, 280–81
  toolbars, 286
MMC (Microsoft Management Console), 44–45
models for hardware, 99, 100, 149
modems
  checking for problems, 34, 150
  command logs, 150
  compatibility, 148, 149, 155
  conference calls and, 256
  detecting, 147, 148–49
  dialing problems, 150–51
  exchanging data over, 146
  external modems, 148
  fax capabilities, 59, 62
  half-duplex and full-duplex, 257
  incoming calls, 147
  installing, 69
  noise problems, 146
  port speed, 147
  sharing voice lines, 61
  speed and slow connections, 106, 146, 154–55
  transferring data over, 152–53
  troubleshooting flowchart, 146–47
  using instead of network connection, 116–17
  waiting for dial tones, 151
  waking computers from hibernation, 66, 199
Modify permission, 86
monitoring network access to files, 6
monitors. *See* multiple monitors; screen display

months
date settings, 15
incorrect display, 13
mouse devices
acting as if button is pressed, 93
buttons and wheels, 93, 156,
160–61
cordless, 162
cursor display, 93
cursor problems, 156, 157,
162–63, 166–67
DirectX software and, 166–67
disassembling and cleaning, 162
disconnecting from
keyboards, 126
drivers, 163
game problems, 88, 92–93, 161
left- or right-handed use, 160
missing pointer on screen,
164–65
nonfunctional devices, 158–59
rollers inside, 162
single- or double-clicking, 157
speed of cursors, 163, 165
switching to keyboard
instead, 124
troubleshooting flowchart,
156–57
wheels on, 156, 160–61
wheel tricks for resizing
fonts, 109
MouseKeys feature, 135
moving
Active Desktop items, 25
encrypted files or folders, 55,
56, 57
files off Desktop, 21
files to network storage or
backups, 39
files to non-NTFS
systems, 81
files with shortcuts, 275
items on screen, 230
multiple-monitor screen
areas, 177
pointers to default dialog box
buttons, 163
taskbar, 282–83
toolbars, 292–93
MS-DOS games
mouse problems and, 92
multiple monitors and, 174
running with boot disk, 89

MS-DOS programs
compatibility list, 228
printing problems, 214, 218–19
problems running, 221, 228–29
versions of MS-DOS, 229
MSN accounts, 35
multicolored squares on screen
after wakeup, 231
multimedia programs, 89, 233
multiple-boot systems. *See* dual-
booting computers
multiple hard drives, 50
multiple monitors
Desktop portions missing, 241
display adapter problems,
170–71
flickering monitors, 177
identifying, 170
monitors are switched,
176–77
mouse pointers and, 166
screen area adjustments,
176–77
taskbar position, 280
troubleshooting flowchart,
168–69
wrong items displayed on
monitors, 174–75
wrong monitor starts up,
172–73
multiple processors, 196
multiple-user computers,
184–85. *See also*
logging on
music. *See* sound features
mute settings, 252, 254, 258
My Computer folder
window, 84
My Computer icon, 22
My Documents folder
hiding files in, 8
missing, 22
moving files into, 21
as Start menu submenu, 273
My Faxes shortcut, 64
My Network Places icon
finding other
computers, 122
ICS host computers, 112
missing, 22
setting up to work
off line, 225
My Pictures folder, 84

names
of fax printers, 75
of folders, 76
on separator pages, 211
navigating with keyboard, 134–35
NetMeeting, 152, 256, 257
Net Start Spooler command, 206
Net Use command, 217, 219
network administrators
control of system, xvi
groups and permissions, xv
permissions for removable
media, 44
shutting down computers, 247
Network And Dial-Up
Connections item, 273
network cards, 30
network connections. *See also*
network administrators;
networks
dial-up connection troubleshooting flowchart, 28–29
Hibernate mode and, 195
ICS connections, 112–15
modem troubleshooting, 146–47
never dialing, 116
remote connections, 29, 30–33
Safe Mode and, 263
secure connections, 31
slow connections, 154–55, 225
taskbar icon, 285
Network Connection Wizard,
31, 35
Network Identification Wizard,
30, 31
networks. *See also* network
administrators; network
connections
access to files on, 2, 6–7
browsing over ICS, 118, 122–23
conference calls and, 256
deleting or renaming folders,
86–87
dial-up connection troubleshooting flowchart, 28–29
disrupting with ICS installation, 120
domains and ICS, 120

slow modem connections, 146,
154–55
slow mouse pointers, 165
slow printing, 202, 208
slow screen performance, 234–35
slow shutdowns, 242, 248–49
slow startups, 260, 266–67
Small Icons view, 80
Small Memory Dump log, 302
small text and items on screen,
231, 238–39
smoothing screen fonts, 19
Softfonts, 209
software
compatibility lists, 34, 167,
221, 228
hardware drivers, 96,
98–99, 101
sorting Start menu items, 277
sound adapters
compatibility lists, 253, 255
DirectX and, 91
sound events, 251
sound features
bandwidth and, 256
choppy voice communications,
251, 256–57
compatibility lists, 253, 255
echoes in voice communications,
251, 256–57
logon music problems, 251
modem speaker volume, 146
music CDs, 258–59
mute settings, 254
nonfunctional sound system,
250, 252–53
playing CDs, 250, 258–59
playing sounds, 254–55
sound files, 253
Sound Recorder program, 253,
254–55, 258
speaker problems, 251, 252
troubleshooting flowchart,
250–51
volume settings, 251, 254
sound files, 254, 258
Sound Recorder program, 253,
255, 258
space on hard drives. *See* free space
on hard drives
spacing icons on Desktop, 18
speaker problems, 251, 252
speaker volume for modems, 146

special characters
international characters on web
sites, 105, 110–11
problems entering with
keyboard, 124, 128–29
special effects for Desktop, 19
speed. *See* performance
speed of repeating characters, 130
spooled print jobs
slow printing and, 208
space for, 207
square blobs on screen after
wakeup, 231
stalled computers. *See* crashes
stand-alone computers, xvi
Standard Buttons toolbar, 82,
290, 291
standard Desktop. *See* Desktop
Standard Mode, 260
Standard PC power manage-
ment, 196
Standby mode
crashing, 199
entering instead of shutting
down, 189
modems and, 199
mouse devices and, 158
network connections and, 201
password protection, 200
problems entering, 198–201
problems waking, 192
requiring passwords, 141
settings for, 191, 200
unavailable, 196–97, 198
unexpected shutdowns and, 246
waking computers slowly
from, 192
waking for fax calls, 59, 66–67
starting environment,
inspecting, 51
starting games, 88–91
starting printers immediately, 208
starting programs
by opening files, 220–21
problems, 220–21
Quick Launch toolbar, 289
running automatically at startup,
266–67
starting Start menu items, 272
starting Windows
after installing hardware, 99, 101
automatic remote
connections, 33

blank screen display, 230
dual booting, 46–47, 48–49
error messages, 47
F8 key, 232
hardware profiles, 262
multiple-monitor problems, 169,
172–73
not requiring passwords, 33
problems starting computers,
264–65
problems starting Windows,
260–61
reconfiguration messages,
268–69
running programs automatically,
266–67
screen crashes at startup, 232–33
Setup disks, 51
slow startups, 260, 266–67
troubleshooting flowchart,
260–61
Windows 2000 Professional
CD, 51
Start menu
adding items to, 272–73
administrative tools on, 273
All Users menus, 277
confusing order of items, 270,
276–77
Control Panel submenu, 273
deleting items, 275
Favorites on, 273
full menus not displayed, 271
logoff command on, 273
missing items, 270, 272–73
My Documents submenu, 273
Network And Dial-Up
Connections submenu, 273
nonfunctional items, 270,
274–75
personalized menus, 271, 277
printer choices on, 273
rearranging items on, 270,
276–77
renaming items on, 272
scroll bars on Programs
submenu, 273
shortcuts for items, 16
sorting items, 277
symbols on submenus, 271
troubleshooting flowchart,
270–71
wrong order for items, 270

X icon, 102
XMS memory (extended), 229

years
    date settings, 15
    incorrect, 13
yellow exclamation-mark icon, 102

ZIP disks, 44
ZIP programs, 39

About the authors

Jerry Joyce has had a long-standing relationship with Microsoft: he was the technical editor on numerous books published by Microsoft Press, and he has written manuals, help files, and specifications for various Microsoft products. As a programmer, he has tried to make using a computer as simple as using any household appliance, but he has yet to succeed. Jerry's alter ego is that of a marine biologist; he has conducted research from the Arctic to the Antarctic and has published extensively on marine-mammal and fisheries issues. As antidotes to staring at his computer screen, he enjoys traveling, birding, boating, and wandering about beaches, wetlands, and mountains.

Marianne Moon has worked in the publishing world for many years as a proof-reader, an editor, and a writer—and sometimes all three simultaneously. She has been editing and proofreading Microsoft Press books since 1984 and has written and edited documentation for Microsoft products such as Microsoft Works, Flight Simulator, Space Simulator, Golf, Publisher, Greetings Workshop, and the Microsoft Mouse. In another life, she was chief cook and bottlewasher for her own catering service and wrote cooking columns for several newspapers. When she's not chained to her computer, she likes gardening, cooking, traveling, writing poetry, and knitting sweaters for tiny dogs.

Marianne and **Jerry** own and operate **Moon Joyce Resources,** a small consulting company. They are coauthors of *Microsoft Word 97 At a Glance, Microsoft Windows 95 At a Glance, Microsoft Windows NT Workstation 4.0 At a Glance, Microsoft Windows 98 At a Glance, Microsoft Word 2000 At a Glance, Microsoft Windows 2000 Professional At a Glance,* and *Microsoft Windows Millennium Edition At a Glance.* They've had a 19-year working relationship and have been married for 9 years. If you have questions or comments about any of their books, you can reach them at moonjoyceresourc@hotmail.com.

The manuscript for this book was prepared and submitted to Microsoft Press in electronic form. Text files were prepared using Microsoft Word 2000. Pages were composed using Quark 3.35 for the Power Macintosh, with text in Adobe Caslon Regular and Gill Sans, and display type in Gill Sans Extrabold. Composed pages were delivered to the printer as electronic prepress files.

Cover designer

Landor Associates

Interior graphic designer

James D. Kramer

Compositor

Blue Fescue Typography & Design

Graphic artist

Sue Cook Visuals

Proofreader/copyeditor

Alice Copp Smith

Indexer

Wright Information Indexing Services

Get to know Me

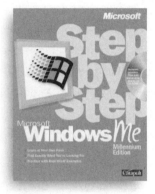

...and have more fun living in the Digital Age!

Do It Yourself Microsoft® Windows® Me
No jargon—just fun, to-the-point explanations, useful tips, and amazing tricks for using the cool features in Windows Me.

Microsoft Windows Me At a Glance
Quick visual solutions—in full color!—help you put Windows Me and your home PC to work.

Microsoft Windows Me Step by Step
The easy way to teach yourself Windows Me! This book-and-CD self-study kit builds new skills—a step at a time.

COMING SOON:
Microsoft Windows Movie Maker Handbook
Learn tips and tricks for making your own movies and videos on the PC and sharing them over the Web.

Microsoft Windows Media™ Player Handbook
Comprehensive guide to exploring and customizing Windows Media Player 7—your all-in-one digital jukebox.

Microsoft Press® products are available worldwide wherever quality computer books are sold. For more information, contact your book or computer retailer, software reseller, or local Microsoft Sales Office, or visit our Web site at mspress.microsoft.com. To locate your nearest source for Microsoft Press products, or to order directly, call 1-800-MSPRESS in the U.S. (in Canada, call 1-800-268-2222).

Prices and availability dates are subject to change.

Microsoft®

mspress.microsoft.com

up! Step Step

STEP BY STEP books provide quick and easy self-training—to help you learn to use the powerful features and tools in Microsoft Office 2000, Microsoft Windows Professional, and Microsoft Windows Me. The easy-to-follow lessons present clear objectives and real-world business examples, with numerous screen shots and illustrations. Put Office 2000 and Windows 2000 Professional, and Windows Me to work today with STEP BY STEP learning solutions, made by Microsoft.

- MICROSOFT® OFFICE 2000 PROFESSIONAL 8-IN-1 STEP BY STEP
- MICROSOFT WORD 2000 STEP BY STEP
- MICROSOFT EXCEL 2000 STEP BY STEP
- MICROSOFT POWERPOINT® 2000 STEP BY STEP
- MICROSOFT INTERNET EXPLORER 5 STEP BY STEP
- MICROSOFT PUBLISHER 2000 STEP BY STEP
- MICROSOFT ACCESS 2000 STEP BY STEP
- MICROSOFT FRONTPAGE® 2000 STEP BY STEP
- MICROSOFT OUTLOOK® 2000 STEP BY STEP
- MICROSOFT WINDOWS® 2000 PROFESSIONAL STEP BY STEP
- MICROSOFT WINDOWS ME STEP BY STEP

mspress.microsoft.com

Stay in the *running* for maximum productivity.

These are *the* answer books for business users of Microsoft software. They are packed with everything from quick, clear instructions for new users to comprehensive answers for power users—the authoritative reference to keep by your computer and use every day. The RUNNING series—learning solutions made by Microsoft.

- RUNNING MICROSOFT® EXCEL 2000
- RUNNING MICROSOFT OFFICE 2000 PREMIUM
- RUNNING MICROSOFT OFFICE 2000 PROFESSIONAL
- RUNNING MICROSOFT OFFICE 2000 SMALL BUSINESS
- RUNNING MICROSOFT WORD 2000
- RUNNING MICROSOFT POWERPOINT® 2000
- RUNNING MICROSOFT ACCESS 2000
- RUNNING MICROSOFT INTERNET EXPLORER 5
- RUNNING MICROSOFT FRONTPAGE® 2000
- RUNNING MICROSOFT OUTLOOK® 2000
- RUNNING MICROSOFT WINDOWS® 2000 PROFESSIONAL

mspress.microsoft.com